JN105569

# 50音順 一日の会話で使う動詞のすべてを英語にしてみる

曽根田憲三
Kenzo Soneda

ベレ出版

# はじめに

英語を無理なく、しかも確実に身に着ける最も手っ取り早く、かつ有効な方法はなんでしょう。その答えのヒントは、私たちが何の苦も無く毎日使いこなしている母語である日本語を獲得してきた過程にあります。誰もが、この世に生を受けた瞬間から、両親を初めとし、まわりの人たちから絶えずかけられる様々な言葉を耳にしていくうちに、自然とそれらを真似、口にするようになっていくのです。そして小学校へ上がるころには、日常生活で使われる言葉や表現を聞き、話すことに苦労することはほとんどなくなっているはずです。クラスメートたちとの会話はもちろん、教師のことばも、理解するにあたって特別な知識が必要なものは別として、分からないと悩む人はいません。日本語の会話教室に通ったわけではないし、塾で日本語を学習をしたわけでもないのに、自分の言いたいことは自由に言えるし、相手の発言も何ら問題なく聞き取れるようになっているのです。それは取りも直さず、ほぼ日本語だけが飛び交う日々の生活の中で常に日本語を聞き、そして話してきたからに他なりません。

このことから一つ断言できることは、言語を習得するための最良の、そして最速の道が、モノにしようとする言語を私たちの日常生活の中で用いるということです。試験のために一夜漬けで覚えたような表現や、人生の中で一度か二度しか使わないような表現ではなく、私たちが日々の暮らしの中で、日常的に繰り返し使っている、すなわち、生活していく上で必要不可欠な日本語の表現を英語で言ってみることなのです。そうすることで、自然に英語を使うことができ、お決まりの表現を頻繁に口にする機会に恵まれるため、たとえ今日、適切な表現が使えなかったり、言い方を間違えたとしても、すぐさま同じ状況が訪れる翌日には訂正し、本来の表現を口にすることができるわけです。言い換えれば、語学学習に最も大切な継続、そして反復が容易に可能となり、結果、私たちの語学力は飛躍的に伸びるのです。

こうした日常生活において使われることばの中で最も重要なものの一つが動

作や変化、状態や存在を表す動詞ということになります。朝「起きる」ときから夜「寝る」ときに至るまで動詞を使わないで私たちの日々の動作、行動、状況、考えを描写することも、まわりの人たちと意思の疎通を図ることもできません。あなたの近くにいる人が、もう一つの重要な品詞である名詞、たとえば「ごはん」と言ったとします。しかし、これだと聞き手にとって、その人がご飯が「欲しい」と言っているのか「食べたい」のか、あるいは「作りたい」と言おうとしているのか、動詞を伴っていなければ聞き手には分かりかねます。「ご飯を食べたい」とか「ご飯を作ろう」と表現して初めて話し手の意図が聞き手に伝わるのです。

そこで本書は、これまで「基本動詞」など、巷にあふれている従来の書籍が取り上げてきた英語の動詞を解説するという方法とは大きく異なり、英語を話すという観点から、私たちにとってより分かりやすく、そしてより使いやすいようにと、日常生活の中で絶えず用いられている「会う」から「笑う」までの日本語の動詞を「あいうえを」順に挙げ、それらが使われる日常表現を英語にして収めたものです。とはいえ英語と日本語の表現方法が異なることから、例えば、「遊ぶ時間はないんだ」をI have no time for fun.、「化粧品で肌が荒れちゃった」をI got a rash from my makeup. といった具合に、必ずしも日本語の「遊ぶ」とか「荒れる」に対応した英語の動詞で表されるわけではありません。また、日本語に多く存在する、発音は同じだが意味が異なる同音異義語もやっかいな問題です。一例として「あげる」です。人に物を「あげる」、手を「あげる」、声を「あげる」、カバンを棚に「あげる」、結婚式を「あげる」、証拠を「あげる」、都合の良い日を「あげる」、天ぷらを「あげる」など、何を「あげる」かによって、当然のことながら、英語の場合は使われる動詞もしくは表現が違ってきます。ここではそうした様々な点を考慮し、一見して違いが分かるように身近な例を引き合いに出して、英語にして掲げています。

なお、本書では読者の便宜を図って、以下のような工夫をこらしています。

★ 日本語表現に対応する英語表現が複数ある場合は I walk to school every day. / I go to school on foot every day. のように / で区切って載せています。
★ 用例で使われた単語や語句で知っておくべき基本的なもの、紛らわしいもの、分かりにくいものなどについては → plan to ~「～するつもりである、～する予定です」のように、意味を載せるとともに、場合によっては簡潔な説明を加えています。
★ 同じような意味を表す単語や言い換え可能な語句がある場合は → There's no need to~ = You don't have to~ のように示しています。
★ ⇒ plain → in a loud voice（大きな声で）、in a whisper（声をひそめて）、in an undertone（小声で、ぼそっと）、in an audible voice（よく聞こえる声で、大声で）、more slowly（もっとゆっくり）のように表示されたものは、用例の中の plain を → 以下の表現に置き換えて使えることを表したものです。

言葉をモノにする方法は人間関係を築く方法と酷似しています。家族や友人を例に挙げるまでもなく、ともに時間を過ごせば過ごすほど親しさが増していくように、言葉も使えば使うほど上達していきます。実際、Practice makes perfect. という諺が教えてくれている通り、ターゲットとしている言語の習熟度は、どれだけその言語と付き合ったかによって決まるものです。無料でダウンロードできる本書用の英語音声を毎日、聞き、口真似するなどフルに活用して、コミュニケーションの手段としての英語に磨きをかけてください。みなさんのご検討をお祈りしています。

曽根田　憲三

〈50 音順〉一日の会話で使う動詞のすべてを英語にしてみる○もくじ

# 音声ダウンロードサービス

本書の音声をベレ出版のホームページより無料でダウンロードできます。こちらのサービスはパソコンからのダウンロードをおすすめします。

スマートフォン、タブレットからのダウンロード方法については、小社では対応しておりません。

## 音声のダウンロード方法

① 「ベレ出版」ホームページ内、『〈50音順〉一日の会話で使う動詞のすべてを英語にしてみる』の詳細ページにある「音声ダウンロード」ボタンをクリック。
（URLは https://www.beret.co.jp/books/detail/801）

② 8ケタのコードを入力してダウンロード。
ダウンロードコード **taJHwVan** ［！大文字、小文字は正確に入力してください］

＊ダウンロードされた音声はMP3形式となります。Zipファイルで圧縮された状態となっておりますので、解凍してからお使いください。

＊iPod等のMP3携帯プレイヤーへのファイル転送方法、パソコン、ソフトなどの操作方法については、メーカー等にお問い合わせいただくか、取扱説明書をご参照ください。小社での対応はできかねますこと、ご理解ください。

※音声の権利・利用については、小社ホームページ内［よくある質問］にてご確認ください。

# あ

## 会う

彼には毎日会っているよ。

今日の夕方彼に会うつもり。

彼女には明日会うけど。

私たち 2 日に一度会うの。

彼女には一週間前に会ったよ。

また会いたいな。

いつ会える？

今日の午後会えます？

明日会いましょう。

どこで会おうか？

駅で朝 10 時に会おう。

11 月のどこかで会おう。

今日は誰に会う予定なの？

あなたに会えてラッキーだわ。

彼に会うのが楽しみだな。

TRACK 001

**I see him every day.** → see は会ったことのある人に使われる。

**I plan to meet him this evening.**
→ plan to~「〜するつもりである、〜する予定です」→ meet は初対面の場合。ただし、時間や場所を決めて話し合う約束をする際には meet。

**I'm going to see him tomorrow.**
→ be going to~「〜しようとしている」

**We see each other every other day.**
→ every other day「一日おきに」

**I saw her a week ago.** → saw は see の過去形

**I want to see you again.**

**When can I see you?**

**Can I see you this afternoon?**

**I'll see you tomorrow.**

**Where will we meet?**

**I'll meet you at the station at ten o'clock in the morning.**

**Let's meet sometime in November.**

**Who will you meet today?**

**I'm lucky to have met you.** ⇒ lucky → glad

**I'm looking forward to meeting him. / I cannot wait to meet him.** → look forward to ~ing は「〜するのが待ち遠しい」 cannot wait to ~ は「〜が待ちきれない」

## 合う

この食べ物は私の口に合うわね。

このワインはこのチーズによく合うな。

そのドレスはあなたに良く合うわよ。

あなたにはショートヘアの方が合うと思うけど。

この赤いネクタイ、僕のジャケットに合うと思う？

日本の気候は合いますか？

このジャケットは私にピッタリだわ。

ピッタリ合うかどうかこのジャケットを着てみたら？

これらの服はもう私の体に合わないんだ。

あなたはこの仕事にピッタリだわね。

学校からの帰宅途中で雨にあっちゃった。

昨日、事故にあっちゃってさ。

私たち、波長が合うわね。

## 上がる

このエレベーターは上に上がります。

エレベーターで上がろうよ。

エレベーターで５階までお上がりください。

TRACK 002

**This food suits my taste.** / This food agrees with me.
→ suit（「食物、気候などが」合う、ふさわしい →「合わない」とする際は… does not suit~、… does not agree with ~ とする。

**This wine goes well with this cheese.**
→ go well with~「～とぴったり合う」

**That dress suits you very well.**
→ ここでの suit は衣服、色などが人、物に「よく合う、似合う」

**I think short hair suits you better.**

**Do you think this red necktie goes well with my jacket?**

**Does the climate of Japan agree with you?**

**This jacket fits me very well.** → fit は（「衣服などのサイズ、形などが人、物、場面などに」ピッタリ合う、ふさわしい）

**Try on this jacket to see if it fits well.**

**These clothes don't fit me anymore.**

**You fit the bill perfectly for this job.** / You are the right person for this job. → fit the bill（「希望、条件などに」ピッタリ合う）

**I got caught in the rain on my way home from school.**
→ get caught in~（～に巻き込まれる）

**I met with an accident.**

**We are on the same wavelength, aren't we?**
→ be on the same wavelength（波長が合う、息が合う、考え方が同じである）

TRACK 003

**This elevator is going up.** → is going up（上がっている）

**Let's go up in an elevator.**

**Please go up in an elevator to the 5th floor.**

二階にお上がりください。

階段はゆっくり上ってね。

そこの高い石段を上がるときは気をつけて。

階段を一度に二段ずつ上がらないで。

物価はまだ上がると思うね。

電車賃が 250 円から 300 円に上がったよ。

消費税がまたまた上がるようだ。

給料が上がるといいんだけど。

給料が上がったよ。

突然、体温が上がっちゃった。

昨日、体温が上がったけど、今日は下がったよ。

天気予報によると午後には温度が上がるって。

今日は全国的に 30 度以上になるらしい。

この価値は上がると思うよ。

今学期の成績が上がったよ。

頑張れば英語のレベルはすぐに上がるよ。

**Go upstairs please.** → 反対は go downstairs（階下へ降りる）

**Go up the stairs slowly.**
→ stairs は室内の「階段」、steps は屋外の「階段」

**Be careful when you go up that long flight of stone steps.**
→ flight of~（「階段や階段状になっているものについて」一続きの～、一連の～）

**Don't go up the steps two at a time.**

**I think prices will go up still higher.**
⇒ go up still higher → go on rising（上がり続ける）

**The train fare went up from 250 yen to 300 yen.**
→ went up は go up の過去形

**The consumption tax will go up again.**

**I wish my salary will go up.**

**My pay went up.** /I got a pay rise. / I had a pay raise. / I got a raise. / I got an increase in salary. / My pay increased. /I had my salary raised. → pay rise= pay raise

**Suddenly my temperature rose.** → my temperature = my body temperature → rose = went up → rose は rise の過去形

**My temperature went up yesterday, but it dropped today.**

**According to the weather forecast, the temperature will go up in the afternoon.**

**The temperature is expected to rise above 30 degrees Celsius nationally today.**
→ is expected to~（～すると思われている、～する見込みである、～するはずである）

**I think this value will go up.** / I think this will go up in value.

**My grades went up this semester.** / I got higher grades this semester.

**Your English level will go up soon if you work hard.**

突然、スピーチを頼まれてあがったよ。

あがっちゃってすっかりセリフを忘れたんだ。

早くプールから上がりなさい。

バッテリーがあがってる。

## あきらめる

彼女のことはあきらめるよ。

あなたのことがあきらめられない。

海外留学のことはあきらめるよ。

あきらめてはだめ。

何であれいったんやり始めたら、絶対にあきらめてはだめ。

なぜ最初からあきらめたりしたの？

それをあきらめるのはまだ早いよ。

ときにはあきらめることも必要だと思うけど。

## あきる

これ、食べ飽きたよ。

同じ料理を 3 日連続で食べるのは飽きたな。

この仕事には飽きたな。

**I got very nervous when I was suddenly called on to make a speech.** → get nervous（あがる、神経質になる、怖がる）→ be called on（指名される、声がかかる）

**I got stage fright and forgot my lines completely.**
→ get stage fright（あがる、落ち着きを失う、硬くなる） → line（セリフ、一節）

**Get out of the pool quickly.** → get out of ~（～から外に出る）

**The battery is dead.** → is dead（死んでいる、だめになっている）

TRACK 004

**I'll give up on her.** → give up on ~（～に見切りをつける、～を断念する）

**I cannot give up on you.**

**I'm going to give up the idea of studying abroad.**
→ study abroad（海外留学、留学）

**Don't give up.** ⇒ give up → give up halfway（途中であきらめる）、give up without a struggle（努力もせずにあきらめる）、give up until the last time（最後の最後まであきらめる（な））、even if you fail（たとえ失敗しても）

**Once you have begun to do anything, never give it up.**

**Why did you give up from the start?**

**It's still too early for you to give up on that.**
⇒ give up on that → give up on your dream（あなたの夢をあきらめる）

**Sometimes it is important to give up, I think.**

TRACK 005

**I'm tired of eating this.** ⇒ this → the same thing（同じもの）
→ be tired of ~= be weary of; get tired of ; get sick of

**I got tired of having the same cuisine 3 days in a row.**
→ cuisine（「特にレストランなどの」特有の料理、調理法）
→ in a row（一列に、連続的に、続けて）

**I'm tired of this work.** / I got bored with this work. / I'm weary of this work. ⇒ this work → watching TV（テレビを見ること）

あの上司のもとで働くのはちょ〜飽きたよ。

君の言い訳を聞くのは飽きたよ。

彼とのデートには飽きたわ。

私たちお互い少し飽きてきたわね。

毎日同じことの繰り返しに飽きてきたよ。

彼女と話していて飽きない？

その映画を繰り返し見ても飽きないわけだ？

それは何度見ても飽きない映画だ。

この眺めは何度見ても飽きないね。

## 開ける

窓を開けて。

ドアを開けたままにしておいて。

カーテンを開けて日光を入れよう。

このドアは引いて開けるのよ。

この引き出しは開けないで。

教科書を開けてください。

本の 30 ページを開けてみて？

この包みを開けてください。

**I'm sick and tired of working for that boss.**
→ be sick and tired of ~　~にはうんざりだ、~にあきあきしている

**I'm tired of hearing your excuses.** ⇒ your excuses → your bragging (あなたの自慢話)、 your complaints (あなたの不満)、 her chatter (彼女のおしゃべり)、 city life (都会の生活)、 my monotonous life (単調な生活)

**I'm tired of going out with him.**
→ go out with ~　~と付き合う、~とデートに行く

**We got a little bored with each other.**

**I'm getting tired of doing the same thing every day.**
⇒ doing the ... day → being alone (一人でいること)

**Don't you get tired of talking to her?**

**You don't get tired of watching the movie again and again, do you?** → again and again (何度も何度も、繰り返して)

**That's a movie you never get tired of watching.**

**I never get tired of this view.**
⇒ this view → looking at that (それを見ること)

TRACK 006

**Open the windows.**
⇒ the windows → all the windows (全ての窓)、the door (ドア)

**Leave the door open.**

**Let's open the curtains and let the sunshine in.**

**You pull this door open.** ⇒ pull → push (押す)

**Don't open this drawer.**

**Please open your textbooks.**

**Will you open your book to page 30?**

**Please open this package.**
→ package (小包、小荷物) → アメリカで使われることが多い。イギリスでは parcel。

この包み紙を開けてもいい？

口を開けて。

このビンどうやって開けるの？

そこのプラスチックボトルのふたを開けてくれる？

この缶ビールのふたを開けたのはだれ？

トイレのふたを開けたままにしないで。

道を空けてくれ。

消防車に道を空けなさい。

週末に家を空けます。

2 時間オフィスを空けます。

隣の人と少し間をあけてください。

濃厚接触を避けるには 2 メートルの間隔をあけることが大切よ。

広がって間隔をあけましょう。

私のためにスペースをあけてくれる？

席を空けていただいてありがとう。

もうすぐ夜が明けるよ。

もう缶ビール 3 本あけたのか？

今度の日曜日を空けておいてくれる？

**Can I open the wrapper?**

**Open your mouth.** ⇒ mouth → mouth wide（口を大きく）

**How do you open this bottle?** ⇒ bottle → can（缶詰）

**Can you uncap that plastic bottle?**
→ uncap（ふたを外す、キャップをはずす）

**Who pulled the tab from this beer can?**
→ tab（「切り離し式用の」引っ張る口金、つまみ、ふた）

**Don't leave the lid up on the toilet.**

**Make way.**

**Make way for a fire-engine.**
⇒ a fire-engine → an ambulance（救急車）、a police car（パトカー）

**I'm going to stay away from home on the weekend.**
→ stay away from（～から離れている、～を避ける）

**I'll be away from my office for 2 hours.**
→ be away from = leave

**Please leave a space between you and the person beside you.** → beside = next to

**It is important to keep 2 meters apart to avoid close contact.** → close contact（濃厚接触）

**Let's spread out and make some space.** → spread out（広がる）

**Could you make room for me?**
→ make room for ~（～に場所を空ける）

**Thank you for making room for me.**

**Day will break soon.**

**Did you already drink up three cans of beer?**
→ drink up（飲み干す）

**Will you keep next Sunday open for me?**
→ keep ～ open（～を空けておく）

行間をもっと開けたほうがいいよ。

## あげる

それ君にあげるよ。

君にあげるものがあるんだ。

庭の花に水をあげてくれる？

手を上げて。

質問のある人は手を上げてください。

賛成の人は手を上げて。

声を上げないで。

私たち、人種差別に対して声を上げるべきよ。

顔を上げなさい。

これを上にあげてもらえますか？

このバッグを上の棚にあげていただけますか？

結婚式はいつ挙げるの？

結婚式は６月に挙げる予定なの。

これって、どうやって揚げるの？

これは180度くらいの油で揚げるんだ。

**You had better leave a bigger space.**

TRACK 007

**I'll give it to you.**

**I have something to give you.**

**Will you give water to the flowers in the garden?**
⇒ give water to = water

**Raise your hands.** / Put your hands up.
⇒ your hands → both your hands（両手）

**People with questions, please raise your hand.** / If you have any questions, raise your hand.

**Those in favor, raise your hands.** / Raise your hand if you agree.

**Don't raise your voice.**

**We should raise our voice against the racial discrimination.** / We should protest against racism.
→ racial discrimination（人種差別）

**Look up.** ⇒ from your book（本から）

**Could you help me put this up there?**
→ help someone do（人が～するのを手伝う） → up there（あの上へ、あそこへ）

**Could you put this bag in the overhead locker for me? / Would you mind putting this stuff in the overhead locker ?**
→ overhead locker 飛行機などで荷物を保管するために座席の上にあるロッカー

**When do you hold your wedding ceremony?**
→ hold（「会食、催しなどを」開催する、行う）

**We plan on having our wedding ceremony in June.**
→ plan on ~ing（～する予定である、～するつもりである）

**How do you fry this?** → fry（油で炒める、揚げる）→ 小麦粉、パン粉などを付けて油に浸して揚げる場合は deep-fry、また French-fry という。

**You should deep-fry this at about 180 degrees Celsius.**

天ぷらをサラッと揚げるにはコツがいるんだ。

その国旗を揚げてください。

子供のころはよく凧を揚げたものだ。

一例を挙げてみて。

好きな俳優の名前を挙げてみて。

東京のおいしい料理を出す店を 2、3 挙げてみてくれる？

候補の日を挙げてみて。

都合のいい日を 2、3 挙げるね。

ハードルをほんの少し上げてみては？

君は名を上げたね。

あなたはいつも自分のことは棚に上げるのよね。

## 味わう

ここでは旬の食べ物が味わえるよ。

本場のフランス料理を味わいたいな。

この酒を一口味わってみて。

昨日パーティで色んな珍味を味わったよ。

自由の喜びが味わえるのはいいね。

**It requires skill to cook crispier tempura.**
→ crispier → crispy（パリパリした、サクサクの）の比較級。

**Please raise the national flag.**
⇒ the national flag → the Japanese national flag（日本の国旗）

**I used to fly a kite when I was a child.**
→ used to do（よく～したものだ、以前は～したものだった）→ 過去のかなり長い期間にわたって行っていた習慣を表す。現在も継続しているかどうかは問われない。

**Give me an example.** ⇒ Give me → Could you give me~（～を挙げてもらえますか） ⇒ an example → evidence（証拠）、your favorite number（好きな数字）、more similar examples（同様の例をもっと）

**Will you name actors you like?** → name（名を言う、名を挙げる）

**Can you name a few great restaurants in Tokyo?**
⇒ great restaurants → historic spots（史跡）

**Would you list the possible days?** → list = give me

**Let me name a couple of dates that would be convenient for me.** → be convenient for ~（～に都合がよい）

**How about raising the bar just a little bit?**

**You became famous.** / You made your name. / You won fame. → make one's name（名を上げる）

**You always shut your eyes to your own faults.** → shut one's eyes to~（～に目をつむる）= are blind to → faults（欠点）= blemishes; shortcomings

TRACK 008

**You can taste seasonal foods here.**
→ seasonal food（旬の食べ物）→ seasonal（特定の季節だけの、季節の）

**I want to enjoy authentic French cuisine.**
→ authentic（正真正銘の、本物の）

**Please take a taste of this *sake*.** → take a taste of = taste

**I enjoyed various kinds of delicacies at the party.**
→ various kinds of（色んな種類の） → delicacy（珍味）

**It's good to be able to taste the joy of freedom.**

もう恋の甘さと苦しさを味わうのはごめんだ。

海外に行くと日本とは違った雰囲気が味わえるよ。

## 遊ぶ

遊ぼう。

外で遊ぼう。

何して遊ぼうか？

いつもどこで遊んでる？

誰と遊ぶの？

明日、友だちと遊ぶ予定なの。

彼女、最近、一郎と盛んに遊んでるよ。

近いうちにまた遊ぼうね。

絶対道路で遊んではだめ。

遊ぶ時間はないんだ。

## 当たる

あなたの予想が当たったわ。

僕の勘はよく当たるよ。

君の勘は当たっているかも。

**I don't want to experience the sweet and bitter aspects of love anymore.** → aspect（側面、面）

**If you go abroad, you can experience a different atmosphere from Japan.** → atmosphere（雰囲気）

TRACK 009

**Let's play.** / Let's hang out.
→ hang out（ぶらぶら時を過ごす、遊ぶ）→ 若者の間で使われる

**Let's play out of doors.**
→ out of doors = outside ⇒ play out of doors → play in the sand（砂場で遊ぶ）、play in the snow（雪の中で遊ぶ）、 play in the park（公園で遊ぶ）、play at home（家で遊ぶ）、play tag（鬼ごっこして遊ぶ）、play cards（トランプして遊ぶ）

**What shall we do for fun?** → for fun（楽しみに、気晴らしに）

**Where do you usually hang out?**

**Whom do you play with?**

**I plan on hanging out with my friends tomorrow.**

**She's been hanging out with Ichiro a lot recently.**

**Let's hang out again soon.**
⇒ hang out again soon → hang out after work（仕事のあと遊ぶ）、hang out at the weekend（週末に遊ぶ）、hang out on Saturday（土曜日に遊ぶ）

**Never play on the road.**

**I have no time for fun.** ⇒ for fun = to play around

TRACK 010

**Your guess was right.** / You guessed right.
⇒ right → wrong（間違った）

**My gut feelings are often right.**
→ gut feeling = instinct; hunch; intuition; feeling

**Maybe your hunch is right.** → hunch = guess; intuition

彼の占いはよく当たるよ。

今日の星占いが当たっていればいいけど。

今日の天気予報は当たった。

宝クジが当たったよ。

福引で２等が当たった。

僕の投げたボールが彼の頭に当たっちゃった。

そんなことをしたらバチが当たるよ。

私、イライラしていたから、彼に辛く当たっちゃった。

## 集まる・集める

みんな、集まれ！

どこへ集まろうか？

何時までに集まればいいですか？

明日、私たち真理子の家に集まるの。

あそこの広場に集まろう。

次はいつ集まろうか？

クリスマスに集まろうよ。

私たちみんな、最低年に一度は集まるようにしてるんだ。

明日、例の新しいプロジェクトについて話し合うために集まれるかな？

**His fortune-telling is often right.**
⇒ is often right → has come true（当たった）

**I hope today's horoscope is right.**

**Today's weather forecast proved right.**
→ prove ~（～であるとわかる、～だと判明する、的中する）

**I won the lottery.**

**I won second prize in the raffle.** → raffle（抽選）

**The ball I threw hit him on the head.**
→ hit someone on the head（人の頭に当たる）

**Heaven will punish you for it.** / You will pay dearly for it.
→ pay dearly for~（～でひどい目にあう、～して高くつく）

**I was feeling irritated and vented my frustration on my boyfriend.** → vent one's frustration on ~= take it out on ~（～に不満を発散させる、～に八つ当たりする）

TRACK 011

**Everyone, gather!** / Gather around, everyone!

**Where shall we gather?** ⇒ gather → meet（会う）

**By what time should we gather?**

**We will gather at Mariko's house tomorrow.**

**Let's gather in the open space there.**

**When shall we get together next?**
→ get together は gather よりくだけた言い方。

**Let's get together for Christmas.**

**We all try to get together at least once a year.** ⇒ get together at least once a year → get together at regular intervals（定期的に集まる）

**Can we meet up tomorrow to talk about that new project?** → meet up は get together よりも更にくだけた言い方。

また集まれたらいいね。

私の趣味は切手を集めることです。

もっとデータを集める必要があるな。

例の会社の情報を集めたかね？

私たちは社長室に集められた。

## 浴びる

ひと風呂浴びるとしよう。

さっとシャワーを浴びなさい。

私、朝食後すぐにシャワーを浴びるの。

日中に日光を浴びると夜ぐっすり眠れるよ。

日光浴することは大量の紫外線を浴びることだよね。

彼って、よく発言で批判を浴びるね。

## 甘やかす

子供を甘やかしてはだめ。

彼を甘やかし過ぎじゃない？

彼女は自分を甘やかし過ぎてるみたい。

私のことを甘やかしてくれるボーイフレンドが欲しいな。

**I hope we can get together again.**

**My hobby is collecting stamps.**
→ collect stamps = make a collection of stamps ⇒ collecting stamps → collecting watches（時計を集める）、collecting butterfly specimens（蝶の標本を集める）

**We need to collect more data.**

**Did you gather information about that company?**

**We were assembled at the president's office.**
→ assemble（集める、招集する）

TRACK 012

**I'm going to take a bath.** → take = have

**Take a quick shower.** → take = have

**I take a shower right after breakfast.**
→ right after~（～の直後に、～するとすぐに）→ ここでの right は副詞、前置詞の前に置いて「ちょうど、まさしく」などの意を表す副詞。

**If you sunbathe during the day, you can sleep soundly at night.** → sunbathe（日光浴をする）→ sleep soundly = sleep well; sleep like a baby; sleep like a log

**The sunbath means exposure to a large quantity of ultraviolet light, doesn't it?** → exposure to ~（～に身を晒すこと）→ a large quantity of~（大量の～、多量の～）→ ultraviolet light（紫外線）

**He is frequently criticized for what he says.**
→ frequently=again and again; repeatedly → be criticized for~（～で批判される）

TRACK 013

**Don't spoil your child.** → spoil（甘やかす、甘やかしてだめにする）

**You spoil him too much, don't you?**

**She seems to spoil herself.**

**I want a boyfriend who spoils me.**

私のこと甘やかさないで！

## 怪しむ

何か怪しいなあ。

それって何か話がうま過ぎじゃない。怪しい感じだなぁ。

絶対あいつを信じちゃだめ。怪しいやつだから。

## 謝る

君に謝らなければいけない。

君に謝るべきことがある。

君に対してしたことを謝りたい。

僕は自分の言ったことを謝る必要はない。

君は私に謝るべきだ。

どうして私が謝る必要があるの？

君が謝る必要はないよ。

どうして謝っているわけ？

これは君が謝ることではない。

もしそれが本当なら、彼が謝るべきだよ。

君は彼女に対する無礼を謝るべきだね。

彼女に謝るつもりだったが、言いそびれてしまったのさ。

You are spoiling me!
→ あなたは私を甘やかしてダメにしている、との意。

TRACK 014

Something is fishy. / I smell a rat.

That sounds too good to be true. It sounds fishy.

Don't ever trust him. He is a shady guy.
→ shady（うさんくさい、いかがわしい）

TRACK 015

I owe you an apology.
→ owe someone an apology（人に謝らねばならない）

There's something I should apologize to you for.
→ apologize（詫びる、謝る、謝罪する）

I want to apologize for what I did to you.

I don't have to apologize for what I said.

You should apologize to me.

Why should I apologize?

You don't need to apologize.

Why are you apologizing?

This is not something you need to apologize for.

If that is true, then he needs to apologize.

You should apologize to her for having been rude to her. → for having being rude → for being rude

I was going to apologize to her, but I missed the chance.

## 洗う

石鹸で手を洗いなさい。

皿を洗うの、手伝ってくれる？

この布地は洗っても大丈夫？

洗うと傷みます。

この色は洗ってもはげないんだ。

## 改める

君は行いを改めるべきだ。

君、過ちを認めて改めたらどうだ？

我々の方針を改めてみてはどうだろう？

## 表す

君の考えを言葉で表しなさい。

これは君の正直さを表しているね。

## 現れる

彼、いつ現れると思う？

あの人、間もなく現れるわよ。

君が現れるのを待っていたよ。

人柄は顔に現れるものよ。

酒を飲むと本性が現れるのさ。

TRACK 016

Wash your hands with soap.

Will you help me wash the dishes?

Is this material washable?

It doesn't wash well. → wash well（よく洗濯が効く、簡単に洗える）

This color is fast when washed. → fast（変色しない、あせない）

TRACK 017

You should mend your ways. → mend one's ways = amend one's conduct; turn over a new leaf（改心する、行いを改める）

Why don't you acknowledge your mistake and correct it? → acknowledge = admit; accept; realize

How about changing our policy?

TRACK 018

Express your thoughts in words.

This shows your honesty. → shows = is the evidence of

TRACK 019

When do you think he will turn up?
→ turn up（「思いがけなく」現れる、姿を現す）

It will not be long before he turns up. / He will turn up soon.

We were waiting for you to show up. → show up = turn up

Your character comes through in your face. / Your personality is revealed in your face. → come through（「隠れていたものが」出てくる） → reveal（明らかにする、漏らす）

Liquor reveals one's true self.

昨日の夜、彼が夢に現れちゃった。

泣かないで。いつか素敵な人が現れるわよ。

その人物は第 7 章に現れると思う。

### 歩く

歩こう。

毎日歩いて学校へ行ってるよ。

学校からずっと歩くの？

そこまで歩くのって遠すぎない？

できるだけ歩くようにしているの。

タクシーなさそうだから、ホテルまで歩かない？

歩くほうがいいよ。

歩いて行こう。そんなに遠くないし。

そこまで歩いてどのくらいかかる？

歩いて 30 分ぐらいかな。

本を読みながら歩かないようにね。

### 荒れる

今日は荒れそうだ。

**He appeared in my dream last night.**
→ appear（出現する、姿を現す、現れる）

**Don't cry. Someday your prince will come.**
→ 女性への表現　⇒ your prince will come → the perfect woman for you might appear（君にピッタリの女性が現れるかも）

**I think the character appears in Chapter 7.**

TRACK 020

**Let's walk.**　⇒ walk → walk slowly（ゆっくり歩く）、walk fast（早く歩く）、walk aimlessly（ぶらぶら歩く）、walk heavily（重い足取りで歩く）、walk barefoot（裸足で歩く）、walk in the rain（雨の中を歩く）、walk with light steps（軽い足取りで歩く）、walk with tipsy steps（千鳥足で歩く）

**I walk to school every day. / I go to school on foot every day.**　⇒ walk to school → walk home（歩いて帰宅する）

**Do you walk all the way from school?**
⇒ from school → from the station（駅から）

**Isn't it too far to walk there?**
⇒ walk there → walk from there（そこから歩く）

**I'm making sure to walk as much as possible.**
→ make sure to~（必ず～する、確実に～する）

**Why don't we walk to the hotel since there doesn't seem to be any taxis?**

**I prefer walking.**　→ prefer（むしろ～を好む、～のほうがよい）

**Let's take a walk. It's not that far.**　→ take a walk = walk

**How long does it take to walk there?**

**It's about a thirty-minute-walk, I guess.**

**Don't walk while reading.**
⇒ while reading → while talking on a cell-phone（携帯電話で話しながら）

TRACK 021

**It looks like it's going to be rough today.**
→ rough（「海、天候などが」荒れた、激しい、荒い）

毎年、今頃は天気が荒れる。

何だか知らないけど肌が荒れちゃった。

ガーデニングで手が荒れちゃった。

化粧品で肌が荒れちゃったわ。

昨夜のパーティは荒れたよ。

君、昨夜は荒れたね。

## あわてる

あわてるな！

あわてる必要はないよ。まだ時間は十分あるんだから。

彼、どうしたんだ？あわてて飛び出していったけど。

僕はどんなときでも慌てないね。

# い

## 言う

本当のことを言いなさい。

全く君の言う通りだよ。

もう何も言うな。

もう言わない。

**We have stormy weather at this time every year.**
⇒ at this time every year → at this time of the year（一年の今頃は）

**I don't know why but my skin got chapped.**
→ get chapped（「皮膚が」荒れる） ⇒ my skin → my lips（私の唇）、my hands（私の手）

**My hands got rough from gardening.**

**I got a rash from my makeup.**
→ get a rash（発疹ができる、かぶれる、吹き出物が出る） → from my makeup = from using makeup

**The party last night was wild.** → was wild = got out of control

**You completely lost control last night, didn't you?**
→ lose control（抑えがきかなくなる）

TRACK 022

**Don't panic!** → panic（慌てる、うろたえる）

**There's no need to rush. We still have plenty of time.**
→ rush（急ぐ、突進する） → plenty of ~（たくさんの～、十分な～）

**What's the matter with him? He rushed out in a panic.**
→ in a panic（慌てふためいて、うろたえて）

**I remain unruffled on any occasion.**
→ remain unruffled（動じない、うろたえない、冷静を保つ）

TRACK 023

**Tell me the truth.** / Speak the truth.

**You're perfectly right.**

**Say no more.**

**I'll say no more.**

誰にも言うなよ。

彼がそう言うのは変だな。

何か言うことがあるかね？

回りくどいことを言うのはやめよう。

いつまでもブツブツ言うんじゃない。

冗談言うなよ。

生を言うんじゃないぜ。

よく言うよ。

言うだけやぼだよ。

君はそう言うと思った。

あなた昨日、寝言を言ってたわよ。

君は言うこととやることが違う。

彼はズケズケものを言う男だ。

君はうまいことを言うね。

## 生きる

自分らしく生きるべきだね。

私のモットーは精一杯生きること。

肩ひじ張って生きたって無駄だよ。

**Don't tell a soul.** / Don't tell anybody. ⇒ a soul → a lie（嘘）

**It's strange that he says so.**

**What is there to say?** / Do you have anything to say?

**Let's stop beating around the bush.**
→ beat around the bush（遠回しに言う）

**Don't keep complaining.** → complain = grumble

**Stop fooling!** / Cut out the fooling! / Talk sensibly, won't you!
→ cut out = stop

**None of your cheek!** → cheek（生意気、図々しさ）

**Don't make me laugh!**

**You would only waste your words.**

**I knew you would say that.** / I knew you were going to say that.

**You were talking in your sleep last night.**

**You say one thing but do another.** / You talk in one way but act in another.

**He says what's in his mind.** / He doesn't mince words.
→ what's in one's mind（頭の中で考えていること） → mince words（慎重に言葉を選ぶ、遠回しな言い方をする）

**You have a way with words, don't you!** / You are good with words. → have a way with words（言葉の使い方がうまい）

TRACK 024

**You should live life your own way.** / You should live life being you.

**My motto is to live as best I can.**
⇒ live as best I can → live in the present（今を生きる）、live freely（自由に生きる）

**It's no use playing tough.** → play tough（強がる）

私は今、全力で生きてるよ。

生きることは苦しむことかな？

つくづく生きるのが嫌になったね。

彼は過去の栄光に生きている人さ。

生きる勇気をくれて本当にありがとう。

100 歳まで生きるぞ。

この一語で文が生きてくると思う。

急ごう。

急げばバスに間に合う。

急いでるの？

急いで宿題を終わらせたよ。

急がないで。

そんなに急いでどこへ行くの？

急ぐことはない。

どうしてそんなに急ぐの？

答えを急ぐ必要はないですよ。

急ぐ必要なんてないよ。まだ時間はあるんだから。

**I'm now living with all my might now.**
→ with all one's might（全力で、精一杯）

**Is to live to suffer?**

**I've become utterly tired of life.** / I'm completely fed up with life. → be fed up with~（～にうんざりしている）

**He lives in the recollection of his past glories.**

**Thank you very much for giving me the courage to live.**

**I'm going to live to be one hundred years old.**
→ to be 100 years old= to the age of 100

**I think this word will make the sentence come to life.**
→ make something come to life=make something more real or exciting

TRACK 025

**Let's hurry.**
⇒ hurry → hurry back（急いで戻る）、hurry home（急いで帰宅する）

**If we hurry, we can catch the bus.**
⇒ catch the bus → overtake them（彼らに追いつく）

**Are you in a hurry?**

**I finished my homework in a hurry.**

**Don't hurry.** ⇒ hurry → hurry so much（そんなに急ぐ）

**Where are you going in such a hurry?**

**There's no rush.** / You don't have to hurry.

**Why are you in such a hurry?** / Why all the hurry? / What's the hurry? → hurry = rush

**There's no need to rush the answer.**
→ There's no need to = You don't have to

**You don't have to hurry. You still have time.**

それは急ぎません。

急ぐ必要はなかったのに。

急がせないで。

急がせちゃってごめん。

## 祈る

君の成功を祈る。

君の幸運を祈る。

あなたの幸せを祈ります。

（誕生日の祝辞）幾久しくご長寿を祈ります。

彼の冥福を祈る。

あなたの早い回復を祈っています。

明日雨が降らないことを祈る。

もう神に祈るしかない。

## 祝う

新年を祝おう。

おばあちゃんの還暦を祝いましょう。

彼女の 20 歳の誕生日をお祝いするために集まりましょう。

**There's no hurry about it.** / It's not urgent. / It can wait.

**You need not have hurried.**

**Don't hurry me.**

**I'm sorry I hurried you.**

TRACK 026

**I wish you success.** / May you succeed. / I pray for your success. / I hope that you will succeed.

**Good luck.** / Good luck to you. / I wish you good luck. / I wish you the best of luck.

**I pray for your happiness.** → pray for ~（～のために祈る）

**May I wish you many happy returns of the day.**

**I pray for his happiness in the next life.** / I pray for the repose of his soul. ⇒ pray for his happiness → pray for Japan（日本のために祈る）、 pray for miracles（奇跡を祈る）

**I wish you a speedy recovery.** / I'm praying for your speedy recovery. → speedy=quick

**I hope it won't rain tomorrow.**

**There is nothing left for me to do but pray to God.**

TRACK 027

**Let's celebrate the New Year.**
⇒ celebrate the New Year → celebrate Christmas（クリスマスを祝う）、celebrate Hallowe'en（ハロウィーンを祝う）、celebrate our wedding anniversary（私たちの結婚記念日を祝う）、celebrate the fiftieth anniversary（50周年記念を祝う）、celebrate your graduation（君の卒業を祝う）

**Let's celebrate our grandmother's sixtieth birthday.**
⇒ sixtieth birthday → longevity（長寿）

**Let's get together to celebrate her 20th birthday.**

彼の結婚を祝うために飲み会を開こうよ。

## 印刷する

印刷するものはありますか？

このページを 10 部印刷したいのですけど。

この USB の中にあるファイルを印刷したいんだけど。

添付したファイルを印刷してください。

A4 で 5 部印刷してください。

この文書をできるだけ早く印刷してくれる？

これをカラーで印刷してもらえます？

片面印刷をしていただきたいのですが。

これを両面印刷したいのですが。

この部分はイタリックで印刷したいんだ。

# う

## 植える

何を植えるの？

庭にバラを植えようと思ってるの。

色んな種類の花を植えたいんだ。

**Let's have a drinking party to celebrate his wedding.**
⇒ celebrate his wedding → celebrate his promotion（彼の昇進を祝う）、celebrate his passing the university entrance examination（彼の大学合格を祝う）、celebrate him on his success（彼の成功を祝う）

TRACK 028

**Do you have anything you need to print?**
⇒ anything you need to → anything you want to（〜したいもの）

**I want to print ten copies of this page.** / I want to print this page ten times.

**I want to print a document from my USB.** / Can I print a file from my USB?

**Please print the attached document.**

**Please print out five A4 sized copies.** / Please print this in A 4. Five copies, please.

**Can you print out this document as soon as possible?**

**Could you make a color copy of this?**

**I would like you to make single-sided copies.**

**I'd like to print this both sided.**

**I want to print this part in italics.**
⇒ print this part in italics → print this part in lowercase letters（この部分は小文字で印刷する）、print this part in boldface（この部分は太字体で印刷する）

TRACK 029

**What are you going to plant?**

**I'm thinking of planting roses in the garden.**
⇒ in the garden → in this pot（この鉢に）

**I want to plant various kinds of flowers.**

花の代わりに野菜を植えようかな。

ジャガイモを植えたところよ。

この種は最低 1 メートル離して植えなきゃいけないのよ。

## 飢える

世界では多くの人が飢えているのよ。

私はいま知識に飢えているのよね。

ここ 2 ～ 3 週間一人だったので、話し相手に飢えているのさ。

## 浮かぶ

空に浮かんでいるあの黒い雲を見て。

ある考えが心に浮かんだよ。

良い考えが一つも浮かんでこないよ。

私の心に浮かぶのは感謝の言葉だけです。

日本と聞いて思い浮かぶものは何ですか？

最初心に浮かんだ花はひまわりです。

朝目が覚めて最初に思い浮かぶのはあなたです。

## 受かる・受ける

君はきっと試験に受かるよ。

**Maybe I will plant vegetables instead of flowers.**

**I just planted seed potatoes.** ⇒ seed potatoes → tomatoes（トマト）、onions（玉ねぎ）、Welsh onions（ネギ）、carrots（人参）

**I have to sow the seeds at least one meter apart.**
→ sow（「種子を」撒く）

TRACK 030

**A lot of people are starving in the world.**

**I'm thirsty for knowledge.**

**I have been on my own for a couple weeks and am starving for conversation.** → be on one's own（独り立ちしている、単独でやっている） → starve for ~（～を切望する、～に飢えている）

TRACK 031

**Look at those black clouds floating in the sky.**

**An idea occurred to me.**
→ occurred to me = came to mind; flashed across my mind

**No good idea occurs to me.** / I cannot think of any bright ideas.

**All that comes to my mind is words of thanks.**
→ come to one's mind（思い浮かぶ、思いつく）

**What comes to mind when you hear "Japan"?**
→ come to mind（頭をよぎる）

**The first flower that came to mind is sunflower.**

**When I wake up in the morning, the first thing that comes to mind is you.** ⇒ you → your happy face（あなたの幸せそうな顔）

TRACK 032

**You'll pass the exam, believe me.** / I have no doubt that you will pass the exam.
→ believe me（本当に、確かに） → exam = examination

試験に受かるかどうかは君次第だな。

テストに受かるように一生懸命勉強しなさい。

そのテストに受かる自信はあるよ。

第一志望の学校に受かったよ。

試験に受かるのは簡単だったよ。

君が試験に受かったのは全然不思議じゃないよ。

今年は英語の授業を受けるつもり。

来週あの授業を受けるのを楽しみにしてるんだ。

あなた、週何回英語の授業を受けてる？

私、いま料理の講習を受けてるの。

健康診断はいつ受ける？

昨日、診察を受けてきたよ。

それちょ～受けるね。

君、ちょ～受けるよ。

僕のジョークは受けたよ。

あの映画は若者にすごく受けたよ。

そこで温かい歓迎を受けたよ。

**It's up to you whether you pass the examination or not.** ⇒ examination → entrance examination（入学試験）

**Study hard so that you can pass the test.**

**I have confidence in passing the test.**

**I got accepted to my first-choice school.**
→ got accepted = was accepted　→ first-choice school（第一志望校）

**It was easy for me to pass the exam.**

**It's no wonder that you passed the exam.**

**I'll take a course in English this year.** / I'll take an English class this year.　→ course は class より少し堅い言い方。

**I'm looking forward to taking that class next week.**

**How many times do you take English lessons a week?**

**I'm taking classes in cooking now.**

**When are you going to get a medical checkup?**
→ medical checkup = medical examination　⇒ a medical checkup → a gastroscope examination（胃カメラの検査）

**I received a medical examination yesterday.**
⇒ a medical examination → an X-ray examination（X 線検査）

**That's so funny!** / That cracks me up!
→ crack someone up（人を大爆笑させる）

**You crack me up!**

**My joke went over very well.**　→ go over（「話、公演などが」受ける、受け入れられる）→ しばしば well、badly などの様態の副詞を伴って使われる。反対に「スベった」は bombed や fell flat とする。

**That movie was a big hit with young people.**

**I received a warm welcome there.**
⇒ a warm welcome → a hearty welcome（心からの歓迎）、an icy welcome（よそよそしい歓迎）

私たちの町は地震で大きな被害を受けたんだ。

## 動かす

体を少し動かしたいな。

私たち老化を防ぐために体を動かすべきね。

あなたは指一本動かそうとしないんだから。

頭を前後に動かしてみてください。

このテーブル動かすのを手伝ってくれない？

この本箱を横に動かしてくれる？

この食器洗い機だけど、どうやって動かすの？

会議を木曜日に動かせませんか？

予定はもう動かせないよ。

この人形は自分で動くんだよ。

音楽にはたしかに私たちの心を動かす力があるね。

愛は世界を動かすってこと？

人の心を動かすのは真心だよ。

君は人の意見に動かされやすいよな。

君は人を動かすのがうまいね。

僕はどんな誘惑にも心動かされないね。

Our town was severely affected by the earthquake.

TRACK 033

I want to get some exercise.

We have to get some exercise to stave off senility.
→ stave off（食い止める、避ける） → senility （老年、老衰、ぼけ）

You wouldn't even lift a finger.
→ lift a finger（指を上げる、努力をする）→ 通例、否定文で使われる。

Please move your head back and forth.
⇒ back and forth → from side to side（左右に）、up and down（上下に）

Will you help me move this table?
⇒ table → chair（椅子）、desk（机）、 furniture （家具）

Can you move this bookcase aside?

How do you run this dishwasher? → run = operate

Could we move our meeting to Thursday?

We cannot change the schedule now. → change = alter

This toy doll moves on its own.
→ move on its own = move by itself（単独で動く）

Music certainly has the power to move our hearts.

Are you saying that love makes the world go round?

Sincerity is what moves people. → moves = touches

You are easily affected by other people's opinions.

You are good at influencing people.
→ influencing = motivating

I am proof against any temptation.
→ proof against ~（～に耐える、～に強い）

動かないで。

私の指示があるまで動かないで。

このエンジンは動きますか？

これはどうやって動くの？

この機械は電気で動くのですね。

この車椅子はモーターで動きます。

この車は太陽電池で動くのさ。

これは電池で動く時計だよ。

このエレベーターは動いてないですよ。

この装置はバネ仕掛けで動くのか？

彼は金の力で簡単に動くって噂だよ。

彼は決して金で動くような人じゃないよ。

## 歌う

歌うのは好き？

風呂でよく歌ってるよ。

いつもギターを弾きながら歌ってるんだ。

私、歌うのが得意なんだ。

どういった歌を歌うの？

TRACK 034

**Don't move.** / Stay put. / Keep still. / Freeze.

**Make no move till you hear from me.**
→ make no more = do nothing

**Does this engine work?** / Is this engine functional?

**How does this thing work?**

**This machine runs by electricity, right?** → run by electricity = run on electricity ⇒ runs by electricity → runs on a fuel cell（燃料電池で動く）

**This wheelchair is propelled by a motor.**
→ propel（駆り立てる、推進する、進ませる）

**This car is powered by solar batteries.**

**This is a battery-operated clock.** / This is a clock powered by a battery.

**This elevator is not working.**

**Does this device work by a spring?**

**Rumor has it that he is influenced easily by the power of money.** → Rumor has it that~（～という噂である）

**He can never be bought.**
→ be bought（金で買われる、金の力になびく）

TRACK 035

**Do you like singing?**

**I often sing in the bathtub.** ⇒ in the bathtub → at home（家で）

**I always sing while playing the guitar.**

**I am good at singing.**
⇒ am good at ~ → am bad at ~（～が苦手だ、～が下手である）

**What kind of songs do you sing?**

あなたが歌うのを聞いたことないんだけど。

歌を聞くより歌うほうが好きだな。

カラオケで歌おうよ。

あなたの歌う番だよ。

歌うのがすごく上手いわね。

あなたは歌うために生まれてきたみたいね。

人前で歌うのは苦手だな。

次は何を歌うの？

## 疑う

どうして私を疑うの？

私の言ったことを疑うの？

それが本当かどうか疑ってるのさ。

僕は自分の目を疑ったね。

彼女の常識を疑いたくなるよ。

彼女の能力を疑わざるを得ないね。

君は夫が浮気をしていると疑っているわけだ。

それについて疑う余地はないけど。

あなたの私に対する愛を一度も疑ったことなんてないわよ。

I never heard you sing.

I prefer singing songs to listening to them. / I like singing songs more than listening to them.

Let's sing at karaoke.

It's your turn to sing.

You are very good at singing. / How well you sing!

It seems like you were born to sing.

I don't like to sing in public.

What are you going to sing next?

TRACK 036

Why do you suspect me? → suspect =doubt → suspect は疑わしい点があることから「疑いを抱く」という意味。一方 doubt ははっきりした証拠がないため、「～ではないかなと疑いを抱く」こと。

Do you doubt what I said?

I doubt whether it is true or not.

I could not believe my eyes. ⇒ my eyes → my ears（自分の耳）

I'm inclined to doubt her common sense.
→ be inclined to~（～する傾向がある、～したい気がする）

I can't help being doubtful of her ability. → can't help ~ing（～せざるを得ない）→ doubtful = skeptical ⇒ ability → humanity（人間性）

You suspect that your husband is cheating on you.
→ cheat on~（～を裏切る、～を裏切って浮気をする）

There is no room for doubt about it.

I have never questioned your love for me.

## 打つ

僕は 3 番を打っているんだ。

この前の試合で 3 塁打を 2 本打ったよ。

痛み止めの注射を打った。

今年、インフルエンザの注射を打つの？

彼女の歌に胸を打たれた。

この関係に終止符を打ちたいんだけど。

あなた、何度も寝返りを打ってたわよ。

残念だが我々にはもう打つ手がない。

## 奪う・奪われる

その地震は数百人もの命を奪った。

誰も私たちの権利を奪うことはできないよ。

あの娘、私のボーイフレンドを奪ったのよ。

ロボットが人間の仕事を奪うと思う？

財布を奪われちゃった。

彼に心を奪われちゃった。

公園のかわいらしい花に目を奪われた。

TRACK 037

**I bat third.**

**I hit two three-base hits in the last game.**
⇒ three-base hit → a single hit（一塁打）、a two-base hit（2塁打）、a foul ball（ファウルボール）、a pop-fly（ポップフライ）、a groundball（ゴロ）、a homerun（ホームラン）、a grand slam（満塁ホームラン）

**I got a shot for a painkiller.** → painkiller（鎮痛剤）

**Are you going to get vaccinated for the flu this year?**
→ get vaccinated（予防接種を受ける）

**Her song moved me to the core. / Her song touched my soul.** → to the core（芯まで、心底まで）

**I want to bring an end to this relationship.**
→ bring an end to~（～に終止符をうつ、～を終わらせる）

**You turned over many times in your sleep.**

**Unfortunately, we've no options left.**
→ have no options left（選択肢が残されていない、他に方法がない）

TRACK 038

**The earthquake took hundreds of lives.**

**No one can deprive us of our human rights.**
→ deprive A of B（AからBを奪う）→ human rights（人権）

**That girl stole my boyfriend.** ⇒ boyfriend → idea（アイディア）

**Do you think robots will steal human jobs?**
→ steal = take; take over

**I was robbed of my purse.** → be robbed of~（～を盗まれる） → purse（「口金付きの」財布、がま口） → wallet （札入れ）

**I was fascinated by him. / He stole my heart.**

**I got captivated by the lovely flowers in the park.**
→ captivate（魅了する、心を奪う）

## 生まれる

どこで生まれたの？

東京で生まれ育ったの。

ここが私が生まれた町よ。

彼女に赤ちゃんが生まれるよ。

彼女の赤ちゃんは４月に生まれる予定だって。

あなたの子はいつ生まれるの？

昨日、私たちの赤ちゃんが生まれました。

彼女は金持ちに生まれたって言ってたわ。

## 生む

彼女はいつ赤ちゃんを生むのだろう？

彼女は昨日、女の子を生んだよ。

この鶏はもう卵を産まなくなっちゃった。

彼は日本が生んだ最も偉大な科学者だ。

これはきっと付加価値を生むだろう。

## 埋める

これを土の中に埋めよう。

空欄を埋めなさい。

この余白を挿絵で埋めるってのはどう？

TRACK 039

Where were you born?

I was born and raised in Tokyo.

This is the town where I was born.

She is going to have a baby.

She says her baby is due in April.
→ be due = be expected to be born

When will your child be born?

Our baby was born yesterday.

She said she was born rich. / She said she was born of rich parents. ⇒ was born rich → was born poor（貧乏に生まれた）

TRACK 040

When will she have a baby? → have a baby = give birth to a baby
→ 彼女が妊娠している場合には the baby とする。

She had a baby girl yesterday.
⇒ a baby girl → a baby boy （男の子）、twins（双子）、triplets（三つ子）

This hen has stopped laying eggs.

He is the greatest scientist Japan has ever produced.

I'm sure this will produce added value.
⇒ added value → a profit（利益）

TRACK 041

Let's bury this in the ground. ⇒ bury this → bury this shallowly（これを浅く埋める）、bury this deep（これを深く埋める）

Fill in the blanks.

How about filling up the blank space with an illustration? → How about ～（～はどうですか、～はいかが）

熱狂した観客がスタンドを埋めた。

赤字を埋めるためにこれらを売らなきゃいけないな。

私はここに骨を埋めるつもりだ。

まず初めに外堀を埋める必要があるね。

## 占う

これから占い師に占ってもらうんだ。

占い師に運勢を占ってもらったの。

おみくじで運勢を占ってみない？

手相で君の運勢を占おうか？

## 恨む

あなたは私を恨んでるの？

あなたに恨まれるようなことは何もしていないけど。

恨んでないよ。

心配しないで。恨んだりしてないから。

## 売る

車を売りたいんだ。

新しい携帯買うために、これ売りたいんだけど。

**The stands were filled with enthusiastic fans.**
→ filled = packed　→ enthusiastic（熱心な、熱狂的な）

**We have to sell these to make up the deficit.**
→ make up（「損失、不足の」埋め合わせをする）　→ deficit（赤字、欠損）

**I wish to be buried here.**

**Firstly, you need to lay the groundwork.**
→ lay the groundwork（根回しをする、外堀を埋める）

TRACK 042

**I'm going to get my fortune told by a fortune teller.**
→ fortune（運勢、財産）

**I had my fortune told by a fortune teller. / I got a fortune teller to tell my fortune for me.**　⇒ by a fortune teller → with cards（トランプで）

**How about drawing a fortune slip to read our fortune?**　→ draw a fortune slip（おみくじを引く）

**Shall I predict your fortune by palm reading?**
→ predict（予知する、占う）→ palm reading（手相）

TRACK 043

**You have a grudge against me, don't you?**
→ have a grudge against~（～に恨みを抱く）

**I don't think I have done anything to incur your resentment.**
→ incur（「好ましくないことを」招く）→ resentment（恨み、憤り）

**I don't resent you.**　→ resent（腹を立てる、憤る）

**Don't worry. I have no hard feelings.**
→ have no hard feelings（悪気はない、悪く思わない、恨みはない）

TRACK 044

**I want to sell my car.**

**I want to sell this to buy a new phone.**

この品は値段の割にはよく売れるね。

あの店では何を売ってる？

あの店では野菜を安く売ってるよ。

それ、幾らで売る？

これ、値段を安くして売るよ。

この本を君に 300 円で売るよ。

彼はいつも上司に媚びを売っている。

油を売ってないでしっかり働きたまえ。

## え

### 描く

友情を描いた小説を読むのが大好きなんだ。

この小説は男子高校生の日常を生き生きと描いているのさ。

これは一人の少女の成長を描いた映画なの。

この映画の日本の描き方はおかしいよ。

**This article sells well for its price.** → article（品物、物品、品目）

**What do they sell at that store?**

**They sell vegetables cheaply at that store.**
⇒ vegetables → utility goods（実用品）、thrifted clothes（古着）

**How much would you sell that for?**

**I'll sell this at a discount.** → sell this at a discount = sell this at a reduced price; sell this cheap ⇒ sell this at a discount → sell this at a cost「原価で売る」、sell this below cost「原価以下で売る」、sell this for cash「現金で売る」、sell this at half price「半値で売る」、sell this at wholesale price「卸値で売る」、sell this at a loss「損して売る」

**I'll sell this book to you for three hundred yen.**

**He always butters up the boss.**
→ butter up（「気に入られようとして」ご機嫌をとる、お世辞を言う）

**Stop loafing around and work hard.**
→ loaf around（ブラブラする、ゴロゴロする）

TRACK 045

**I love to read novels portraying friendship.**
→ portray =depict; describe; illustrate

**This novel vividly portrays daily life of a high school boy.** → vividly =movingly; dramatically; eloquently

**This movie tells a story of a young girl growing up.**
**/ This is a movie about a young girl growing up.**
→ grow up（成長する、成人する、大人になる）

**The depictions of Japan in this movie are inaccurate.**
**/ Japan is not depicted accurately in this movie.**
→ depiction = portrayal → inaccurate = not correct, or not exact; wrong → depicted = portrayed → not depicted accurately = depicted inaccurately

## 選ぶ

あなたは誰を選ぶ？

僕は多分彼女を選ぶだろう。

このカタログの中から一つ選んで。

A と B のどちらを選びます？

どちらでも選ぶことができるよ。

A と B なら、A を選ぶわね。

B より A を選ぶわ。

好みのものを選べば。

この中から選ぶわけね？

4 つの中から一つ選べるよ。

いくつでも選んでいいよ。

選べない。あなたにまかせる。

これを選ぶべきだと思うけどな。

私だったら量より質を選ぶけどね。

どれを選んだ？

いいものを選んだね。

友人を選ぶときは気をつけることね。

TRACK 046

**Who will you choose?** ⇒ choose → choose for the new student council president（新しい生徒会長「に誰を」選ぶ）⇒ who → Which（どれを）、What（何を）

**I will probably choose her.**
⇒ her → this（これを）、the latter（後者を）

**Choose one item from this catalog.** → Choose → You may choose；You can choose；Please choose → item（項目、品目）

**Which one do you choose, A or B?**

**You can choose either one.**

**Between A and B, I'd choose A.**

**I choose A over B.** → over~（～を超えて、～よりも）

**You can choose your favorite one.** / Take your choice. / Pick whatever you want. → pick = choose; select

**Do I have a choice among these?**

**You can choose one out of the four.**

**You can pick as many as you like.**

**I can't choose. I'll leave it to you.**

**I think you should choose this.**

**If I were you, I would choose quality over quantity.**

**Which one did you choose?**

**You made a good choice.** /You made the right choice.

**You should be careful in choosing your friends.**

夫を選ぶ際にはどんなに気をつけても気をつけすぎるってことはないわよ。

容姿だけで夫を選ぶのは賢明じゃないわね。

彼女は一万人の応募者の中から選ばれたんだ。

君に選ぶ権利はない。

### 得る

やっと教員の職を得ることができたよ。

この部屋に入るためには許可を得る必要があるよ。

彼の賛成を得るためにはどうしたらいいかな？

この話からどんな教訓を得ることができました？

僕はその辛い経験から教訓を得たよ。

この本を読んで大いに得るところがあったね。

彼の話は何も得るところがない。

## お

### 追いかける

夢を追いかけて！

夢を必死で追いかけて実現させなさい。

もう彼女を追いかけるのはやめたほうがいい。

**You can't be too careful in choosing your husband.**
→ can't be too careful in~（～においていくら用心してもしすぎることはない）

**It's not wise to choose a husband merely for his looks.**
→ merely=only; solely; just

**She was selected out of ten thousand applicants.**
→ applicant（応募者、出願者、候補者）→ select（選抜する） → choose より少し硬い表現

**You have no right to choose.**
→ have no right = do not have the right

TRACK 047

**I finally got a post as a teacher.**
→ got a post as a teacher = got a teaching job; found a job in teaching

**You need to gain permission to enter this room.**

**What should we do to secure his approval?**
→ secure = receive; get; obtain; acquire; gain

**What lesson did you learn from this story?**

**I learned a lesson from the bitter experience.**
→ bitter = hard; painful; heart-breaking

**I could learn a great deal from this book.**
→ a great deal（かなりの量、相当量、ずいぶん）

**There's nothing to be learned from his stories.**
→ his stories = the things he says

TRACK 048

**Chase your dream!**

**Chase your dreams and make them come true.**

**You had better stop chasing her anymore.**

私は追うより追いかけられるタイプかな。

私、追いかけられる立場になりたいな。

## 追い越す

あの車を追い越そうよ。

スマートフォンの売り上げがパソコンの売り上げを追い越したんだって。

## 追いつく

先に行って。すぐ追いつくから。

クラスのみんなに追いつくのは簡単じゃない。

やっとライバルに追いつくことができたよ。

日本は１分を残して同点に追いついた。

## 追う

(諺) 二兎を追うものは一兎も得ず。

それ順を追って説明して。

あの娘はいつも最新の流行を追ってるよ。

両親は私が夢を追うのを励ましてくれてるの。

いま学校の予習に追われているんだ。

いま仕事に追われているんだ。

ごめん。時間に追われているんだ。

**I'm more of a catcher than a chaser.**
→ more of A than B（B というより A）

**I want to be the one being chased.**

**TRACK 049**

**Let's overtake that car.**
→ overtake（追い越す、追いつく）= pass; go by; catch up with

**They say smartphone sales surpassed PC sales.**
→ surpass = excel; exceed; go beyond

**TRACK 050**

**Go ahead. I'll catch up with you soon.**
→ go ahead（先へ進む、お先にどうぞ）→ catch up with ～（～に追いつく）

**It's not easy for me to catch up with my classmates.**

**I finally could catch up with my rival.**

**Japan tied the game with one minute remaining.**
→ tie the game（同点にする）

**TRACK 051**

**He who runs after two hares will chase neither.**
→ hare（野ウサギ） → chase（追う）

**Explain them in order.** → in order（順番に）

**She is always following the latest fashion.**
→ following = following after

**My parents are encouraging me to follow my dream.**

**I'm busy with preparations for school.**

**I'm swamped with work now.** → swamped = pressed; busy

**Sorry. I'm pressed for time.**
→ be pressed for~（～が足りなくて困る）

日を追って暖かくなってきたね。

彼女は日を追うごとに美しくなるね。

## 終える

それ、なるべく早く終えてちょうだい。

夕食前に宿題を終えるようにしてね。

あと 30 分ほどで宿題を終えるよ。

それを時間通りに終えるように頑張っています。

期限内に終えるようできる限り頑張ってみるね。

簡単な課題を先に終えてしまおうよ。

今日は何時に仕事を終えるの？

5 時に仕事を終えるよ。

この仕事を明日までに終えるなんて無理よ。

その仕事を終えるのにまだ十分時間があるわよ。

今日その仕事を終える必要はないよ。

その本読み終えた？

この小説を読み終えるのにまる一日かかっちゃった。

これで討論を終えよう。

**It's getting warmer day by day.**
→ day by day（日ごとに、一日一日と）

**She gets beautiful as the days go by, doesn't she?**
→ as the days go by（日を経るに従って）

TRACK 052

**Finish that as quickly as possible.**

**See that you finish your homework before supper.**
→ see that~（～するよう取り計らう、～するよう気をつける）

**I'm going to finish my homework in about thirty minutes.**

**I'm breaking my neck to finish that on time.**
→ break one's neck =work hard　→ on time=punctually; according to schedule; when you should

**I'll try to finish that in time as best I can.**
→ in time（時間内に、間に合って）

**Let's get the easy task done first.**

**What time do you finish today's work?**

**I'll finish work at 5 o'clock.**
⇒ at 5 o'clock → by 5 o'clock（5 時までに）、 as soon as possible（できるだけ早く）

**It's not possible to finish this work by tomorrow.**
⇒ by tomorrow → in such a short time（そんな短い時間内に）

**There is still enough time for you to finish that work.**

**It's not necessary for you to finish that job today.**

**Did you finish reading that book?**

**It took me a whole day to finish reading this novel.**
⇒ a whole day → a whole afternoon（午後ずっと）、five hours（5 時間）

**Let's wrap up the discussion.**
→ wrap up = put an end to; end; stop; finish

試験を終えるのに時間が足りなかった。

彼女は僕が話し終える前に電話を切っちゃった。

コーヒーを飲み終えるまで待って。

ヒロインの死でその物語は終わるわけね？

お互いの将来のためにこの関係を終わらせましょう。

“-ly” で終わる副詞は多いね。

予定より早く宿題を終えることができてよかった。

あなたのおかげで仕事を早く終えることができてよかった。

彼は先月 90 歳で生涯を終えた。

## 起きる

何時に起きるつもり？

起きる時間よ！

いつも何時に起きるの？

私、毎朝、早く起きるの。

早く起きるのは慣れているんだ。

早く起きるのは苦手だな。

6 時に起きるべきだった。

日本では地震がよく起きる。

**I didn't have enough time to complete the exam.**
→ complete = finish

**She hung up before I finished.**

**Wait till I have finished my coffee.**

**The heroine's death terminates the story, right?**
→ terminate =end; stop; finish; put an end to

**Let's end our relationship for both of our futures.**

**Many adverbs terminate in "-ly".**

**I'm glad that I could finish my homework sooner than I expected.**

**Thanks to you, I was able to finish my work quickly.**
⇒ quickly → on schedule（予定通りに）、on time（時間通りに）、by noon（正午までに）、safely（安全に）、without mishap（無事に）

**He died last month at the age of ninety.**

TRACK 053

**What time will you get up?** → get up（起床する）

**Time to get up!** / It's about time you get up!

**What time do you usually get up?**

**I get up early every morning.** ⇒ early → before 7（７時前に）
⇒ every morning → in the morning（朝に）

**I'm accustomed to getting up early.** → be accustomed to~（~に慣れている、~が習慣になっている）= be used to~ → こちらは少しくだけた表現。

**I have trouble waking up early.**
→ have trouble = have a hard time → wake up（目を覚ます）

**I should have got up at 6 o'clock.**
→ should have ＋過去分詞（～すべきだったのにしなかった）→ 後悔の念を表す。

**Earthquakes often happen in Japan.** → happen = occur

大きな地震が起きるかもよ。

100 年に一度起こるといわれているよ。

最近は色んなことが起きているね。

明日は何が起こるか誰にもわからないさ。

何か悪いことが起こる気がするな。

事故は起きるもの。

交通事故はよく不注意から起こるんだ。

言うまでもなく文化的偏見は無知から起こるものさ。

この病気は偶発的に起きるんだよ。

## 置く

鉛筆を置きなさい。

これはどこに置こうか？

そこに置いておいて。

これ、ここに置くよ。

それはテーブルの上に置かないで。

それは所定の場所に置いて。

その本は元の棚に置きなさい。

その皿はそこに重ねて置いてね。

荷物は下に置いて。

A big earthquake might occur. ⇒ big → strong（強い）

They say that it occurs once every one hundred years.
⇒ every one hundred years → every week（毎週）、every two weeks（2週間ごとに）

A lot of things are happening lately.

Nobody knows what may happen tomorrow.

I get a feeling of something evil to come.

Accidents will happen.

Traffic accidents often arise from carelessness.
→ arise = occur

Needless to say, cultural prejudices come from ignorance. → needless to say=of course; obviously

This disease occurs episodically.
→ episodically（偶発的に）=accidentally; occasionally

TRACK 054

Put down your pencils. / Stop writing. ⇒ pencils → chopsticks（箸）

Where shall I put this?

Leave it there.

I'll put this here.

Don't put it on the table. ⇒ on the table → at the center of the table（テーブルの中央に）、at the edge of the table（テーブルの端に）

Put it in place.

Put the book back on the shelf where it belongs.
→ it belongs = you found it

Stack up those plates there. → stack up（積み重ねる）

Put your baggage down.

通路に物を置かないで。

スマートフォンを枕元に置いて寝るわけ？

わたし、しばらく彼と距離を置くつもりなの。

私たち、お互いに距離を置くことにしたわ。

君は外見に重点を置きすぎだよ。

## 起こす

明日の朝は何時に起こして欲しいの？

朝７時に起こして。

今朝、地震で起こされたよ。

あわや事故を起こすとこだった。

行動を起こす時だ。

口で言うのは簡単だが、実際に行動を起こすのは大変だよ。

余計なもめ事を起こすんじゃないよ。

彼女には気をつけろ。よくヒステリーを起こすから。

あいつ、また気まぐれを起こしてる。

## 惜しむ

労を惜しんではいけない。

寸暇を惜しんで勉強しなさい。

Don't put your things in the passage.

Do you sleep with a smart phone beside the pillow?

I'm going to keep my distance from him for a while.
→ keep my distance=stay away → for a while=for a short time

We both decided to place some distance between us.

You place too much emphasis on external appearances. → external =outer; outside; visible

TRACK 055

What time do you want me to wake you up tomorrow morning?

Wake me up at seven. ⇒ at seven → like always（いつものように）

I was awoken by the earthquake this morning. / The earthquake woke me up this morning.

I almost caused an accident.

It's time to take action. → take action = make a move

It's easy to say, but hard to actually take action.

Don't rock the boat. → rock the boat=cause trouble; cause problems

Watch out for her. She often goes into hysterics. → go into hysterics = fall into hysterics; has hysterics → lose her temper（癇癪を起す）

He is being whimsical again.
→ whimsical（気まぐれな、移り気な）

TRACK 056

Spare no pains. → spare no pains =make every effort → spare は労力、費用などを惜しむ、けちるの意で、通例、「惜しまない」のように否定文で使われる。

Devote every minute to your study.
→ devote A to B（A を B に捧げる、充てる）

夢を叶えるためだったら努力はおしまないよ。

君ってお金を惜しまないね。

欲しいものにはお金を惜しまないのさ。

この企画を成功させるための経費は惜しまない。

## 押す

押さないで。

後ろから押すのはやめて。

そんなに押さないでくれる。

私は押してないよ。

最初にこのスタートボタンを押して。

このボタンを押すと機械は動き出すよ。

横断歩道のボタンを押してもらえる？

まずい。間違ったボタンを押してしまった。

ここを押すと痛い？

## 落ちる

この絵が棚から落ちたよ。

花瓶が手から落ちちゃった。

私の名前が落ちてるじゃない。

**I'll spare no effort to make my dreams come true.**
→ I'll spare no effort = I don't spare any effort

**You don't spare money.** / You are generous with your money.

**I don't mind spending money on things I want.**

**I'll spare no expense to make this project a success.**

TRACK 057

**Don't push me.** / Don't push against me. / Don't jostle me.
→ jostle =shove; push; thrust

**Stop pushing me from behind.**

**I wish you wouldn't squeeze me so.**
→ squeeze（押し込む、強く押す）

**I'm not jostling.**

**First press this start button.**
⇒ this start button → the Enter key（エンターキー）、the mouse button（マウスボタン）、Ctrl-Space（スペースキー）

**If you press this button, the machine will start.** / The machine works at the push of this button.
⇒ the machine will start → the door will open（ドアが開く）

**Can you press the button for the pedestrian crossing for me?** → pedestrian crossing（横断歩道）

**Oh no. I pressed the wrong button.**

**Does it hurt when I press here?**

TRACK 058

**This picture fell off the shelf.** → fell off = fell from

**The vase fell from my hand.** → fell = dropped

**My name is missing.** → missing = left out

庭の木に雷が落ちたんだ。

試験に落ちちゃった。

運転免許試験に落ちたのか？

成績が落ちちゃった。

彼女の人気も落ちたね。

このカメラはあれより品質が落ちるよ。

彼の仕事の質も落ちたね。

一目で恋に落ちたんだ。

## 脅かす

脅かさないでよ。

脅かすつもりはないが、10 万円かかるよ。

コロナウイルスは世界経済を脅かす最悪の伝染病だね。

大気汚染は私たちの生存を脅かすものだ。

喫煙が健康を脅かすということに誰もが賛成するよ。

それは子供たちの安全を脅かすものだ。

## 落とす

財布を落としちゃった。

**Lightning hit the tree in the garden.** → hit = struck

**I failed the exam.** / I did not pass the exam.
→ exam = examination

**Did you fail the driving test?**

**My grades went down.**

**Her popularity declined.** → decline= diminish; reduce; decrease

**This camera is inferior to that one.**
→ be inferior to~（～に劣っている、～に及ばない）

**The quality of his work has fallen off.**

**I fell in love at first sight.**
→ at first sight = on sight; immediately

TRACK 059

**Don't scare me!** / Don't scare me like that! / Don't scare the shit out of me!

**I don't mean to scare you, but it will cost you one hundred thousand yen.**

**Coronavirus is the worst epidemic that threatens the global economy.** → threaten=scare; endanger; jeopardize

**Air pollution is a threat to our survival.**
⇒ Air pollution is → Nuclear weapons are（核兵器は）

**We all agree that smoking is a health hazard.**
→ health hazard（健康被害、健康を害するもの） ⇒ smoking → drinking alcohol（飲酒）

**It's a menace to the children's safety.**
⇒ children's safety → peace and order in society（社会の平和と秩序）

TRACK 060

**I lost my purse.** → lost（なくした）
⇒ purse → purse somewhere around here（どこかこの辺りで）

箸を落としました。新しいのをもらえますか？

何か落としましたよ。

コンタクトレンズを落としたの？

皿を落とさないで。

もう少しでこの皿を落とすとこだった。

これを床に落としたのはだれ？

手を洗って汚れを落としなさい。

このシミがどうしても落ちないんだけど。

Tシャツ洗ったら、赤い文字が落ちちゃった。

この色はなかなか落ちない。

寝る前にメイクは落としてる？

肌呼吸させるためにメイクは落としたほうがいいよ。

体重を落としたいな。

体重を落とすために朝食を抜き始めたの。

余分な体重を落とすためにジョギングをすることにしたわ。

体重を落としたいなら、間食を減らすべきね。

速度を落として！

**I dropped my chopsticks. Could you give me new ones?**

**You dropped something.**
⇒ something → a handkerchief (ハンカチ)、some coins (小銭)、this (これを)

**Did you drop your contact lenses?**

**Don't drop the dish.** → dish は料理を盛りつけてテーブルに置く皿ののこと。この語が「料理」の意を表すのはそのため。

**I almost dropped this plate.**
→ plate は食べ物が載っていない皿、料理をとるための取り皿。

**Who dropped this on the floor?**

**Wash your hands clean of dirt.** / **Wash the dirt off your hands.**

**This stain won't wash off.** → wash off = come off; come out

**The red letters in my T-shirt ran when I washed it.**
→ run (「衣類などの染料が」落ちる、脱落する)

**This color won't fade.**
→ fade (「色、光などが」次第に薄れていく、消えていく)

**Do you take off your makeup before going to bed?**

**I think you should take off your makeup to let your skin breathe.** → breathe (呼吸する、息をする)

**I want to lose weight.**

**I have started skipping breakfast with a view to losing weight.** → with a view to ~ing (～する目的で)

**I decided to jog to get rid of my excess weight.**
→ get rid of = remove; eliminate; lose → excess weight (過剰体重)

**If you want to lose weight, you should cut down on between-meal snacks.**
→ cut down on ~ (～を減らす) → between-meal snacks (間食)

**Drop your speed!** / **Slack off speed!** / **Slow down!**

これ、会社の伝票で落とせますか？

これは会社の経費で落ちますよね？

テレビの音を落としてくれる？

声を落としていただけますか？

一語読み落としたよ。

この報告書で重要な項目を書き落としてるよ。

60 点未満の人は落とします。

英語の科目を落としちゃった。

木々がすっかり葉を落としているね。

君は例の件ですっかり信用を落としちゃったね。

いま体調を落としているんだ。

## 踊る

踊ろう。

踊りましょうか。

どんな音楽で踊ってみたい？

どんなダンスを踊ります？

わたしダンスを習い始めたの。

**Can I pay this with a company chit?**
→ chit（伝票、飲食物の伝票）

**I can put this on the expense account, can't I?**
→ put this on the expense account（これを経費勘定に入れる）

**Can you turn down the volume of the television?**
→ turn down the volume of the television = turn down the television

**Could you lower your voice, please?**

**You skipped a word.**

**You left out an important item in your report.**

**Those who get under 60 will not pass.** → not pass = fail

**I failed my English class.**

**The leaves have all fallen from the trees.**

**You've completely lost your credibility as a result of that affair.** → affair（事件、出来事） ⇒ lose your credibility → lose your good reputation（評判を落とす）

**I'm in poor health now.** / I'm not in good condition now. / I lost my health. → スポーツ選手の場合は I'm not my best. とする。

TRACK 061

**Let's dance.** ⇒ dance → dance to the music（音楽に合わせて踊る）、dance to the music of the piano（ピアノ伴奏で踊る）、dance in a ring（輪になって踊る）、dance the waltz（ワルツを踊る）、dance the jitterbug（ジルバを踊る）、dance cheek to cheek（チークダンスを踊る）

**Shall we dance?** / Do you want to dance?
⇒ Shall we → Why don't we ～（～しませんか）

**What music do you want to try dancing to?**

**What kind of dance do you do?**
⇒ do you do → are you learning now（今習ってる）

**I've started to learn how to dance.**
→ started to learn how to dance = started taking dance lessons

踊るのは久しぶりよ。

## 衰える

近頃、体力が衰えていくのを感じるんだ。

気力も衰えちゃったよ。

歳をとるにつれて記憶力も徐々に衰えちゃうね。

しばらく体を鍛えてないから、筋力が衰えてしまった。

英語力が衰えてきてるんだ。

## 驚かす

誕生日プレゼントで彼女を驚かそうよ。

驚かさないで！

驚いた。

あなたにはいつも驚かされるわ。

驚かせてごめん。

別に驚かそうとしたわけじゃないのよ。

## 覚えている

私のこと、覚えてる？

君に最初に会った日のことを昨日のことのように覚えてるよ。

君と一緒にここへ来たことをまだ覚えてるよ。

**This is the first time for me to dance in a while.**
→ first ~ in a while（久しぶりの～）

TRACK 062

**These days I feel my strength declining.**
→ I feel my strength declining = I feel I'm getting weaker

**I have lost my vigor, too.** → lose one's vigor（気が衰える）

**As we grow older, our memory becomes weaker.**

**I haven't trained for a while so I've lost my muscle.**

**My English is getting rusty.** / My English is starting to slip away. → rusty（さび付いた、なまった）→ slip away（逃げる、徐々になくなる、低下する）

TRACK 063

**Let's surprise her with a birthday present.**

**Don't surprise me like that!** / Don't scare me!

**You surprised me!** / I was surprised! You scared me! / You shocked me! / You frightened me! / You frightened the life out of me! / You gave me a fright!

**You always surprise me.**

**Sorry that I scared you.** / Sorry I startled you.

**I didn't mean to surprise you.**
→ mean to = intend to → surprise = startle

TRACK 064

**Do you remember me?**

**I remember the first day I met you like it was yesterday.**

**I still remember coming here with you.**

そのとき何があったか覚えてる？

## 覚える

もっと英単語を覚えるようにしましょう。

新しい単語を覚えるのは大変。

一日に英単語 10 個覚えることにしてるんだ。

難しい英語のスペルを覚えるのは苦手です。

この表現は覚える価値があるよ。

覚えることがたくさんあるわぁ。

明日のテストのためにこのページを覚えなきゃいけないんだ。

リンカーンの演説を覚えた？

それ覚えたよ。

英語の歌を覚えている最中なの。

私、YouTube で歌を覚えるんだ。

それって覚えにくいよね。

物事を覚えるのに繰り返しが役に立つよ。

車の運転を覚えるのにしばらく時間がかかったよ。

これだけは覚えていて。

皆さんに覚えておいてほしいことが 5 つあります。

Do you remember what happened then?

TRACK 065

Try to memorize more English words.

It's difficult to memorize new vocabulary. → memorize = remember ⇒ difficult = not easy

I make it a rule to memorize ten English words a day.
→ make it a rule to~（～するのを習慣にしている、いつも～することにしている）=always try to ~

I'm bad at memorizing difficult English spellings. / I'm weak on difficult English spellings. ⇒ English spellings → new vocabulary（新しい単語）、idiomatic phrases（熟語）、people's names（人の名前）

This expression is worth memorizing.

I have so many things to learn.

I've got to memorize this page for tomorrow's test.

Did you memorize Lincoln's speech?

I remembered it.

I'm now memorizing English songs.

I learn songs on YouTube.

That's not easy to remember. / That's not an easy one to remember. ⇒ not easy → easy（「覚え」やすい）

Repetition helps you remember something.

It took me some time to learn how to drive a car.

Be sure to keep this in mind. / Never forget this.
→ be sure to~（必ず～するように）

There are five things that you have to bear in mind.

仕事のために多くのことを覚えなくっちゃ。

## 思い出す

いま思い出した。

何を思い出したの？

今でもそれを思い出すわ。

いつも彼女を思い出すんだ。

彼女が何て言ったか思い出せない。

彼女の言ったことを思い出すと吹き出しそうになるよ。

彼の顔は覚えているけど、名前が思い出せないんだ。

もしかして彼の名前を思い出せないんじゃない？

この写真を見ると楽しかった昔を思い出すなぁ。

## 思う

君、どう思う？

かっこいいと思うな。

私もそう思う。

そうは思わないけど。

どうしてそう思う？

私、痩せすぎだと思う？

I have to memorize a lot of things for work.

TRACK 066

I just remembered.

What did you remember?

I still remember that now. ⇒ that now → his name（彼の名前）

I always remember her.
⇒ her → him（彼を）、her smile（彼女の笑顔）

I can't recollect what she said. → recollect = remember; recall

Remembering what she said makes me want to laugh.

I can remember his face, but not his name.

You don't happen to recall his name, do you?
→ happen to~（ひょっとして～、もしかして～）

This picture reminds me of the good old days. → remind A of B（A に B のことを思い出させる） ⇒ good old days → my home town（私の故郷）、my younger days（私の若い頃）、my college days（大学時代の頃）

TRACK 067

What do you think? ⇒ think → think of him（彼のことを「どう」思う）

I think he is cool.
⇒ cool → handsome（ハンサムな）、amazing（すごい）、smart（頭がいい）、rich（金持ち）、a good man（善人）、right（正しい）、wrong（間違い）、super bad（ちょ～悪）

I think so, too. ⇒ so, too → you are right（君は正しい、君の言う通り）

I don't think so.

Why do you think so? / What makes you think so?

Do you think I am too thin? ⇒ I am too thin → she will come（彼女は来る）、my English is terrible（私の英語はひどい）

明日は雨だと思う？

俺様をバカだと思ってるのか？

どれが似合うと思う？

その考えは間違いだと思う。

彼はそれをわざと言ったんじゃないかと思っている。

彼がそんなことをわざと言ったとは思わない。

## 降りる・下りる

どこで電車を降りるの？

ここで降ります。

私たちどこで降りるの？

降りるときは教えてあげるよ。

バスを降りる場所を間違えちゃった。

ダイエット中なので、途中で降りて歩いて帰るわ。

車から降りるとき携帯落としちゃった。

タクシーを降りたとき車内にカバンを忘れてしまった。

（エレベーター）10階で降ります。

1階まで階段を使って降りようよ。

**Do you think it will rain tomorrow?** ⇒ it will rain → it will snow（雪が降るだろう）、it will be cloudy（曇になるだろう）、it will be fine（晴れるだろう）

**Do you think I'm stupid? / Do you take me for a fool?**
→ take A for B（A を B だと思う）

**Which do you think suits me?**

**I think the idea is wrong.** ⇒ the idea is wrong → this is absurd（これは馬鹿げている）、this is a good idea（これはいい考えだ）、it is realistic（それは現実的だ）、friends are important（友人は大切だ）

**I suspect that he said that on purpose.**
→ I suspect~（～ではないかと疑う、～だろうと思う）→ on purpose = purposefully; intentionally; deliberately

**I doubt that he said such a thing on purpose.**
→ I doubt ~（～を疑問に思う、～ではなさそうだと思う）

TRACK 068

**Where do you get off the train?**

**I get off here.** ⇒ here → at the next station（次の駅で）、at the last station（終点で）

**Where are we getting off?**

**I'll tell you where to get off.**

**I made a mistake about where to get off the bus.**
**/ I got confused about which bus stop to get off at.**

**As I'm on a diet, I'll get off before my stop and walk home.**
⇒ I'm on a diet → I want to stretch my legs（足を延ばしたい、体を動かしたい）

**I dropped my cellphone when I got out of the car.**
→ get out → 自家用車やタクシーから降りる場合は get out。電車、バス、飛行機、エレベータなど大型で公共性が高い乗り物は get off が使われる。

**When I got out of the taxi, I forgot my bag in there.**

**I'm getting off at the 10th floor.**

**Let's use the stairs to go down to the first floor.**

やっとビザが下りたよ。

彼は健康の問題から CEO の地位から降りるそうだ。

### 降ろす・下す

どこで降ろしましょうか？

その角のところで降ろして。

そのスーツケースを下ろすの、手伝いましょうか？

棚からその赤い箱を下ろして。

ブラインドを下ろしてもいい？

手を下ろしてください。

銀行からお金を下ろさなくちゃ。

あのコンビニの ATM でお金を下ろすことにしよう。

彼女は主役から降ろされた。

## か

### 買う

何買いたいの？

何か買いたいの？

My visa has been issued at last.

I've heard he is going to step down from CEO due to his health issues.
→ CEO = Chief Executive Officer（最高経営責任者） → due to~（~のため、~の結果）= owing to; because of → health issues = health problems（健康問題）

TRACK 069

Where would you like to be dropped off?

Drop me at the corner over there.
→ drop me = drop me off ⇒ at the corner → in front of the station（駅の前で）、after the traffic signal（信号を過ぎたところで）

Shall I help you take that suitcase down?

Please take down that red box from the shelf.

Can I pull the blinds down? → pull ~ down = draw ~ down

Please put your hands down.
→ put your hands down= lower your hands; drop your hands

I've got to withdraw some money from the bank.
→ withdraw = take out

I'll take out some cash from the ATM at the convenience store. → some cash = some money

She was removed from the leading role.
→ leading role= central character; star role; principal part ⇒ the leading role → the starting lineup（先発メンバー）

TRACK 070

What do you want to buy?

Do you want to buy something?

これ買いたいんだ。

今から春物の新しいスカートを買うの。

ジャケットはどこで買うの？

これ買うの、買わないの？

これさ、買うべきだと思う？

これ、いま買うと安いよ。

この DVD はアマゾンで買ったんだ。

昼食に何買った？

昼食に寿司を買ったの。

これ幾らで買った？

これ 3 割引きなら買うわ。

あの店でこのテレビを安く買ったんだ。

このコンピュータを高く買っちゃった。

これ 1000 円で買ったんだ。

これ競売で買ったんだ。

何を買うか考えてるんだ。

一体どっちを買うつもりよ？

どっちを買うか迷うな。

**I want to buy this.** ⇒ this → a new computer（新しいコンピュータ）

**I'm going to buy a new skirt for the spring.**

**Where will you buy your jacket?**
⇒ will you buy → did you buy（買ったのか）

**Are you going to buy this or not?**

**Do you think I should buy this?**

**This is cheap if you buy now.** ⇒ cheap → expensive（高い）

**I bought this DVD from Amazon.** → from Amazon = on Amazon

**What did you buy for lunch?**
⇒ for lunch → at the store（あの店で）

**I bought *sushi* for lunch.**

**How much did you pay for this?**
→ did → would にすると「幾らで買いますか」といった意になる。

**I'll buy this at a 30 percent discount.**

**I bought this TV set cheap at that store.**
→ cheap = cheaply ⇒ cheap → at a discount（割引で）

**I paid too much for this computer. / I paid more than the actual price for this computer.**

**I bought this one for one thousand yen.**
⇒ buy something for ~（物を～で買う）

**I bought this at an auction.** ⇒ at an auction → on an online auction（ネットオークションで）、for cash（現金で）、outright（即金で）、on trust（クレジットで）、on a credit card（クレジットカードで）、on time（月賦で）

**I'm thinking about what to buy.** ⇒ what → which（どれを）

**Whichever do you intend to buy?** → whichever → which の強調形として「一体どちらを」の意を表す → intend to~（～するつもり、～しようと思う）

**I can't decide which to buy.**

私、よく考えずに物を買うもんだから。

あなたはやたらとバッグを買うんだから。

何かを買う前には価格を比べたほうがいいわよ。

これ買うことにした。

これ買う余裕なんてないわよ。

ビール１缶買ってきてくれるかな？

これ買ってあげようか？

愛情は金では買えないよ。

私、彼の恨みをかうようなことは何もしてないんだけど。

彼は彼女の歓心をかうためなら何でもするやつさ。

## 飼う

ペットを飼ってる？

今どんなペットを飼っている？

猫をペットに飼ってるよ。

学校でウサギを５匹飼ってるよ。

鶏を飼いたいな。

ペットは飼っていないの。

家ではペットを飼うことができないんだ。

**I buy things without thinking about it.**

**You buy bags indiscriminately.**
→ indiscriminately = at random; randomly; aimlessly　⇒ bags → makeup（化粧品）

**You had better compare prices before you buy anything.**

**I decided to buy this.**
⇒ buy this → buy this for my personal use（私個人が使うために買う）

**I can't afford to buy this. / I don't have enough money to buy this.**　→ can't afford to ～（「経済的、時間的に」～する余裕がない）

**Will you go get a can of beer?**
→ go get = go and get; go to get　→ get = buy

**Shall I get this for you?**　→ Shall I ～（～しましょうか）

**Money can't buy love. / Love cannot be bought with money.**

**I certainly haven't done anything to earn his enmity.**
→ earn someone's enmity（人の恨みをかう、人の敵意をかう）

**He does everything to win her favor.**
→ win someone's favor（人の好意を得る、人に気に入られる）

TRACK 071

**Do you have any pets?**

**What kind of pet do you have now?**　⇒ have → want（欲しい）

**I have a cat as a pet.**　⇒ cat → dog（犬）、parrot（オーム）、rabbit（ウサギ）、hamster（ハムスター）、parakeet（インコ）、common pet parakeet（セキセイインコ）　⇒ as a pet → called Jack（ジャックという）

**We have five rabbits at school.**　⇒ at school → at home（家で）

**I want to have a chicken.**
⇒ chicken → chick（ひよこ）、hen（めんどり）、cock/ rooster（おんどり）

**I don't have any pets.**　⇒ any pets → even one pet（一匹も）

**I can't keep a pet in my house.**　→ keep a pet（ペットを飼う）
⇒ in my house → in this apartment（このアパートでは）

私、猫アレルギーなので、飼えないんだ。

風変わりなペットを飼うのが流行ってない？

## 帰る

家に帰りたい。

帰ろうよ。

もう家に帰る。

もう家に帰る時間だ。

家に帰る準備はできた？

どうやって家に帰るの？

歩いて家に帰るんだ。

電車で帰るの。

もう帰るね。

もう帰るの？

家に帰る途中？

いま家に帰っている途中よ。

すぐに帰ってきなさい。

今夜は帰るのが遅くなるよ。

何時に帰ってくる？

お帰りなさい。

**I have an allergy to cats, and so I can't have any.**

Isn't it fashionable to keep an exotic pet?

TRACK 072

**I want to go home.** → go home は話し手が聞き手から離れていく時や外出先から自宅、オフィスに帰るとき。

**Let's go home.**

**I'm going home now.** ⇒ I'm going → I've got to go (「家に」帰らなきゃ)

**It's already time for me to go home.**
→ go home = go back home

Are you ready to go home?

**How are you going back home?**

I walk home. / I walk back home. / I go home on foot.

**I go home by train.** ⇒ by train → by car (車で)、by bus (バスで)

I'm leaving now.

**Are you leaving so soon?**

Are you going back home now?

**I'm on my way home.** → be on one's way ~ (~への途中にいる)

Come right home. → come home は話し手が聞き手に近づいていくとき。こうした命令文の場合は話し手が聞き手に対して近づくよう命じるとき。

**I'll come home late tonight.** ⇒ late tonight → soon (すぐに)

What time are you coming home? ⇒ What time → When (いつ)

**Welcome home!**

家に帰る途中、にわか雨にあっちゃった。

## 変える

考えを変えたよ。

他人は変えられないが、自分を変えることはできるじゃない、でしょ？

この本は私の人生を変えたんだ。

髪型を変えたね？

仕事を変えたいわけ？

いつ住所を変えたの？

席を変えよう。

私と席を変えて欲しいんだけど。

これを米ドルに換えてもらえますか？

円をアメリカドルに換えたいのですが。

1万円札を小銭に換えてもらったよ。

チャンネル変えてもいい？

言い方を変えるね。

このシャツをもう一つ上のサイズのものに替えたいのですが。

## 抱える

赤ちゃんを抱えている女性はだれ？

僕は髪の毛に多くの悩みを抱えてるんだ。

On my way home, I got caught in a sudden shower.
→ get caught in~（「雨、嵐、ひどい目など」に遭う、襲われる）

TRACK 073

I changed my mind. ⇒ mind → opinion（意見）、policy（方針）

You can't change others, but you can change yourself, right?

This book changed my life. ⇒ my life → my world（私の世界）

You changed your hairstyle, didn't you?

You want to change your job, don't you?

When did you change your address?

Let's change seats. ⇒ seats → the subject（話題）

I'd like you to change seats with me.

Could you change this into US dollars?

I'd like to change Japanese yen into American dollars.

I had one ten-thousand-yen bill broken into small change.

Can I change the channel?

Let me rephrase that. → rephrase（言い換える）

I'd like to exchange this shirt for one a size larger.

TRACK 074

Who is that woman carrying a baby in her arms?
→ carrying = holding

I have many problems with my hair.

私たちはみんなそれぞれ悩みを抱えているのよ。

うちの会社は解決しなきゃいけない多くの難問を抱えているんだ。

日本が抱える問題の一つに少子高齢化があるんだ。

## かかる

この仕事は時間がかかりそうだね。

この本を日本語に翻訳するには時間がかかるだろう。

それ、何時間かかります？

長くはかからないよ。

30 分程度かかるかもね。

最低 1 週間はかかるんじゃないかな。

留学にはかなりお金がかかるね。

駅へ行くには何分かかる？

ここへ来るのに 2 時間かかったよ。

このドアには鍵がかかっているよ。

このドアは自動的に鍵がかかるんだ。

出かけるときは鍵をかけることを忘れないで。

壁にかかっている美しい絵は誰が画いたの？

**All of us have our problems, you know.**

**Our company has a lot of difficult problems to solve.**

**One of the problems Japan has is the declining birthrate and aging society.**

TRACK 075

**This work seems to take time.**

**It will take time to translate this book into Japanese.**

**How many hours does it take?**
⇒ How many hours → how many days（何日）、How long（どのくらい）

**It will not take long.**

**It may take somewhere around thirty minutes.**
→ somewhere around~（およそ～、～くらい）

**It might take a minimum of one week.**
→ might → may とほぼ同じ意味だが、might の方が可能性が低い。⇒ a minimum of one week → three months at least（少なくとも 3 か月）、a couple of days at the soonest（早くても 2 ～ 3 日）、5 months at the longest（長くて 5 か月）

**Studying abroad costs a lot of money.**

**How long does it take to get to the station?**
→ How long = How much time

**It took two hours for me to come here.**
→ took two hours for me=took me two hours

**This door is locked.**
⇒ is locked → won't lock（鍵がかからない）、文尾に from within（内側から）

**This door locks by itself.**

**Don't forget to lock the door when you go out.**
/ Remember to lock the door before you go out.

**Who painted that beautiful picture hanging on the wall?**

煙草を吸いすぎると重い病気になるかもよ。

彼は重い病気にかかっているんだ。

インフルエンザにかかっちゃった。

いつからその病気にかかっているの？

この病気からの回復は長くかかる。

詐欺にかからないようにね。

彼女、結婚詐欺にかかったの、知ってる？

彼女、振り込み詐欺にかかったんだって。

友だちのお母さんがオレオレ詐欺の被害にあったんだ。

ブレーキがかからない！

## 書く

なに書いてるの？

友だちに手紙を書いてるんだ。

君、左手で書くんだ。

綺麗な文字を書くのね。

美しい文章を書くわね。

**If you smoke too much, you may get a serious disease.**

**He is suffering from a serious disease.** → suffer from（〜に苦しむ、〜を患う）→ serious disease =severe illness ⇒ a serious disease → food poisoning（食中毒）

**I caught flu.** → flu = the flue=influenza

**How long has it been troubling you?**

**It takes long to recover from this disease.**

**Be careful not to get scammed.** → get scammed（詐欺に遭う）

**Do you know that she was swindled out of money under a false promise of marriage?** → was swindled out of money（金を巻き上げられた、金をだまし取られた）→ false promise（うその約束）

**She said she was defrauded by a money transfer scam.** → defrauded = tricked; cheated → money transfer（送金）

**My friend's mother has fallen victim to the "Hey, it's me" telephone scam.**
→ fall victim to~（〜の犠牲になる、〜の被害者になる）

**The brakes won't work!**

TRACK 076

**What are you writing?**

**I'm writing a letter to my friend.**
⇒ a letter to my friend → a poem（詩）、a novel（小説）、a report（レポート）、a book report for homework（宿題の読書感想文）、a term paper（期末レポート）、about Japan – U.S. relations（日米関係について）、a diary in English（英語の日記）

**You write with your left hand.** ⇒ left hand ⇒ right hand（右手）

**You have good handwriting.**
⇒ good handwriting → bad handwriting（汚い字）

**You write in a beautiful style.**
⇒ in a beautiful style → good English（立派な英語）、bad English（下手な英語）、in English（英語で）、in large characters（大きな文字で）、in a cursive style（草書体で）

英語を書くことも話すこともできます。

ここはカナ文字で書いたらどう？

わたし書くのが遅いんだ。

何か書くもの持ってる？

何も書くものがないんだ。

書く紙がないんだ。

何が書いてあるの？

このボールペンは良く書けるね。

英語で手紙が書けますか？

英語が少し書けるようになったよ。

## 描く

僕は絵を描くのが趣味なんだ。

私が描いたこの絵はどう？

私は風景画を描くのが得意なんだ。

人物画を油絵で描く方法を教えてよ。

## 隠す

何で君は年齢を隠すのかわからないな。

手で顔を隠したって無駄よ。

**I can both write and speak English.**

**How about writing this in *kana* letters?**
⇒ in *kana* letters → in Chinese characters（漢字で）、in capital letters（大文字で）

**I'm slow at writing.** ⇒ slow at writing → fast at writing（書くのが早い）

**Do you have something to write with?** → write with は「～で書く」なので筆記用具のこと。なお、この文は yes を想定したもの。相手が yes か no のどちらで答えるか分からない場合は something が anything に代わる。

**I have nothing to write with.**
→ write with → write on にすると「～の上に書く」なので、書くための紙のこと。また write about にすると「書くネタ」のこと。

**I have no paper to write on.**

**What does it say?** / What's written there?

**This ballpoint pen writes well.**

**Can you write a letter in English?**

**I became able to write English a little.**

TRACK 077

**My hobby is drawing pictures.**
→ draw は鉛筆やペンなどで絵を描くこと。

**Do you like this picture I drew?** → drew は draw の過去形。

**I'm good at painting a landscape.**
→ paint は絵の具で絵を描くこと。

**Can you teach me how to paint a portrait in oil?**
⇒ in oil → in watercolor（水彩画で）

TRACK 078

**I don't understand why you hide your age.**
→ hide your age= conceal your age; make a secret of your age

**It's no use covering your face with your hands.**
**/ It's no use hiding your face in your hands.**

ミスを隠さないように。

彼女は何かを隠している気がする。

君は僕に何か隠しているよね？

僕に何を隠しているんだ？

あなたには何ひとつ隠してないわよ。

この笑いジワを隠したいんだけど。

コンシーラーで笑いジワ隠せるかな？

### 隠れる

どこに隠れているの？

鼻まで隠れるようにマスクをして下さい。

### かける

2 × 4 は 8

この窓にブルーのカーテンをかけるのはどう？

このテーブルにはおしゃれなテーブルクロスをかけましょう。

彼は常識に欠けるね。

君に欠けているのは勇気だよ。

私、毎月、本にかなりのお金をかけているんだ。

私は自分にお金をかけてるわ。

**Don't hide your mistakes.** ⇒ Don't hide → You tend to hide（君は隠す傾向がある） ⇒ your mistakes → the fact that is inconvenient（都合の悪い事実）

**I feel she's hiding something.**

**You're hiding something from me, aren't you?**

**What are you hiding from me?**

**I'm not hiding anything from you.** / I have no secrets from you.

**I want to hide my laugh lines.**

**Can I conceal these laugh lines with concealer?** ⇒ these laugh lines → these blemishes（これらのシミ）、these acnes（これらのニキビ）

TRACK 079

**Where are you hiding?** ⇒ Where → Why（どうして）

**Please wear your mask so that it covers your nose.**

TRACK 080

**Two times four is eight.** / Two multiplied by four make eight. / Four twos are eight. → make = makes; is; equals

**How about hanging blue curtains in this window?**
→ in this window=over this window

**Let's cover this table with a fancy tablecloth.**

**He lacks common sense.**
⇒ lacks commonsense → lacks in intelligence（知性に欠ける）

**What you lack is courage.** / What you need is courage.

**I spend a lot of money on books**
⇒ spend → can't spend（かけられない）

**I spend money on myself.**
⇒ money → much money（かなりのお金）

この皿はふちが欠けてるわよ。

これには醤油をかけたほうがいいわよ。

それには少し塩をかけることがおすすめね。

頻繁にブレーキをかけないで。

エンジンをかけてください。

あの眼鏡をかけた女性を知ってる？

6時に目覚まし時計をかけて。

これに食事を賭けないか？

## 飾る

部屋を飾りたいんだ。

このテーブルを季節の花で飾るのはどう？

我が家には有名な画家の絵がいくつか飾ってあるわ。

彼女のようにうわべを飾る人は嫌いだな。

彼女、いつも着飾ってるね。

彼は言葉を飾るのが好きだな。

## 貸す

お金貸して。

**This plate has a chip on the edge.**
→ chip（かけら、切れ端） → edge （淵、端）

**You had better put soy sauce on this.** → put = pour

**I recommend sprinkling a bit of salt on that.**

**Don't put on the brakes too often.** → put on = apply

**Please start the engine.**

**Do you know that lady wearing glasses?**
→ wear glasses は「眼鏡をかけている」、put on one's glasses は「眼鏡をかける」

**Set the alarm clock for six o'clock please.**

**Why don't we bet a dinner on this?**

TRACK 081

**I want to decorate my room.** / I want to put up decorations in my room.

**How about decorating the table with seasonal flowers?** → seasonal flowers = flowers that fit the season

**My house is decorated with a couple of pictures by famous painters.** → a couple of（2 つの、2 ～ 3 の）

**I don't like ostentatious people like her.**
→ ostentatious = showy; gaudy; pretentious

**She's always dressed up in fine clothes.** / She is always dressed beautifully. ⇒ dressed up in fine clothes → dressed up in modish clothes（流行の服で飾っている）、dressed up to the nines（華やかに着飾る、完璧に着飾る）

**He uses flowery style.** / He uses fine language. / He uses fair words. ⇒ uses flowery style → writes in a showy style（文章を飾る）

TRACK 082

**Please lend me some money.** → lend は貸す行為に対して料金の発生はない。タダで貸すことで、loan と同じ。 ⇒ some money → ten thousand yen（1 万円）

お金は貸せないよ。

金を借りるのも貸すのも嫌なんだ。

彼に 3 万円貸したんだ。

彼に金を貸すなんて君も馬鹿だな。

僕は彼に金を貸すほど愚かじゃないよ。

電話貸してくれる？

明日、車貸してもらえるかな？

彼にお気に入りの小説を貸したんだけど、まだ返してもらってないんだよ。

## 固まる

これ常温で固まるの？

この接着剤は 3 分で固まるんだよ。

この液体は熱すると固まるんだ。

それが固まるまで冷蔵庫に入れておいて。

## 勝つ

勝つぞ。

僕は勝つためには何でもするよ。

僕に勝てるかな？

病気に勝ってやる。

**I can't lend you money.**

**I don't like to lend or borrow money.**

**I lent him thirty thousand yen.** → lent = loaned

**It's stupid of you to lend him the money.**
→ the money（そのお金）

**I know better than to lend him money.**
→ know better than ~（～するほどバカじゃない、～しないだけの分別がある）

**Can I use your phone?**

**Could you lend me your car tomorrow?**
⇒ car → bike（自転車）、CDs（CD）

**I lent my favorite novel to him and I haven't got it back yet.** → get ～ back（～を返してもらう、～を取り返す）

TRACK 083

**Will this get hard at normal temperature?**

**This glue hardens up in three minutes.**
⇒ in three minutes → in an instant（一瞬で、たちまち）、in a moment（瞬間に、瞬く間に）

**This liquid turns solid when you heat it.**

**Will you put it in the refrigerator until it firms up?**
→ firms up = sets

TRACK 084

**I'm going to win.** ⇒ win → win an election（選挙に勝つ）、win a game（競技に勝つ）、win in an argument（議論に勝つ）、win a victory over adversity（逆境に打ち勝つ）、win against him（彼に勝つ）、win against myself（自分自身に勝つ）

**I will do anything to win.**

**Can you win against me?**

**I will overcome my illness.**
→ overcome = get better of; conquer; defeat; beat

（諺）地道なものが勝つのさ。

結局は実力が勝つわけさ。

長い目で見れば僕は勝つ。

僕にとって勝つことが全てさ。

誰が勝つと思う？

勝つも負けるも運ね。

勝つ者もいれば負けるものもいる。

人生は勝つか負けるかだ。

勝とうが負けようが関係ないね。

彼女が勝つ可能性はごくわずかだ。

勝って学ぶより負けて学ぶことのほうが多いよ。

私たちは 5 対 2 で勝った。

## 借りる

これ借りていい？

この本はいつまで借りられます？

本を借りるには ID カードが必要だよ。

この車はいくらで借りられます？

学校の近くに部屋を借りたいな。

**Slow and steady wins the race.**

**Real ability wins in the end.** → in the end（最後は、結局は）

**I will win in the long run.** → in the long run = eventually; in the end

**Winning is everything to me.**

**Who do you think will win?** → will win = will get the victory ⇒ win → win the Presidential election（大統領選挙に勝つ）

**Victory or defeat is all a matter of chance.**

**Some will win and others will lose.**

**It's win or lose in life.**

**Win or lose, it doesn't matter.**

**There's little chance of her winning.** / She has little chance of winning.

**You can learn more from losing than winning.**

**We won with a score of five to two.**
⇒ won with a score of five to two → won by a hair; won by a narrow margin（僅差で勝った）、won unexpectedly（思いがけず勝った）

TRACK 085

**Can I borrow this?** → borrow は借りる際の料金は発生せず、基本的に持ち運べるものを借りる時に使われる。⇒ this → your pencil（君の鉛筆）、your dictionary for a while（しばらく辞書を）

**Until when can I borrow this book?**

**You need your ID card to borrow a book.**

**How much will it cost to rent this car?**
→ rent はお金をもらって貸す、お金を払って借りる際に使われる。

**I want to rent a room near school.**

いつからこの部屋を借りられますか？

むやみに友人たちからお金を借りるべきじゃないよ。

これらのDVDはツタヤから借りたんだ。

## 枯れる

この木が枯れてきた。

この花だけど、1週間で枯れちゃった。

定期的に水をやらないと、この花は枯れちゃうよ。

出張旅行で家を空けていた間に鉢植えの植物が全部枯れちゃった。

風邪を引いて声が枯れちゃった。

喉が枯れちゃって、殆ど声が出ないよ。

## 乾かす

今、髪の毛をドライヤーで乾かしてるの。

私はいつも髪の毛は自然乾燥させてるわよ。

洗濯物はどうやって乾かしてる？

私は洗濯物は日に当てて乾かしてるわ。

## 乾く

このシャツ、乾くのが早いわね。

From when can I rent this room?

You shouldn't borrow money from your friends indiscriminately. → indiscriminately = at random; randomly; aimlessly

I rented these DVDs from *Tsutaya*.

TRACK 086

This tree is dying.
⇒ This tree → This pine tree（この松の木）、This persimmon tree（この柿の木）、This apple tree（このリンゴの木）、This pear tree（この梨の木）、This plant（この植物）

This flower withered in a week. → wither（しおれる、枯れる）

These flowers will die if you don't water them regularly.

All my potted plants withered while I was away from home on a business trip.

I have a cold and my voice is hoarse. / I lost my voice because of a cold. → hoarse=coarse; husky; throaty; harsh → lose one's voice（声が出なくなる、声がつぶれる）

I'm hoarse and I can barely talk.
→ barely（かろうじて、やっと、どうにかこうにか）

TRACK 087

I'm drying my hair with a hair dryer now.

I always air-dry my hair. / I let my hair air-dry.
→ air-dry（空気乾燥させる）

How do you dry your laundry?

I dry my washing in the sun. → washing=laundry; wash

TRACK 088

This shirt dries quickly. ⇒ shirt → cloth（布地） ⇒ dries quickly → has dried（乾いた）、doesn't dry（乾かない）、hasn't dried yet（まだ乾いていない）

今日は天気がいいから、きっと洗濯物が良く乾くわよ。

雨だから洗濯物が乾くにはしばらく時間がかかるわね。

今日は目が乾くわ。

口がカラカラに乾いちゃうんだけど。

マニキュアが乾くまで待って。

## 考える

それについて考えてみて。

その件については考えさせて。

そのことについては良く考えるよ。

自分のことだけ考えないで。

それについては彼女の観点から考えてみよう。

弱者の立場に立って考えてみて。

まず第一に自分の幸せを考えるべきだよ。

決断する前によく考えることね。

それについて考える時間をもう少しもらえるかな？

考えれば考えるほど理解できないわね。

年配者はそう考える傾向があるね。

**I'm sure the laundry will dry well because the weather is nice today.**

**It's going to take a while for the laundry to dry because of the rain.** → take a while（しばらく時間がかかる）
⇒ because of the rain → because it is very damp today（今日は湿気が多いので）

**I have dry eyes today.**

**My mouth gets dry as a desert. / My mouth dries up.**

**Wait till the manicure gets dry.**
→ the manicure gets dry = the nail polish is dry

TRACK 089

**Think about it.** ⇒ Think → Think hard（真剣に考える）、Think carefully（慎重に考える）、Think seriously（まじめに考える）→ Think about your future.（自分の将来について考えなさい）、Don't think about it（そのことは考えるな）

**Let me think about it.**
⇒ about it → about it positively（それについては前向きに）

**I often think about that.**

**Don't think only of yourself.**

**Let's think about it from her point of view.**
→ from someone's point of view（～の視点から）

**Put yourself in the position of the weak and think.**
→ put yourself in the position of~（～の立場に身を置く） → the weak = weak people

**You should think about your happiness first.**

**You should think carefully before you make up your mind.** ⇒ think carefully → think long and hard（じっくりと考える）

**Can I have a little more time to think about that?**

**The more I think, the less I understand.**
→ The more~, the less…（～すればするほど…しなくなる）

**Elder people tend to think so.** ⇒ so → like that（そんな風に）

あなたがそう考えるのも自然だわね。

そう考えるのは私一人じゃないわ。

そう考える人もいるかもね。

それはあなたが考えるほど単純じゃないよ。

あなた考えすぎよ。

それについて考えるのやめたわ。

それについて考えると頭が痛いよ。

今はもう何も考えたくないわ。

国のために自分に何ができるかを考えてみなさい。

彼女の年齢を考えると、彼女は若く見えるね。

あなたが考える優れた日本文化ってなに？

君は何でもお金で考えるんだね？

## 感謝する

感謝します。

あなたの協力に感謝します。

あなたの親切に感謝しています。

家族に感謝しています。

その感謝する気持ちを忘れないで。

**It's natural for you to think so.**

**I'm not alone in thinking so.**

**Some people might think like that.**
⇒ Some people might → Let's not（～はよしましょ）

**It's not as simple as you think it is.** / It's not as simple as that. ⇒ simple → easy（簡単な）

**You are thinking too much.**

**I stopped thinking about that.**

**My head hurts when I think about that.**

**I don't want to think about anything now.**

**Think what you can do for your country.**
⇒ for your country → for your family（家族のために）

**She looks young considering her age.**
→ considering（考えると、考慮すると、～の割には）

**What do you think is a superior culture of Japan?**
→ superior=remarkable; awesome; splendid

**You do think of everything in terms of money, don't you?** → in terms of ~（～の観点から）

TRACK 090

**I appreciate it.** / I'm grateful. / Thank you.

**I appreciate your cooperation.**

**I'm grateful for your kindness.**
⇒ your kindness → your support（あなたのご支援）

**I'm thankful for my family.** ⇒ my family → my parents（両親）、the food（食べ物）、an ordinary day like this（このような日常）

**Don't forget the feelings of gratitude.**

## 消える

データが消えた！

ラインのデータが全部消えちゃった！

それは目の前で消えたよ。どこへ行ったのかな。

これらの字が消えていて読めないよ。

私の給料のほとんどは洋服代に消えちゃうの。

突然、明かりが消えた。

キャンドルの火が消えかけている。

サインが消えるまでおタバコはご遠慮ください。

地面の雪はすぐに消えるだろう。

それはどのくらいの時間で消えますか？

その症状はしばらく消えないでしょう。

それは何か月経っても消えることはないよ。

このお笑い芸人はすぐ消えると思うよ。

彼は芸能界から消えちゃったね。

TRACK 091

**The data is gone! / I lost the data!**
⇒ The data → All the data（全てのデータ）

**All my LINE data disappeared.**

**It vanished right in front of my eyes. I wonder where it went.** → vanished = disappeared

**These characters are defaced and unreadable.**
→ character（文字） → defaced（外観を損なっている、読みづらくなっている）
→ unreadable = illegible; incapable of being read

**Most of my salary goes to clothes.**
⇒ goes to clothes → goes to pay my rent（家賃の支払いに消える）

**Suddenly the light went out.** / All of a sudden, the lights went out.

**The candle flame is going out.**

**Please refrain from smoking until the sign is turned off.** → refrain from ~（～を控える、～をやめる） → turn off ~（「栓をひねって」消す、止める）

**The snow on the ground will soon disappear.**
→ disappear = melt away

**How long will it take for that to disappear?**

**The symptom will not disappear for a while.**
⇒ will not disappear → did not disappear（消えなかった）

**That will not disappear no matter how many months go by.**
→ no matter how…（どんなに…しても） → go by（過ぎ去る、通り過ぎる）

**I think this comedian will disappear soon.**

**He disappeared from the entertainment industry, didn't he?**

## 聞く

ちょっと聞いていい？

聞いて、聞いて。

人の話を聞きなさい！

最後まで聞いてよ。

聞こえる？

ちゃんと聞いてる？

聞いてなかったでしょう。

あなたは私の言うことを聞こうとしないのよね。

私の話をもっと注意深く聞くべきだったわよ。

人の話を聞いてないからわからないんだよ。

もうそれ聞くのはウンザリだよ。

あなたの不平は聞きたくないわ。

その話を聞くたびにぞっとするわ。

まずはあなたの意見を聞いてみましょう。

なんで聞くの？

そんな決まりきったことは聞かないでよ。

あなたは聞くもの全てを信じるんだから。

見ると聞くとは大違いよ。

TRACK 092

**Can I ask you something?**

**Listen to me.**

**Listen to me when I'm talking!** / Listen to what people have to say!

**Hear me out.**

**Can you hear me?**

**Are you listening?**

**You weren't listening, were you?**

**You won't listen to me.** / You turn a deaf ear to me.

**You should have listened to me more carefully.**

**You don't understand because you weren't listening to me.** → listening to = paying attention to

**I'm already tired of hearing that.** → be tired of = be bored of

**I don't like to hear you complaining.** → don't like = hate

**I shudder every time I hear that story.**

**We will hear your opinion first.**

**Why do you ask?**

**Don't ask me such an obvious question.**
→ obvious=plain; evident; clear; distinct

**You believe everything you hear.**

**What you see is quite different from what you hear.**
/ There is a great difference between what you hear and what you actually see.

あなたの話を聞くのを楽しみにしています。

彼のことは聞いています。

悲しいときはいつもこの歌を聞くんだよ。

この歌を聞くと青春時代に戻れるんだ。

英語を話すことと聞くことは苦手なんだ。

あの教授の講義は聞く価値があるよ。

その知らせを聞くと、彼女、泣き出しちゃってさ。

## 効く

この薬はよく効くよ。

この薬は何に効くの？

これは痛みに効くのさ。

風邪に効く薬はありますか？

この薬は風邪に驚くほどよく効きますよ。

薬が効いてきたみたい。

この薬は効かなかったな。

私におだては効かないよ。

## 聞こえる

私の声、聞こえる？

よく聞こえるよ。

**I'm looking forward to hearing your story.**
→ look forward to~（～を楽しみにしている、～を待ち焦がれている）

**I've heard about him.** ⇒ I've heard → I've never heard（聞いたことがない）

**When I'm sad I listen to this song.**

**Listening to this song takes me back to my youth.**

**I'm very bad at speaking and listening to English.**
→ be bad at = be not good at

**It's worth listening to that professor's lectures. / His lectures are worth listening to.**

**On hearing the news, she began to cry.**
→ On hearing=As soon as she heard

TRACK 093

**This medicine works well.** → works well = is quite effective

**What is this medicine effective for?**
→ effective for = good for; effective against

**This is effective against pain.** → be effective against = acts on
⇒ pain → colds（風邪）、high blood pressure（高血圧）

**Do you have anything for colds?**

**This medicine works wonders for colds.**
→ works wonders= acts like magic

**It looks like the medicine is working.**
⇒ is working → worked（効いた）

**This medicine didn't work.** → didn't work = had no effect

**Flattery won't work with me.**

TRACK 094

**Can you hear me? / Do you hear me?**

**I can hear you clearly.** → clearly = very well

なんとなく聞こえる。

なにか聞こえるよ。

今の物音だけど、聞こえた？

どこから聞こえる？

台所から聞こえたよ。

うるさくて君の声がよく聞こえないよ。

最近よく聞こえないんだ。

君の言うことは皮肉に聞こえるよ。

あなたの発音はあまり英語らしく聞こえないな。

## 着せる

着物を着せてもらいに美容院へ行ってくるね。

どうして犬に服を着せるの？

## 鍛える

ときどきジムで鍛えてるんだ。

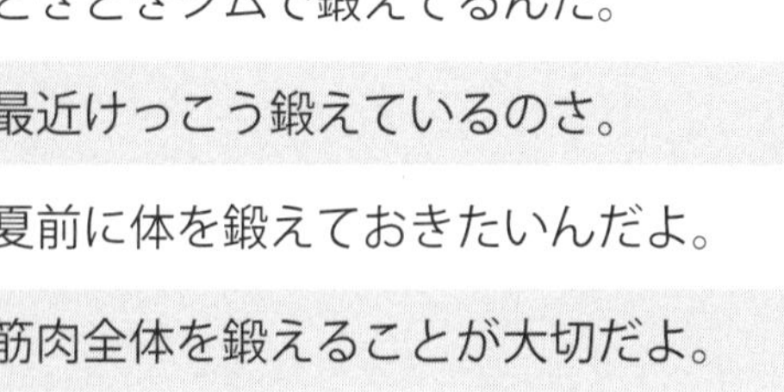

最近けっこう鍛えているのさ。

夏前に体を鍛えておきたいんだよ。

筋肉全体を鍛えることが大切だよ。

心身ともに鍛えることを忘れないで。

俺、腹筋をもっと鍛えないとな。

**I can somewhat hear you.** → you= your voice

**I can hear something.**
⇒ something → music（音楽）、someone singing（誰か歌っているのが）

**Did you hear that noise?**

**Where can you hear it from?**

**I heard it coming from the kitchen.**

**It's so noisy I can't hear you well.** → hear you =hear your voice
⇒ hear you → hear the television（テレビの音が聞こえる）

**I can't hear well these days.**

**What you say sounds sarcastic.** ⇒ sarcastic → false（嘘っぽく）
→ sound~（〜らしく聞こえる、〜に思われる）

**Your pronunciation doesn't sound much like English.**

TRACK 095

**I'll go to a beauty salon to have them put my *kimono* on.**

**Why do you put clothes on your dog?**

TRACK 096

**I work out at the gym sometimes.**
⇒ sometimes → on weekdays（平日に）

**I've been working out a lot these days.**

**I want to get in shape before summer.**
→ get in shape（体を整える、体を鍛える）

**It's important to train all of your muscle groups.**

**Don't forget to train both the body and mind.**
→ the body and mind= the mind and body

**I've got to work out my abs more.**
→ abs = abdominal muscles（腹筋） ⇒ abs → back（背中）、biceps（上腕二頭筋）

君は精神力を鍛える必要があると思うけどな。

## 決める・決まる

はやく決めてよ。

それは誰が決めるの？

それはあなたが決めることよ。

これを決めるのはあなたじゃないわ。

決める前によく検討したいんだけど。

まだ人生の目標が決められないんだ。

次に会う時間を決めよう。

留学するかどうか決めた？

まだそれ決めてない。

誕生パーティにはこのドレスに決めたわ。

結婚式の日取りを 11 月 20 日に決めたよ。

これで決まりだ。

まだ決まってない。

これは私の運命が決まる大切な試験なんだ。

彼女は成功するに決まっているよ。

価格は需要と供給によって決まるのさ。

I think you need to develop your mental strength.

TRACK 097

**Make up your mind now.** → make up one's mind=decide; determine
⇒ Make up your mind → I can't make up my mind（決められない）

**Who decides that?** → decide　意思をもって判断、選択すること。

**It's up to you to decide.**
→ It's up to you to~（～するのはあなた次第である）

**You are not the one to decide this.**

**I want to consider carefully before I decide.**
⇒ consider carefully → consult with my mother（母に相談する）

**I still can't determine my life goal.**
→ determine　様々な条件などを考慮し判定、確定する、決める。

**Let's decide on a time to meet next.**
→ decide on a time = fix a time

**Have you decided whether you should study abroad or not?**

**I haven't decided it yet.**

**I decided on this dress for my birthday party.**

**We have fixed November 20 as the date of our wedding.**

**That settles it.** / Now it's official.

**It's not official yet.**

**This is the examination that will determine my future.**

**She is sure to succeed.** → sure= certain; bound

**Price depends on supply and demand.**
→ demand and supply とすることもあるが稀。

## 嫌う

彼、私のことを嫌ってると思う。

彼に嫌われたくないよ〜。

友だちに嫌われるのが怖い。

嫌われてなくてよかった。

理由はわからないが、僕は上司に嫌われているんだ。

彼はいつも自慢するから嫌いなんだよ。

ツンツンした女は嫌いだな。

彼のこと好きだったけど、急に嫌いになっちゃった。

あなたが彼を嫌うなんて思ってもみなかったわね。

彼を嫌う人なんて誰もいないよ。

もう私のこと嫌いになった？

嫌いになって欲しいの？

## 切る

そのトマトを切ってくれる？

このレモンを薄切りに切ってくれるかな？

その人参を半分に切ってね。

このパンを薄く切ってちょうだい。

このキュウリを４分の１に切ってもいい？

TRACK 098

I think he hates me. / I feel he hates me.

I don't want him to hate me.

I'm afraid of being hated by my friends. / I'm afraid of my friends disliking me. → hate = dislike; don't like

I'm glad I wasn't hated.

I don't know why, but my boss doesn't like me.

I hate him because he brags all the time.
→ brag=boast; blow one's own horn

I hate a girl who is a snob. → snob（お高くとまった人、気取り屋）

I liked him, but I suddenly started to dislike him.

I thought you were the last person to hate him.
→ the last person to~（~するとはとても思えない人、最も～しそうにない人）

Nobody hates him.

You don't like me anymore? / Do you hate me now?

Do you want me to hate you?

TRACK 099

Will you cut the tomato?

Can you slice this lemon thin?

Will you cut the carrot in half? → in half = into halves

Please cut this bread thin.

Can I cut this cucumber into quarters? ⇒ cut into quarters
→ cut into thirds（3 分の 1 に切る）、cut into bite-size chunks（一口大に切る）

この大根を小さく花形に切ろうか？

皿を洗ったら水をよく切ってちょうだい。

これらの野菜だけど水を切ってからフライパンに入れてよ。

コンピュータの電源を切ってください。

彼女、突然、電話を切ったんだ。

電話は切らないでお待ちください。

トランプをよく切ってください。

爪を切らなくっちゃあ。

髪を切ったほうがいいかなぁ。

期限を切るべきだと思う？

マラソンで 2 時間を切る時が来るのかなぁ？

遂に彼、100 メートル競技で 9 秒を切ったね。

私、彼と手を切ったわ。

彼女は彼と切っても切れない関係にあるみたい。

## 着る・着替える

服を着なさい。

今日は何を着たらいい？

**Shall I cut this *daikon* into small florets?**
⇒ cut this *daikon* into small florets → dice this *daikon*（この大根をさいの目に切る）、slice this *daikon*（この大根を薄切りにする）、chop this daikon finely（大根をみじん切りにする）

**Wash the dishes and drain them well, please.**
→ drain（水気を切る、排水する）

**Drain off the water from these vegetables before dropping them into the frying pan.**

**Please turn off your computer.**
⇒ your computer → the television（テレビ）、the switch（スイッチ）

**She suddenly hung up.** → hung → 現在形は hang

**Hold the line, please.**

**Please shuffle the cards well.**

**I've got to clip my nails.** → clip= cut

**Maybe I had better have my hair cut.**
→ have my hair cut（髪を切ってもらう）= have a haircut

**Do you think we should set a deadline?** → set = fix

**I wonder if the time will come when somebody breaks two hours for the marathon.**

**Finally, he ran 100 meters in less than nine seconds.**
/ Finally, he broke the nine-second mark in the 100-meter race.
→ in less than = under

**I broke it off with him.**
→ break it off with = break off relations with ~（～と関係を切る、縁を切る）

**She seems to be closely bound up with him.**
→ closely = inseparably; intimately → be bound up with ～（～と密接な関係にある、～と深く関係している）

TRACK 100

**Put on your clothes.** ⇒ clothes → clothes quickly（急いで服を）

**What should I wear today?**

この派手な服を着るわ。

私、その日の気分にあった服を着るんだ。

これは外出するときに着る服なんだ。

スーツを着るようにって言われたわ。

これ、どういうふうに着るの？

着物を着たのって久しぶりだわ。

そのドレスを着るとすごくかわいい。

もっとスリムに見えたかったら、黒いものを着るといいわよ。

着るものを決めるときは、TPO を考えて決めたほうがいいよ。

もうコートを着るの、やめたほうがいいと思う？

この暑さではコートなんて着ていられないよ。

服を着たままで寝ないの！

パジャマを着たまま外へ出てはだめよ。

シャツを裏返しに着てるわよ。

これに着替えて。

着替えてくる。

すぐに普段着に着替えるから。

I'll wear these flashy clothes. → flashy = showy

I wear clothes that match the day's mood.

These are my clothes when I go out. / I wear these when I go out. ⇒ when I go out → for a special occasion（特別なときの）

I was told to wear a suit.

How do you wear this? ⇒ How → When（いつ）

It's been a while since I wore a *kimono*.

You look very pretty in that dress.
⇒ look very pretty → look better（〜より見栄えがする）

If you want to look slimmer, you should wear something black.

When you decide what to wear, you had better take the time, the place, and the occasion into consideration. → take ~ into consideration （〜を考慮に入れる）

Do you think I'd better leave off my coat now?
→ leave off （脱いだままでいる、着るのをやめる）

I can't keep my coat on in this heat.

Don't sleep with your clothes on. / Don't sleep in your clothes.

Don't go outside in your pajamas.

You are wearing your shirt inside out.
→ inside out = wrong side out

Change into this.

I'll go get changed. ⇒ I'll go → I have to（私、着替えなきゃあ）

I'll change into my regular clothes in a second.

## 記録する

これを記録して。

私は日々の出来事を日記に記録することにしているの。

私がこの会議の要約を記録する担当です。

これ記録するのを手伝ってもらえる？

その文書はヘミングウエイが 1899 年 7 月 21 日に生まれたと記録している。

# く

## 腐る

この肉をすぐ冷蔵庫に入れなさい。でないと腐るよ。

このケーキは、4 日は腐らないだろう。

塩は食物が腐るのを止めるのに役立つよね？

彼は根性が腐ってるよ。

## 崩れる

明日は天気が崩れそうだね。

天気予報によると今週末から天気が崩れるって。

千円札が崩れますか？

このシャツは形が崩れないんだ。

TRACK 101

**Make a record of this.** → make a record of = record ⇒ this → the meeting（会議）

**I make it a rule to record daily events in my diary.**
→ make it a rule to~（～することを習慣にしている）

**I'm in charge of recording a summary of this meeting.**
→ be in charge of~（～を担当している）

**Could you help me record this?**

**The document records that Ernest Hemingway was born on July 21, 1899.**

TRACK 102

**Put this meat in the refrigerator soon, or it will rot.**

**This cake will keep for four days.**
→ keep（「飲食物が」保存がきく、長持ちする）

**Salt helps stop food from going bad, doesn't it?**
→ go bad = rot; decay; spoil

**He is corrupt at heart.** → corrupt（堕落した、腐敗した）

TRACK 103

**The weather is likely to get worse tomorrow.** / **It is likely to start raining tomorrow.** → start raining（雨が降り始める）

**According to the weather forecast, the weather will change for the worse this weekend.**

**Can you break a thousand yen note?**

**This shirt will hold its shape.** → hold = keep; retain

雨で我が家の後ろで崖が崩れたんだ。

## 配る

この紙をみんなに配ってください。

プリントを各自一枚取って残りを配ってください。

このパンフレット配るのを手伝ってくれる？

彼女はあらゆる細かい点に気を配るね。

## 組む

次の試合で私と組まないか？

僕たち、チームを組む機会があるかもね。

あの脚を組んでる女性はだれ？

腕を組んで歩こうよ。

## 悔やむ

それを今さら悔やんだって無駄さ。

悔やんでも悔やみきれない。

あのとき彼に嘘をついたことを悔やんでいるの。

彼と結婚したことを本当に悔やんでいるのよ。

**The rain caused a landslide behind my house.**
→ cause a landslide（地滑りを引き起こす）

TRACK 104

**Please hand out the papers to everyone.** → hand out = give out; pass; distribute ⇒ the papers → these handouts（これらのプリント）、these documents（これらの資料）、these questionnaires（これらのアンケート用紙）

**Please take a handout and pass the rest along.** → pass along（手渡す）

**Can you help me pass out these brochures?**
→ pass out（配る、配布する） → brochure（パンフレット、小冊子）

**She is attentive to every detail.**
→ be attentive to~（～に注意を払う、～に気を配る）

TRACK 105

**Will you be my partner in the next game?**

**We might have a chance to team up.**

**Who is that lady crossing her legs?**
⇒ crossing her legs → crossing her arms（腕を組んで）

**Let's walk arm in arm.**

TRACK 106

**It's no use regretting it now.** / What is done cannot be undone.

**I cannot regret enough.**
→ cannot ~ enough（いくら～しても十分ではない、いくら～しても足りない）

**I regret having told a lie to him then.**

**I really regret that I married him.** ⇒ that I married him → my own words（自分の言葉）、what I did to her（彼女にしたこと）

## 暮らす

安楽に暮らしたいな。

何不自由なく暮らしています。

年金で暮らしています。

どこで暮らしてるの？

私は田舎でひっそり暮らしています。

いつからここで暮らしてる？

5 歳から 10 歳までは大阪で暮らしていたんだ。

生まれたときからずっとここで暮らしているんだ。

ここで暮らすようになってもう 5 年になるよ。

一人きりで暮らしたくないよ～。

ここで暮らすには幾らかかる？

月 20 万円で暮らせる？

そんなわずかな金では暮らせないよ。

## 比べる

何かを買う前には価格を比べたほうがいいよ。

私、前に比べると元気よ。

TRACK 107

**I want to live in comfort.** ⇒ live in comfort → live in luxury（贅沢に暮らす）、live well（裕福に暮らす）、live happily（幸せに暮らす）、live in style（派手に暮らす）、live free and easy（のんびり暮らす）、live frugally（質素に暮らす）、live straight（地道に暮らす）、live in nature（自然の中で暮らす）

**I'm living without any inconvenience.**

**I'm living on a pension.**
⇒ on a pension → on a small salary（安月給で）

**Where do you live?** / Where have you been living?

**I am living quietly in the country.** ⇒ live quietly in the country → live out in the country（町を離れて田舎で暮らす）、live alone in the country（田舎で一人暮らす）、live in the urban area（都会で暮らす）、live in a big city（大都会で暮らす）、live alone away from my family（家族と離れて一人で暮らす）

**Since when have you been living here?** / From when have you lived here?

**I lived in Osaka between the ages of 5 and 10.**

**I have lived here since I was born.**

**It's already five years since I came to live here.**

**I don't want to live all by myself.**

**How much does it cost to live here?**

**Can you live on two hundred thousand yen a month?**

**I cannot live on such a small sum of money.**

TRACK 108

**You had better compare prices before you buy anything.** → had better~（～した方がいい）

**I'm healthier compared to before.**
→ compared to~（～に比べて、～と比較して）

彼女、昔と比べるとまるで別人だわね。

自分を他人と比べる必要はないよ。

他人と比べて何の意味があるわけ？

あのコンピュータと比べると、このコンピュータのほうが機能的に優れているな。

## 狂う

予定が狂っちゃった。

夜勤してから体内時計が狂っちゃったよ。

病気のせいで計画が狂ったよ。

大阪の支社に転勤させられて人生設計が狂ってしまった。

かわいそうに。あいつ、とうとう狂っちゃった。

あなたのこと好きすぎて、気が狂っちゃう。

## 苦しむ

私、花粉症に苦しんでるのよ。

このところわが社は売り上げの低下に苦しんでいるんだ。

この夏は水不足で苦しんでいるよ。

そんなことで苦しむ必要はないさ。

She looks like a completely different person compared to what she was before.

You don't need to compare yourself with others.

What's the point of comparing with others?

Compared with that computer, this computer is functionally better.

TRACK 109

My schedule is messed up.
→ is messed up = has been thrown off

My body clock is messed up after working the night shift.
⇒ after working the night shift → after the trip（旅行の後で）

My plan fell apart because of my illness.
→ fall apart（崩壊する、崩れる）

Being transferred to a branch in Osaka has messed up my life plans.

Poor man! He's gone insane at last.

I'm going crazy because I love you so much.

TRACK 110

I'm suffering from pollen allergies. → suffer from ~（～に苦しむ、～を患う） ⇒ pollen allergies → toothache（歯痛）、bulimia（過食症）、arthritis（関節炎）、a frozen shoulder（五十肩）、a lower back pain（腰痛）

Our company has suffered from poor sales.

We are suffering from a lack of water this summer.
→ lack = shortage

Don't agonize over such a thing.
→ agonize over~（～のことで苦しむ）

## 加える

彼の名前をリストに加えて欲しいんだけど。

彼を仲間に加えたらどうだ？

補足的な説明を加えましょう。

遠慮なく必要な変更は加えてください。

アメリカは北朝鮮に圧力を加えると思うよ。

## 加わる

君に我々の新たなプロジェクトチームに加わって欲しいんだ。

私は彼らのプロジェクトチームに加わることにしたよ。

君が我々に加わってくれるとは思ってもみなかったよ。

# け

## 経験する

有難う。いい経験をすることができました。

アメリカにいた時に経験したことを話して。

そこで多くのいろんな経験をしたんだ。

忘れられない経験をしたよ。

TRACK 111

I want you to add his name to the list.

**Why don't we let him join us?** → Why don't we~（~しませんか、~しましょうよ）⇒ let him join us → include him in our team（彼を我がチームに加える）

**Let's add a supplementary explanation.**
→ supplementary（補足の、付録の）

**Please don't hesitate to make necessary changes.**
→ don't hesitate to~（遠慮なく～する）

**I think the USA will put pressure on North Korea.**
→ put pressure on = apply pressure to ⇒ will put pressure → has imposed the economic sanctions（経済制裁を加えている）

TRACK 112

I want you to join our new project team.

**I decided to join their project team.**
⇒ I decided to → I don't want to（～したくない）

I never expected you would join us.

TRACK 113

**Thank you. I was able to have a good experience.**
⇒ good experience → bad experience（ひどい経験）、disagreeable experience（不快な経験）、many experiences（多くの経験）

Tell me about your experiences while you were in America.

**I experienced a lot of different things there.**
⇒ a lot of … things → racism（人種差別）

I had an unforgettable experience.

10歳の時に手術を経験したんだ。

生まれて初めてとてもつらい経験をしたよ。

それは誰もが人生で少なくとも一度は経験するよ。

そんな経験はしたことないなぁ。

スポーツ選手はみな少なくとも一度は好調不調を経験するものだよ。

## 計算する

私、計算するのが得意なんだ。

これは計算するの難しいね。

費用がどれくらいかかるか僕、計算してみよう。

減量のためにカロリー計算しなきゃいけないんだ。

合計を計算してくれる？

これ暗算で計算しよう。

クラスの平均点を計算してください。

## 消す

明かりを消して。

出かける前にすべてのものを必ず消すようにしてね。

**I went through a surgery when I was ten years old.**
→ go through（「困難、辛いことなどを」経験する、体験する）

**I experienced great hardship for the first time in my life.** → hardship（苦難）

**Everybody experiences that at least once in their life.**

**I have never experienced such things.**
⇒ such things → spiritual things（心霊体験）

**All athletes experience ups and downs at least once.**
→ ups and downs（浮き沈み）

TRACK 114

**I'm good at calculating.** ⇒ be good at → be bad at ~（~が不得意である）、be slow at ~（~が遅い）、be quick at ~（~が早い）

**It is difficult to calculate this.** → calculate= figure up

**Let me calculate how much it will cost.**
⇒ it will cost → we need（「幾ら」必要か）

**I have to count calories to lose weight.**

**Will you calculate the total?**

**I'll calculate this mentally.**
→ calculate mentally = do a sum in mental arithmetic ⇒ this → the total（合計）

**Please calculate the average mark of the class.**
→ average mark（平均点）

TRACK 115

**Turn off the light.** ⇒ the light → the television（テレビ）、the radio（ラジオ）、the computer（コンピュータ）、the power（電源）、the gas（ガス）、the music（音楽）、the light when you go to bed（寝るときは明かり「を消して」）

**Make sure you turn everything off before you leave.**
→ make sure ~（忘れずに~する、確実に~する）⇒ turn everything off → put out the fire（火を消す）

このビデオテープから雑音を消すことって可能ですか？

今の言葉、取り消すよ。

前言を取り消させて頂きます。

あの嫌な記憶を消したいよ。

この単語を棒線で消してください。

この部分は二重線で消してくれる？

この動画は消さないでよ、いいね？

このモザイクを消す方法を知ってる？

データを消さないで。

検索履歴はどうすれば消せる？

彼の名前をリストから消しましょ。

私の名前がリストから消されちゃった。

壁の落書きを消してくれる？

黒板を消してください。

間違いは消しゴムで消して。

この悪臭はどうやったら消せる？

部屋の臭いを消すために窓を開けましょ。

予約を取り消せますか？

**Is it possible to remove the noise from this videotape?**

**I'll take that back.** / I take back my word. → take back（「言葉などを」取り消す） ⇒ take that back → take back all I said（言ったことを全て取り消す）

**Let me withdraw my previous statement.**
→ withdraw = take back; take away; remove

**I want to erase that unpleasant memory.**
→ erase= blot out; forget; delete; cancel

**Please cross out this word.** ⇒ cross out → delete （削除する）

**Will you cross out these parts with double lines?**

**Don't delete this video, OK?**

**Do you know how to get rid of this tessellation?**
→ get rid of~（～を取り除く）→ tessellation（モザイク細工、モザイク）

**Don't erase the data.** ⇒ data → file（ファイル）

**How do I delete my browsing history?**

**Let's remove his name from the list.**
→ remove =take off; get rid of; cut

**My name was taken off the list.**
→ taken off= struck off; removed from

**Can you clean off the graffiti on the wall?**
→ clean off =erase; remove → graffiti（落書き）

**Please erase what's on the blackboard.** / Please clean the blackboard.

**Erase your mistakes with an eraser.**
⇒ mistakes → spelling mistake（スペルミス）

**How can you remove this bad smell?** ⇒ remove = get rid of

**Let's open the window to free the room of the smell.**
→ free A of B（A から B を取り除く）

**Can I cancel the reservation?**

その会合への参加を取り消したいのですが。

彼女どこへ行ったんだ？突然、姿消しちゃったね。

彼女なら裏口から姿を消したよ。

## 削る

鉛筆をこのナイフで削っていい？

この 15 条は削ったほうがいいと思う。

給料が大幅に削られたよ。

## 結婚する

30 歳前に結婚したいな。

お金持ちの男性と結婚したいよ。

彼女と結婚することにしたよ。

いつ結婚するの？

来月、結婚するよ。

どうして彼と結婚する気になったわけ？

私、彼と結婚するつもりはないわ。

彼と結婚するくらいなら死んだほうがましよ。

彼と結婚するかまだ気持ちがふらついているんだ。

私より彼の方が結婚を焦っているの。

**I'd like to withdraw my participation in the meeting.**
→ withdraw = cancel

**Where did she go? She suddenly disappeared.**

**She disappeared out the back door.** ⇒ back door → exit（出口）、front door（玄関）、main entrance（「大きな建物の」玄関）

TRACK 116

**Can I sharpen my pencil with this knife?**
→ sharpen my pencil= point my pencil

**We had better delete this Article 15.**

**My salary has been slashed.** → slash（大幅に切り下げる、削除する）

TRACK 117

**I want to get married before the age of thirty.**
→ get married = marry

**I want to get married to a rich man.**
⇒ rich man → doctor（医者）、lawyer（弁護士）、soccer player（サッカー選手）

**I decided to marry her.**

**When are you going to get married?**

**I will get married next month.** ⇒ next month → in June（6月に）

**What made you want to marry him?**

**I don't intend to marry him. / I have no intention of marrying him.**

**I would rather die than marry him.**

**I'm still unable to make up my mind to marry him.**
→ make up my mind=decide; determine

**He is more eager to get married than I am.**
→ be eager to~（しきりに〜したがっている、〜したくてたまらない）

結婚するより仕事をしたいな。

彼女は結婚するタイプじゃないよ。

どうして私と結婚したいわけ？

## 欠席する

会議を欠席できますか？

病気のため会議は欠席するよ。

残念ですが、先約があるので欠席します。

私が会合を欠席することで生じる問題はありますか？

あなたが学校を欠席するなんて珍しいわね。

彼女はよく無断欠席するね。

彼女がどうして学校を欠席しているか知ってるか？

私、授業を欠席したことは一度もないわ。

## 見学する

美術館を見学する予定なの。

お寺の中を見学することはできますか？

少し授業を見学することはできますか？

保育園を見学したいな。

今日は体育の授業を見学するんだ。

I want to work more than get married.

She is not the marrying type.

Why do you want to marry me?

TRACK 118

Can I be absent from the conference?
⇒ the conference → work（仕事）、your class（あなたの授業）

I'll absent myself from the conference because I'm ill.
→ absent oneself from = be absent from ⇒ because I'm ill → because of urgent business（急用で）、due to my personal reasons（個人的な理由で）

I'm afraid I will be unable to attend because of prior commitments. → prior commitments（先約）

Are there any problems that would occur if I were absent from the meeting? → occur=happen; arise

It's very unusual for you to be absent from school.

She is often absent without leave.
→ absent without leave（無断欠席）

Do you know why she has been absent from school?

I have never been absent from class.

TRACK 119

I plan to observe the museum. → observe（観察する、見学する、観測する）⇒ museum → factory（工場）、castle（城）

Can I observe the inside of the temple?

Can I observe the class a little? → class = lessons

I want to view a nursery.
→ view a nursery = go to visit a nursery; look at a nursery

I'm going to sit out of P.E. → sit out of ~（「活動などに」参加しない、加わらない）→ P. E = physical education（体育）

## 喧嘩する

わたし、ボーイフレンドとよくケンカするの。

友だちと電話で喧嘩しちゃった。

なんで喧嘩したわけ？

お金のことで喧嘩になっちゃってさ。

くだらないことでよく喧嘩するの。

わたし、夫と喧嘩したことは一度もないわね。

もう君と喧嘩はしたくない。

## 研究する

いま何を研究してる？

シェークスピアを研究してるところ。

気候変動の影響について研究しようと思っているんだ。

君は薬の研究をしてたよね。

ガンの治療法を研究してるんだ。

## 検索する

なにを検索すればいい？

インターネットで「わびさび」を検索してみて。

チョコレートアイスクリームの作り方を知りたいんだけど、
検索してくれない？

TRACK 120

**My boyfriend and I argue a lot.** → argue（「自分の意見を主張して」口論する、口げんかする）

**I had a fight with my friend on the phone.**
→ fight（口論、言い争い、なぐり合い）⇒ on the phone → by email （メールで）

**Why did you quarrel?** → quarrel（口げんかする、口論する）

**We got in a fight over money.**
→ over ~（〜について、〜のことで）→ over trifles（くだらないことで） ⇒ We got in a fight → I got in a fight with my husband（夫と喧嘩になった）

**We quarrel a lot over trivial things.**
→ over trivial things = over trifles; over trifle things

**I have never had a fight with my husband.**

**I don't want to argue with you anymore.**

TRACK 121

**What are you studying now?**

**I'm studying William Shakespeare.**

**I plan to study the effects of climate change.**

**I understand that you have been researching medicine.** → researching medicine = doing research on medicine ⇒ researching medicine → researching pharmacy（薬学の研究をしている）

**I'm researching ways to fight cancer.** → ways to fight cancer（ガンと戦う方法）⇒ ways to fight cancer

TRACK 122

**What should I google?** → google= search; research; explore

**Will you find what "*wabi*" "*sabi*" means on the internet?**

**I want to know how to make chocolate ice cream, can you google it?**

「デザートのレシピ」を検索してみる。

ネットでちょっと検索してみる。

ネットで彼について検索してるところさ。

もしその意味が知りたいんだったらネットで検索するといいよ。

それネットで検索した？

手元にトラッキングナンバーがあるから、荷物が今どこにあるか検索してみよう。

## 検討する

ご検討ください。

私たちの提案をご検討ください。

前向きに検討して頂けますようお願い致します。

あなたの提案を前向きに検討致します。

可能性を検討し、追って連絡します。

社に持ち帰って検討させてください。

あなたの提案を同僚たちと検討させてください。

もう少し検討させてください。

もう少し検討する時間をください。

検討していただけましたか？

**I'll try googling "deserts recipes."**

I'll do some research on the internet.

**I'm searching about him on the internet.** ⇒ searching about him = checking him out → check ~ out（～をよく調べる、～を調査する）= go over; look into; research; examine

If you want to know the meaning, you can search on the internet.

**Did you look it up online?** → online = on the internet

I have the tracking number with me, so let's check where our parcel is now.

TRACK 123

Please take it into consideration. / I would appreciate if you could consider it.
→ take ~ into consideration（～を考慮する、～を考慮に入れる）

**Please consider our proposal.**

Please give it some serious consideration.
→ give consideration（考慮する、配慮する）

**We will consider your proposal positively.**
⇒ positively → seriously（真剣に）、in a comprehensive way（総合的に）

We will consider the possibility and get back to you.
→ get back to you（改めて連絡する）

**Let me take it back to the office and think about it.**

I need to discuss your proposal with my colleagues.
→ colleague=fellow worker; coworker; partner

**Let me look into it a little more.**
→ look into=check; investigate; research; go over

Please give me a little more time to consider.

**Did you get a chance to consider it?**

その提案は現在検討中です。

検討していただいて有難うございます。

## こ

### 合格する

君はきっと試験に合格するよ。

試験に合格する自信はあるよ。

試験に合格するような気がする。

試験に合格したよ。

入学試験に合格するように頑張ります。

あなたが試験に合格することを願っているわよ。

このままだと第一志望校入試に合格できないよ。

僕、試験に合格するにはまだほど遠いな。

試験に合格することはあきらめているよ。

英検 2 級に合格した。

ハーバード大学に合格したんだ。

### 凍らせる

このケーキを凍らせてみてはどう？

**The proposal is now under consideration.**
→ be under consideration（検討中である）

**Thank you very much for your consideration.**

TRACK 124

**I'm sure you will pass the examination.** / You are sure to pass the examination.
→ be sure to= be certain to → examination=exam; test

**I'm confident of passing the exam.**
→ be confident of~（～に自信がある、～を確信している）

**I have a feeling that I will pass the exam.**

**I passed the examination.** ⇒ the examination → the interview（面接）、the oral test（口頭試験）、my first-choice school（第一志望校）

**I will do my best to pass the entrance examination.**
→ do one's best（全力を尽くす、精一杯頑張る）

**I hope that you will pass the exam.**

**I can't pass the entrance exam of my first-choice school like this.**

**I'm still a long way from passing the exam.**
→ be a long way from~（～からかけ離れている、～からはほど遠い）

**I have given up on passing the exam.**
→ give up on~（～に見切りをつける、～を断念する）

**I passed grade 2 of the English proficiency test.**
/ I passed the Eiken grade 2 test.

**I got accepted to Harvard.** → get accepted to = get accepted into

TRACK 125

**How about frosting this cake?**
→ frost（霜で覆う、凍らせる）=chill; freeze

ヨーグルトを凍らせると美味しいよ。

私、凍らせたいものは何でも凍らせるの。

ジュースも氷用トレイに入れて凍らせるんだ。

豆乳は凍らせることができるのかなぁ。

## 凍る

凍えちゃうよ。

骨の髄まで凍えてるよ。

水道管が凍っちゃった。

水は華氏 32 度で凍るの、知ってる？

俺、幽霊を見たとき恐怖で凍りついたよ。

## 志す

私は医者を志しています。

## 試みる

誰かがシステムへの侵入を試みているぞ。

ジョンソン氏との接触を試みてみましたか？

それを再び試みることを決めたよ。

これは試みる価値があるよ。

## 超す

今日は気温が 30 度を超している。

Yogurt is very tasty when you freeze it.

I freeze anything I want to.

I put juice in ice cube trays and freeze them, too.

I wonder if soy milk can be frozen.

TRACK 126

I'm freezing.

I'm frozen to the bone.

The water pipe froze up.

Do you know that water freezes at 32 °F? (F = Fahrenheit)

I froze with terror when I saw a ghost.

TRACK 127

I aim to be a doctor. → aim to = aspire to; intend to ⇒ doctor → scientist（科学者）、writer（作家）、diplomat（外交官）、lawyer（弁護士）

TRACK 128

Someone is trying to hack into the system.
→ hack into~（～に侵入する）

Did you attempt to contact Mr. Johnson?

I made up my mind to try it again.

This is worth trying.

TRACK 129

Today the temperature is above 30℃. (C = Celsius)

今年は入学志願者が 5 千人を超したよ。

彼女は 40 を越しているに違いない。

## 答える

私の質問に答えて。

この質問に答えられる人はいますか？

答える前によく考えて。

急いで答える必要はないよ。

あなたが答える番ですよ。

どう答えていいかわからないよ。

その質問に答えるのは不可能だよ。

これらはイエスかノーで答える質問です。

「はい」か「いいえ」で答えてみて。

あなたの期待に応えられるよう頑張ります。

私の要求に応えてくれてありがとう。

## 異なる

（諺）趣味は異なる。

服装の好みは人によって異なるものよ。

**The number of applicants for admission exceeded five thousand this year.** → exceeded = was over

**She must be over forty.**

TRACK 130

**Answer my question.**

**Who can answer this question?**

**Consider before you answer.**

**You don't have to answer quickly.**

**It's your turn to answer.**

**I don't know what answer I ought to give.** / I'm at a loss for an answer. / I don't know what to say in reply.
→ ought to ～ （～するべき、～すべきである） → in reply （答えとして）

**It's impossible to answer that question.**

**These are the questions that can be answered with "yes or no."**

**Answer with "yes" or "no."**

**I'll do my best to live up to your expectations.**
/ I'll work hard to meet your expectations.
→ live up to ~ （「期待などに」応える、に沿う）

**Thank you for accepting my request.**
⇒ request → sudden request （突然の要求）

TRACK 131

**Tastes differ.** ⇒ differ → differ from person to person （人によって異なる）

**Tastes in clothing vary from person to person.**
→ vary= differ ⇒ Tastes in clothing → Opinions （意見）

習慣は国によって異なるものよ。

あなたの意見は私のとは多くの点で異なるわね。

そこが私たちの異なるところよ。

このテーマに関する意見は年齢によって異なるでしょうよ。

この世論調査は自分の実感とは異なっているね。

日本語と英語は多くの点で異なるなぁ。

これは原作とは異なるね。

ここの気候は私の国の気候とは異なりますね。

## 断る

あの申し出は断るよ。

嫌なことは断るべきよ。

それを断るべきかなぁ？

とても断ることはできないんだ。

どうしてもそれを断ることができなかったよ。

彼女を食事に誘ったが、彼女断ったよ。

10 か所に応募したが、全部断られちゃった。

どうか断らないで。

**Customs differ with countries. / Customs vary from country to country.** → differ with countries = differ from one country to another ⇒ Customs → Eating habits（食習慣）、Table manners（テーブルマナー）

**Your opinion differs from mine in many ways.** ⇒ differs from ... ways → doesn't differ much from mine（私のとはたいして異ならない）

**That's where we differ.**

**The opinion on this subject may vary according to age.**

**This public opinion poll is different from my perception.** → perception（知見、見識、感じ方）

**Japanese differs from English in many ways.**

**This differs from the original story.**

**The climate here varies from that of my country.**

TRACK 132

**I'll turn down that offer.** ⇒ turn down = decline; refuse; reject ⇒ I'll → I could not（できなかった）⇒ that offer → this job offer（この内定を）

**You should refuse anything you hate.**

**Should I refuse that?**

**I can't very well refuse.**
→ cannot very well（「状況などから」～しにくい、～するわけにもいかない）

**I could not bring myself to refuse that.**
→ cannot bring oneself to~（～するに忍びない、～する踏ん切りがつかない、～する気になれない）

**I asked her to dinner, but she declined.**

**I applied to ten places, but was rejected by them all.**
→ apply to ～（「会社など」に応募書類を出す）

**Please don't turn me down.**

## 困らせる

もう困らせるのはやめてよ。

そんな質問で私を困らせないで。

君はいつも難しい質問で私を困らせるね。

人を困らせるような質問はしないで。

人を困らせるような質問ばかりする人っているよね。

君を困らせちゃったかな？

あなたを困らせていなければよいのですが。

あなたを困らせてごめんなさい。

他人を困らせるようなことはしないで。

## 困る

困ったなぁ。

それは困った。

君には困るよ。

それだから困るよ。

そんなくだらないことで私を困らせないで。

彼がいなくては困るよ。

それを私のせいにされては困るわ。

私はそれが一番困るわ。

TRACK 133

**Stop bothering me now.**

**Don't embarrass me with such a question.**
⇒ with such a question → with trifles（つまらないことで）

**You always perplex me with a difficult question.**
→ perplex =puzzle; baffle; perturb

**Don't ask embarrassing questions.**

**Some people only ask questions that bother others.**
→ bother =annoy

**Did I put you on the spot?**
→ put someone on the spot（人を質問で困らせる）

**I hope I didn't bother you.** / I'm sorry if I bothered you.

**I'm sorry I bothered you.** / I'm sorry I've troubled you.

**Don't do anything that may embarrass others.**
→ embarrass= shame; mortify; upset

TRACK 134

**I'm in trouble.** / I'm at a loss.

**That stumps me.** / You've got me stumped.
→ stump（「質問などが人を」悩ます、困らせる）

**You annoy me.** → annoy =trouble; bother; disturb; irritate

**That's what troubles me.**

**Don't bother me with those trifles.**
→ bother = disturb; annoy; trouble; torment

**We cannot do without him.**

**It will put me in trouble if I am blamed for it.**
→ be blamed for~（～で非難される、～を自分のせいにされる）

**That troubles me most.**

困ったことがあったら、いつでも私のところへ来てね。

## 懲らしめる

誰が彼を懲らしめる？

俺様がやつを懲らしめてやる。

やつをたっぷり懲らしめてやろうじゃないか。

## 懲りる

失敗に懲りたよ。

彼は懲りないね。

## 転ぶ

私ってよく転ぶの。

足がもつれて転びそうになっちゃった。

今朝、道で転んじゃった。

掃除機につまずいて転んじゃった。

氷の上で滑って転んで尻もちついちゃった。

石につまずいて前にころんだの。

階段を踏み外して転んじゃってさ。

昨日、膝から転んで、まだ膝が痛いよ。

俺は転んでもただでは起きないぞ。

Come to me whenever you have a problem.

TRACK 135

Who will punish him?

I'm going to teach him a lesson.
→ teach ~ a lesson =punish ~; discipline ~

Let's teach him a lesson that he won't soon forget.

TRACK 136

I learned a lesson from my failure.
⇒ from my failure → through the accident（事故を通して）、from a gambling（ギャンブルから）、from my mistakes （自分のミスから）

He never learns his lesson. / He never changes.
→ learn a lesson（教訓を得る、懲りる）

TRACK 137

I often fall down.

I tripped and nearly fell.

I fell down on the street this morning.
⇒ this morning → and cut my knee（そしてひざをケガした） ⇒ I fell down → I had an epic fall（派手に転んだ）

I fell over the vacuum cleaner.

I slipped on the ice and fell on my bottom.
→ bottom = rear; rump; rear end; buttocks; cheeks

I tripped over a stone and fell on my face.
→ fall on one's face（うつ伏せに倒れる）

I missed a step and tumbled down the stairs.
→ tumble down（転がり落ちる、転落する）

I fell down on my knee yesterday and it still hurts.

I take advantage of every situation.
→ take advantage of~（~をうまく利用する、~に乗じる）

## 壊す

窓を壊したのは誰だ？

誰か窓を壊した人物を見たものは？

お前たちのうち、どちらがこのカメラを壊したのか言いなさい。

おもちゃを壊さないで。

飲みすぎると体を壊しちゃうよ。

食べ過ぎてお腹を壊さないように。

実は今、胃を壊してるのさ。

昼夜を問わず働くと体を壊すよ。

これは生態系を壊してしまうよ。

偏見の壁を壊す必要がありますね。

## 壊れる

これは壊れやすいね。

パソコンが壊れていて使えないんだ。

これは保証が切れたわずか 2 日後に壊れたんだ。

壊れるまでこの自転車は使うつもりさ。

地震で我が地区では多くの家が壊れたんだ。

電話をかけなおせなくてごめん。携帯壊れちゃってさ。

TRACK 138

**Who broke the window?**
⇒ the window → this camera（このカメラ）

**Did anyone see who broke the window?**

**Tell me which one of you broke this camera.**

**Don't break your toys.**

**Excessive drinking will ruin your health.** ⇒ Excessive drinking → Overworking（働きすぎ）、Smoking（喫煙）、Anxiety（不安） → ruin one's health（体を壊す、健康を台無しにする）

**Don't hurt your stomach by eating too much.**
→ hurt =injure; mess up

**As a matter of fact, I have stomach trouble now.**
**/ I have a bad stomach now.**

**If you work day and night, you'll lose your health.**
→ day and night=all the time; night and day; constantly → lose one's health（体を壊す、健康を損なう）

**This will destroy the ecosystem.**

**We need to break down walls of prejudice.**

TRACK 139

**This is very fragile, isn't it? / This breaks easily, doesn't it?**

**I can't use my computer because it's broken.**

**This broke down just two days after the guarantee expired.** → expire（「契約などの」有効期限が切れる、満了する）

**I intend to use this bike until it breaks down.**

**Many houses in our district were destroyed by the earthquake.**

**Sorry I couldn't call you back. My cell phone broke.**

# さ

## 探す

何を探しているんだい？

携帯電話を探しているの。

携帯電話を落としたんだけど、探すの手伝ってくれない？

それ一日中探してるんだけど、まだ見つからないんだ。

家の中をくまなく探したけど、見つからなかったのよ。

このスーツに合うネクタイ探すの、手伝って欲しいんだけど。

これぞ、僕が探していたネクタイだよ。

仕事を探すのって簡単じゃないね。

ネットでもっと情報を探したらどうかな？

## 下がる・下げる

下がってよろしい。

一歩下がってください。

この携帯電話の値段が下がったよ。

私の車の価値が半分まで下がっちゃった。

TRACK 140

**What are you looking for?**

**I'm looking for my cellphone.** ⇒ cellphone → keys（鍵）、purse（財布）、 bag（バッグ）、 glasses（眼鏡）、a job（仕事）

**I lost my cellphone. Could you help me look for it?**

**I've been searching for it all day long, but I still can't find it.** → search for ~（～を探す）→ all day long（一日中） ⇒ searching → searching the whole house（家中を探して）

**I searched all over the house, but I could not find it.**

**I'd like you to help me pick a tie to go with this suit.**
→ pick（念入りに選ぶ、精選する） → go with ~（～と調和する、～とつり合う、～に似合う）

**This is the tie I've been looking for.**

**It's not easy to search for a job.** ⇒ search for = hunt for; look for

**How about searching for more information on the internet?**

TRACK 141

**You may leave.**

**Please take a step backward.**
→ take a step backward=move back one step

**The price of this cell phone went down.** / This cell phone went down in price. ⇒ went down → is coming down（下がってきている）

**My car has dropped in value by half.** / The value of my car depreciated to 50% of its market value.
→ depreciate （「価値、価格などが」下がる）

物価が下がり続けているわね。

米ドルの価値が 100 円に下がった。

温度が下がった。

冬が近づいてきているので、温度が下がっているんだ。

熱が下がった。

今朝、体温は正常に下がったよ。

成績が下がっちゃった。どうしよう？

どうして成績が下がったの？ゲームのしすぎかな？

全然勉強しなかったので、英語の成績がめちゃ下がっちゃったよ。

前回の点数は 970 点だったが、今回は 890 点に下がっちゃった。

今度の試験でクラスの順位が 7 番下がってしまった。

成績が下がるといけないので、一生懸命勉強しないといけないな。

やっと水位が 1 メートル下がった。

あの大きな地震でこの辺の地盤が下がってしまった。

その値段、下げることはできません？

これ以上値段を下げることはできませんね。

どのくらいその値段を下げることができますか？

**The prices continue to go down, don't they?**
→ go down = decline

**US dollar value dropped to one hundred yen.**

**The temperature fell.** → fell = dropped ⇒ fell → fell to minus three Celsius（マイナス 3 度まで下がった）

**Winter is coming, so the temperature is dropping.**

**My fever broke.** → broke = died down ; is gone

**My temperature went down to normal this morning.**

**My grades fell. What should I do?** → fell = dropped ⇒ fell → fell this year（今年は下がった）、are falling（下がり続けている）

**Why have your grades dropped? Too much gaming, I guess?**

**I did not study at all, so my English grades dropped significantly.** → significantly = considerably ; greatly ; notably

**Last time my score was 970, but this time it dropped to 890.**

**I dropped seven places in class after the last examination.** → the last examination（この前の試験、今度の試験）

**I cannot have my grades fall, so I've got to study hard.**

**Finally, the water level dropped one meter.**

**The ground here sank as a result of the big earthquake.**

**Can't you lower that price?**

**I can't make the price any lower.** / This is the best price I can offer.

**How much of that price can you reduce?** → reduce =lower

エアコンの温度を１度下げてくれる？

音量を下げるか消すかにしなさい。

声を下げて頂けますか？

車を少し下げて頂けますか？

椅子をもう少し後ろに下げてくれる？

感染リスクを下げるために距離をとっていてください。

先生の英語の授業のレベルを下げて頂けませんか？

これらの皿を下げてもらえますか？

## 咲く

この花はいつ咲くの？

この花は早春に咲くんだ。

これは花が咲く木だよ。

この木は秋に花が咲くのさ。

桜がまだ咲いてないね。

この桜は近いうちに咲くでしょう。

桜がこの時期に咲くとは不思議だね。

あと一週間で桜は満開に咲くわよ。

桜が咲くのが待ち遠しいね。

**Can you lower the temperature on the AC by one degree?** → AC = air conditioner

**Either turn down that volume or turn it off.**

**Could you lower your voice, please?**

**Could you back up your car a little?**
→ back up（バックする、後退する）

**Can you move your chair a bit more back?**
→ back = backward ⇒ chair → desk（机）

**Please keep a distance to lower the risk of infection.**

**Could you lower the level of your English class?**

**Would you take these dishes away, please?**

TRACK 142

**When does this flower come out?**
→ come out（「植物が」発芽する、開花する）= bloom

**This flower comes out in early spring.** ⇒ early spring → late spring（晩春）、summer（夏）、autumn/fall（秋）、winter（冬）

**This is a flowering tree.**

**This tree blooms in the fall.** → bloom = blossom; flower ⇒ in the fall → twice a year（一年に 2 回）

**The cherry blossoms still haven't bloomed.**

**It won't be long before this cherry blossom comes out.** → come out= bloom

**It's strange that cherry blossoms should bloom at this time of year.**

**The cherry blossoms will be in full bloom in a week.**

**I can't wait for the cherry trees to bloom.**

梅は3月に咲くんだっけ？

今年は梅の花が早く咲いたね。

チューリップが見事に咲いているじゃない。

## 叫ぶ

声を限りに叫んでみなさい。

大声で叫ぶのはよしなさい。

## 避ける

悪友は避けなさい。

私、彼に避けられてるような気がする。

あなた、私のこと避けてるでしょう。

どうして私を避けるわけ？

コロナウイルスにかからないように人込みは避けなきゃあね。

3密を避けることを忘れないで。

私はいつもマスクをして人込みを避けるようにしているわ。

高血糖食品は避けるべきね。

日向を避けて日陰に座りましょ。

Do the *ume* trees blossom in March?

The *ume* trees blossomed early this year.

The tulips are in magnificent bloom, aren't they?
→ magnificent=splendid; spectacular; glorious; wonderful; superb

TRACK 143

Shout at the top of your voice.
→ at the top of one's voice（声を限りに）

Don't shout in a loud voice. / Stop yelling.
⇒ in a loud voice → in the library（図書館で）

TRACK 144

You should avoid bad company. / Try to avoid bad company. → avoid= keep away from; stay away from

I feel like I'm being avoided by him. / I think he's avoiding me.

You're avoiding me, aren't you?

Why are you avoiding me?

We've got to avoid a crowd of people not to catch a coronavirus. → coronavirus（コロナウイルス） ⇒ a crowd of people → crowded trains（満員電車）

Don't forget to avoid the "Three Cs.": Closed spaces, Crowded places, Close contact settings.

I always wear a mask and stay away from a crowd of people.

You should avoid high glycemic foods.
⇒ high glycemic foods → fried foods（揚げ物）、direct sunlight（直射日光）

Let's sit in the shade to keep out of the sun. → keep out of~（～を避ける）

## 刺す

（注射）刺しますよ。

腕を刺された。119 番に電話して！

蜂に刺された。

蚊に刺されちゃった。

今日は肌を刺すような寒さだね。

## 指す

それは何を指していますか？

これが何を指しているのかわかりません。

「it」は文章の中で何を指していると思いますか？

私を指さすのはやめてよ。

人を指さすのは失礼よ。

## 誘う

彼女をデートに誘おうと思ってるんだ。

君をランチに誘ってもいいかな？

誘ってくれてありがとう。

他に誰か誘う？

何人誘おうか？

TRACK 145

**It's going in.** / I'm going to inject you now.

**I was stabbed in the arm. Call 119, please!**

**I was stung by a bee.**
→ sting（「針、トゲなどで」刺す）→ stung は過去形、過去分詞形。

**I was bitten by a mosquito.**
→ bite（かむ、食いつく）→ 蚊に刺される際は bite が使われる。bitten は過去分詞形。

**It's bitingly cold today, isn't it?**

TRACK 146

**What does it indicate?** → indicate=point out; suggest; show

**I don't know what this indicates.**

**What do you think the word "it" refers to in the sentence?** → refer to~（～に触れる、～に言及する）

**Stop pointing your finger at me.**

**It's rude to point at people.**

TRACK 147

**I'm thinking of inviting her on a date.**
→ invite her on a date= ask her on a date ; ask her out

**Can I invite you to lunch?**
⇒ lunch → dinner（食事）、a dance（ダンス）

**Thank you for inviting me.**

**Is there anyone else you'd like to invite?** / Would you like to invite anyone else?

**How many people are we going to invite?**

あなた、パーティに誘われた？

私、誘われてない。

彼、私をパーティに誘ってくれなかったわね。

彼からデートに誘われたけど、その気になれなかったの。

私、一度もデートに誘われたことないんだ。

## 悟る

彼はもう私を愛してなんかいないことを悟ったわ。

ことの重大さを悟りたまえ。

君は自分の間違いを悟るだけの分別がない。

## 去る

（諺）去る者は日々に疎し。

日本を去る前に何をしたいですか？

夏が去り、秋が来た。

彼はこの世を去った。

## 参加する

英語の授業に参加する？

あのイベントに参加するつもりよ。

そのセミナーに終日参加する必要がありますか？

**Were you invited to the party?**
⇒ to the party → on a day trip（日帰り旅行に）

**I haven't been invited.**

**He didn't invite me to the party.**
⇒ to the party → to the wedding（結婚式に）、to the drinking party（飲み会に）

**He asked me out, but I wasn't in the mood for it.**
→ ask someone out（人をデートに誘う）= ask someone for a date

**I have never been asked for a date.**

TRACK 148

**I realized that he doesn't love me anymore.**

**You should realize the seriousness of the problem.**

**You don't have enough sense to realize your mistakes.**

TRACK 149

**Out of sight, out of mind.**

**What do you want to do before you leave Japan?**
⇒ to do → to eat（食べる）

**Summer has passed and autumn is here.**

**He departed this life.** / He passed away. /He died.

TRACK 150

**Are you going to attend the English class?**
→ attend（出席する）

**I intend to take part in that event.**
→ take part in~（〜に参加する）→ 参加して役割を果たす ⇒ that event → the meeting（会議）、the training camp（合宿）

**Do I need to participate in that seminar all day?**
→ participate in~（〜に参加する）→ 参加して活動などに関与する。

あの練習には参加しないよ。

飲み会に参加していい？

君はそれに参加する必要はないと思うよ。

参加することに意義があるとは思わない？

## 残業する

今日は残業？

どのくらい残業する？

今日は 2 時間残業の予定だな。

一週間ずっと残業さ。

週 3 回残業してるよ。

いつもサービス残業さ。

残業はなんかしたくないよ。

## 賛成する

その提案に賛成します。

彼の計画に賛成です。

あなたの意見に賛成よ。

私たち全員、その計画に賛成です。

大賛成です。

**I'm not going to participate in that practice.** ⇒ that practice → that seminar（あのセミナー）、tonight's drinking party（今夜の飲み会）

**Can I join the drinking party?** → join（加わる）

**I don't think you need to participate in that.**

**Don't you think there is meaning in participating?**

TRACK 151

**Are you going to work overtime today?**
→ work overtime（残業する、時間外労働する）

**How much overtime do you work?**

**I plan to work overtime for two hours today.**

**I have been working overtime all week.**

**I work overtime three times a week.**

**I'm always working overtime without pay.**

**I don't want to work overtime.**

TRACK 152

**I favor the proposal.**
→ favor ～（～への支持を表明する、～に賛意を示す）

**I agree to his plan.** → agree to ~（～に合意する、同意する）→ 提案、要求、命令などに対して同意するとき。人に対しては使われない。

**I agree with your opinion.**
→ agree with ~（～に同意する）→ 相手と同じ気持ち、思いを持っているという意味で、人、意見のどちらにも使われる。⇒ opinion → plan（計画）、decision（決定）

**We all agree to the plan.**

**I totally agree. / I couldn't agree more.**

その点については全く君に賛成だよ。

君は私に賛成するよね？

彼の提案に賛成する？

君にはおおむね賛成だよ。

その計画には賛成できないね。

その計画にはなかなか賛成できないね。

### 散歩する

散歩に行こう。

散歩するってのはどう？

今は散歩する気分じゃないな。

公園を散歩してくる。

朝食前に犬を散歩させてくれない？

僕自身の運動不足解消のために毎日、ポチを散歩させてるのさ。

## し

### 叱る

私、いつも息子を叱ってるわ。

息子が部屋を片付けないので叱ったの。

**I completely agree with you on that point.**

**You do agree with me, don't you?**

**Do you approve of his proposal?**
→ approve of ~（～を認める、～に賛成する）

**I agree with you in the main.** → in the main =on the whole; mainly; mostly; for the most part ⇒ you in the main → one of your points（君の言いたい点の一つに）

**I cannot agree to the plan.** ⇒ cannot agree → could not agree（賛成できなかった）、cannot agree with your opinion（君の意見には賛成できない）

**I can hardly agree with that plan.**
→ can hardly~（ほとんど～できない）

TRACK 153

**Let's go for a walk. / Let's have a walk. / Let's take a walk.**

**What do you say to going for a walk?**
→ What do you say to~（～はどうですか、～はいかがですか）

**I don't feel like taking a walk just now.**

**I'll go for a walk in the park.** ⇒ I'll go for → I took（「散歩」をした）

**Could you walk the dog before breakfast?**

**I walk *Pochi* every day to make up for my lack of exercise.** → make up for~（～を埋め合わせる、～を補う）

TRACK 154

**I always scold my son.**

**I scolded my son because he didn't tidy up the room.**
→ tidy up（片づける）

お母さんに叱られたの？

そんなことをしたら、わたし、両親にめちゃ叱られちゃうよ。

遅刻したので先生に叱られちゃった。

今月のノルマを達成できなかったので、上司に叱られちゃったよ。

わたし、両親に叱られたことは一度もないわ。

## 沈む

太陽は東から昇り、西に沈む。

もうすぐ日が沈むよ。

最近は日が沈むのが早いね。

どうした。今日は沈んでるね。

## 慕う

彼女は君を慕ってるよ、知ってる？

子供たちは担任の先生を慕っているんだよ。

君は後輩たちから慕われてるなぁ。

## 従う

(諺) 郷に入らば、郷に従え。

私たちはみな法律に従うべきだ。

法律に従うのは我々の義務だろう？

**Did your mother tell you off?** → tell ~ off = scold~

**If I do such a thing, my parents will give me a good telling-off.** → telling-off（こごと、叱責）

**I was scolded for being late by my teacher.**
⇒ for being late → because I forgot something（忘れ物をしたので）

**I was called on a carpet because I couldn't meet the quota for this month.** → be called on a carpet（呼びつけられて叱られる） → meet the quota（ノルマを達成する）

**I have never been scolded by my parents. / My parents never told me off.**

TRACK 155

**The sun rises in the east and sets in the west.**

The sun will go down soon.

**The sun sets early these days.**

What's the matter with you? You look depressed today. → depressed = blue; melancholy; miserable

TRACK 156

She loves you, you know that?
→ loves you = is deeply attached to you

**The children love their homeroom teacher.** → love = adore

You are loved by younger colleagues.
→ colleague（同僚） ⇒ younger colleagues → many students（多くの生徒たち）

TRACK 157

When you are in Rome, do as the Romans do.

**We all should obey the law.**
⇒ the law → the regulations（規則）、the constitution of our country（国の憲法）

It's our duty to obey the law, isn't it?

交通ルールに従わなきゃだめじゃない。

会社のルールには従うように。

係員の指示に従ってください。

私たち世間の慣行に従わねばなりませんか？

どうして服装規定に従わないといけないんですか？

## 失敗する

失敗した。

試験に失敗しちゃった。

仕事で失敗してしまった。

最近失敗してばかりなんだよ。

失敗したらどうする？

失敗することを恐れないで。

## 質問する

質問していいですか？

遠慮なく質問してください。

きわどい質問をしますね。

そんな馬鹿な質問をするのはやめなさい。

**You must obey the traffic rules.**
→ the traffic rules=the traffic regulations; the rules of the road

**Try to follow the company's rules.** → follow = obey; observe

**Please follow the instructions from the staff.**

**Do we have to follow the ways of the world?**
→ ways of the world（慣例、世の習わし、世の常）

**Why do we have to follow the dress code?**
→ dress code（服装規定）

TRACK 158

**I failed. / I messed up. / I made a mistake. / I screwed up.**
⇒ made a mistake → made a huge mistake（大失敗した）、made a foolish mistake（間の抜けた失敗をした）

**I failed the exam. / I made a mistake on the test.**
⇒ the exam → the university entrance exams（大学入試）

**I made a blunder in my work.**
→ make a blunder（失敗する、ぽかをする、ドジを踏む）

**I keep messing up these days.**
→ these days（最近）→ この表現は現在形の文で使われる。

**What will you do if you fail?**

**Don't be afraid to fail.**

TRACK 159

**Can I ask you a question? / Do you mind if I ask you a question?** → Do you mind if ~（～してもいいですか） ⇒ a question → one more question（もう一つ質問）、another question（もう一つ質問、別の質問）

**Don't hesitate to ask me a question.**
→ Don't hesitate to ~（遠慮なく ~ する）

**You ask a delicate question.**
→ delicate（デリケートな、難しい、扱いにくい） ⇒ delicate → hard（難しい）

**Don't ask such a silly question.**

日本語で質問してもいい？

## 死ぬ

死ぬかと思った。

危うく死ぬところだった。

まだ死にたくないよ。

死ぬにはまだ早いよ。

畳の上で死にたいんだ。

人は必ず死ぬのさ。

僕の友人は若くして死んだよ。

暑くて死にそうだよ。

## 渋る

彼は金を払うのを渋るやつだ。

あの銀行は貸し渋るんだ。

## 仕舞う

これらのおもちゃをこの箱に仕舞いなさい。

この本は本箱に仕舞うのよ。

布団はたたんで押し入れに仕舞ってね。

これどこに仕舞ったらいい？

ケーキはどこに仕舞った？

**Can I ask questions in Japanese?**
⇒ in Japanese → in English（英語で）

TRACK 160

**I thought I was going to die.**

**I very nearly died.**

**I don't want to die yet.**

**I'm too young to die.**

**I want to die in my bed.** ⇒ in my bed → in peace（安らかに）= a peaceful death

**Man is mortal.**

**My friend died young.** ⇒ young → of pneumonia（肺炎で）、of apoplexy（卒中で）、of cancer（ガンで）、of disease（病気で）、of hunger（飢餓で）、of natural causes（老衰で）、from overwork（過労で）

**The heat is killing me.**

TRACK 161

**He is reluctant to pay money.**
→ be reluctant = be unwilling; hesitate

**That bank is reluctant to lend money.**

TRACK 162

**Put these toys in this box.**

**Put this book back in the bookcase.**

**Fold up the *futon* and put it in the closet.**
→ *futon*= bedding

**Where should I put this?**

**Where did you put the cake?**

ケーキは冷蔵庫に仕舞ったよ。

## 閉まる・閉める

このドアは閉まっている。

このドアは勝手に閉まるんだ。

ドアが閉まりますので、離れてお立ちください。

このドアはちゃんと閉まらないじゃない。

窓がちゃんと閉まっているか確認して。

台風のせいで私たちの学校は閉まってるんだ。

この店は何時に閉まるのかな？

郵便局は何時に閉まるかおわかりになりますか？

郵便局は５時に閉まります。

カーテンを閉めてくれる？

窓をきちんと閉めて。

ドアを静かに閉めて。

万が一に備えて、チェーンをかけてドアを閉めなさい。

ドアを乱暴に閉めないで。

出かける際に窓を閉めること、忘れないで。

急いでいたので、ドアを閉めるの、忘れちゃった。

**I put the cake in the fridge.** → fridge = refrigerator

TRACK 163

**This door is closed.** → closed= shut

**This door closes by itself.** / The door shuts automatically.

**The doors are closing. Please stand clear of them.**
→ stand clear of~（～から離れて立つ）

**This door won't close properly.**
→ properly=rightly; appropriately

**Make sure the windows are shut.**
→ make sure ~（～を確認する）

**Our school is closed due to the typhoon.**
⇒ the typhoon → heavy snow（大雪）

**What time does this store close?**
⇒ this store → the bank（銀行）、the post office（郵便局）

**Do you have any idea when the post office closes?**
→ Do you have any idea = Do you know

**The post office closes at five.** ⇒ The post office → This restaurant（このレストラン）

**Will you close the curtains?** → closeは静かにゆっくり閉めること。

**Shut the window tightly.** → shut は素早くぴしゃりと閉めること。

**Close the door softly.** → softly= quietly

**Chain shut the door, just in case.**
→ just in case（万が一に備えて、念のために）

**Don't slam the door.** / Don't shut the door violently.
→ slam=shut forcefully and loudly

**Don't forget to close the windows when you go out.**

**I was in a hurry, and so I forgot to close the door.**

ガスの元栓を閉めてね。

キャップを閉めるの、忘れないで。

ペットボトルのキャップはしっかり閉めて。

シートベルトを締めてね。

## 染みる

これ、目に染みる～。

玉ねぎが目に染みちゃった。

この目薬は目に染みるな。

冷たいものを食べると歯が染みるんだ。

汗がこのＴシャツに染みちゃった。

醤油がこの白いシャツに染みちゃったよ。

この大根は醤油の味がしっかり染みている。うまいよ。

## 占める

中国人は世界人口の何割を占めてるか知ってる？

中国人は世界人口の25%前後を占めているんじゃない？

女性がうちの顧客の大半を占めています。

うちの学校では男子が60%を占めているんだ。

僕の部屋は本が大部分を占めている。

**Please close the gas tap.** → gas tap = gas cock

**Remember to screw the cap back on.**
→ Remember = Don't forget

**Close the cap on the plastic bottle tightly.**
⇒ close the cap → close the lid（蓋を閉める）

**Fasten your seat belt, please.**

TRACK 164

**This stings my eyes.** → sting（「刺激で」ひりひりさせる、ズキズキさせる）

**This onion made my eyes water.**

**These eye drops smart.** / These eye drops make my eyes sting. → eye drops = eye medicine → smart（「薬などが」しみる、うずく）

**My teeth hurt when I eat something cold.**

**The sweat soaked my T-shirt.** → soak（「液体が」染み込む）

**The soy sauce sank into this white shirt.**
→ sink into~（～に染み込む）

**The flavor of the soy sauce has soaked right through this Japanese radish. Delicious.** → soak through（染み込む）

TRACK 165

**Do you know what percentage of the world's population do Chinese people account for?**
→ account for ~（～の割合を占める）

**Chinese people account for around 25% of the world population, right?**

**Women account for the majority of our customers.**

**Boys account for 60% of the students at our school.**
⇒ Boys → girls（女子）、⇒ 60% → one thirds（3 分の 1）

**Books occupy most of my room.** → occupy（占める、占有する）

## 就職する

卒業したらすぐ就職する予定よ。

大学かそれとも就職するか、まだ決まってないんだ。

新聞社に就職するつもりさ。

東京にある会社に就職することにしたの。

銀行に就職したんだ。

大手企業に就職したよ。

大学へ進学するつもりだったが、就職したんだ。

## 修理する

この時計、修理する必要があるな。

君、これ修理できる？

この時計は修理する価値なんかないよ。

コンピュータを修理する店を探してるんだけど。

これは修理するより買ったほうが安いよ。

これ修理するのに費用はいくらかかりますか？

このエアコン修理するのに何日かかります？

## 出席する

万障お繰り合わせの上、ご出席ください。

TRACK 166

**I'll start working as soon as I graduate.** / I plan on starting my career as soon as I graduate.

**I'm not sure yet if I'll go to university or get a job.**

**I'm going to take a job at the newspaper company.**
⇒ newspaper company → publishing firm（出版社）

**I made up my mind to work for a company in Tokyo.**
→ make up one's mind（決心する）

**I got a job in a bank.** → in a bank ＝at a bank

**I landed a job with a major company.**
→ land a job（仕事にありつく）

**I intended to go to university but I got a job instead.**
→ instead（代わりに、そうしないで）

TRACK 167

**This watch requires repairing.** / I need to get this watch repaired.

**Can you fix this?**

**This watch isn't worth repairing.** / It's not worth repairing this watch.

**I'm looking for a shop that repairs computers.**

**It's cheaper to buy a new one than to fix this.**
→ fix =repair ⇒ new one → new computer（新しいコンピュータ）、new air conditioner（新しいエアコン）

**How much will it cost to repair this?**

**How many days will it take to repair this air conditioner?** ⇒ How many days → How long（どれくらい）

TRACK 168

**Your attendance is requested.**

この会議に出席されることを歓迎致します。

パーティに出席できるかどうか教えてください。

この授業はきちんと出席することが重要です。

授業に出席することで単位が取れますか？

あなた、式に出席するつもり？

一郎は今日の授業に出席した？

彼、3週間英語の授業に出席していないよね。

誰がその会議に出席するか知ってる？

わたし、おそらく出席する。

僕は、その学会に出席するのは難しいと思う。

私は会議に出席する資格がないの。

健康がすぐれないのでその会議には出席できないんだ。

それ、仕事の都合で出席できないのよ。

私たち、それに出席する必要なんてないよ。

## 出張する

ニューヨークへ出張することになったよ。

明日、出張するんだ。

今週末から4日間学会出張します。

**We welcome your attendance at this conference.**

**Please let me know if you are able to attend the party.**

**Regular attendance is important in this class.**

**Can I obtain credits by attending the class?**
→ obtain = get; earn

**Are you going to attend the ceremony?**
⇒ ceremony → meeting（会合）、conference（会議）、party（パーティ）、 high-school reunion（高校の同窓会）、class reunion（クラスの同窓会）

**Did Ichiro attend today's class?**

**He hasn't attended English class for three weeks, has he?**

**Do you know who will attend the meeting?**

**I'll probably attend.**

**I think it's difficult for me to attend the academic meeting.**

**I'm not entitled to attend the meeting.**
→ be entitled to do（~する権利がある）

**My health is not good so I can't attend that meeting.**

**I won't be able to attend that because of work.**
→ because of = owing to; due to

**There is no need for us to attend that.**

TRACK 169

**I have to go on a business trip to New York.**
→ go on a business trip = make a business trip

**I'll make a business trip tomorrow.**

**I'll be on an academic study trip for four days from the end of this week.**

金曜日まで出張する。

先週、日帰り出張をしたよ。

今回は長期出張に行っていたんだ。

## 出発する

いつ出発するの？

間もなく出発する。

一週間後に出発する予定よ。

明日、旅行に出発するんだ。

私たち、出発する時間ね。

出発する準備はできてる？

ちょうど自宅を出発したところです。

この列車は何時に出発しますか？

この列車は定刻通りに出発します。

## 準備する

明日の授業の準備でもするか。

試験の準備をしなくっちゃ。

試験の準備はしっかりやったよ。

急いで、学校の準備をしなさい。

**I'll be on a business trip until Friday.**

**I made a one-day business trip last week.**
⇒ a one-day business trip → a three-day business trip（3 日間の出張）

**I was on an extended business trip.**
⇒ an extended business trip → a short business trip（短期出張）、an international business trip（海外出張）、a domestic business trip（国内出張）

TRACK 170

**When are you off ?** → off = moving away ⇒ off → leaving home（家を出発する）

**I'm going to depart soon.** → depart= leave; go off ; start

**I intend to leave in a week.** ⇒ in a week → within a few days（数日以内に）、on the twenty-eighth of March（3 月 28 日に）

**I'm leaving for vacation tomorrow.**
→ leave for vacation（休暇で出かける）

**It's time for us to go.** ⇒ go → leave Japan（日本を出発する）

**Are you ready to depart?**

**I just left my house.**

**What time does this train depart?**

**This train departs on schedule.** → on schedule =on time; as planned; as expected ⇒ on schedule → at nine a. m.（午前 9 時に）

TRACK 171

**I think I'll prepare for tomorrow's lessons.**

**I've got to prepare for the exam.**
→ exam= examination; test ⇒ for the exam → for employment（就職の）、for my trip（旅行の）、to study abroad（留学するための）

**I prepared thoroughly for the exam.**

**Hurry up and get ready for school.** → get ready = prepare

旅行の準備をしているとこさ。

前もって準備する必要があるものはありますか？

何を準備すべきですか？

何か準備する資料はありますか？

木曜日までにその資料は準備できません。

5 人分の食事の準備をしておいてくれる？

## 招待する

彼をうちに招待するんだ。

来たい人は誰でも招待するつもりよ。

高校時代の友人を招待しようと思ってるんだ。

あなたの結婚式には何人ぐらい招待するつもり？

彼を家に招待するつもりはないわよ。

彼は招待しなかったんだ。

私、彼女の結婚式に招待されなかったわよ。

彼を招待すべきだったわ。

あなたの誕生会に招待してくれてありがとう。

私、招待されたけど、出席できなかったんだ。

## 知らせる

彼の電話番号、知らせるね。

I'm getting ready for my trip.

Is there anything that I need to prepare beforehand?
→ beforehand = in advance; previously

What should I prepare? ⇒ What → What materials（どういう資料を）

Are there any materials to prepare?

I can't prepare that material before Thursday.

Will you prepare meals for five people?

TRACK 172

I'll invite him to my place. → my place= my house

I'll invite whoever wants to come.

I'm thinking of inviting my high school friends.

How many people are you planning to invite to your wedding?

I have no intention of inviting him to my house.
→ have no intention of ~（～するつもりはない）

I didn't invite him.

I wasn't invited to her wedding.

I should have invited him. → should have ＋過去分詞（～すればよかった）→すればよかったのにしなかった、という後悔、または非難の意を表す。

Thank you for inviting me to your birthday party.

I was invited, but I couldn't attend.

TRACK 173

I'll let you know his telephone number.

メールで知らせて。

私にできることがあったら知らせて。

あなたの都合がいい時を知らせてくれる？

そのことだけど、あなたにいつまでに知らせる必要がある？

私たちの到着時間を彼に知らせた？

彼にはすぐ知らせるわ。

それが決まり次第あなたに知らせるね。

ずいじ知らせるね。

その件については彼に知らせる必要はないよ。

## 調べる

わからないことがあったら調べてみて。

ちょっと調べてみます。

ちょっと待って。調べてあげるわ。

その件については調べてみます。

どうやってそれを調べるつもり？

この単語の意味を辞書で調べなさい。

それ、ネットで調べてみる。

わからない単語はいつもコンピュータで調べてるよ。

**Let me know by e-mail.** → by = via ; through

**If there's anything I can do, let me know.**

**Could you inform me of your availability?**
→ inform A of B（A に B を知らせる） → your availability（あなたの都合）

**When do I need to notify you about that by?**
→ notify = inform; tell; let someone know

**Did you inform him about the time of our arrival?**

**I'll inform him right away.**
→ right away = soon ⇒ right away → as soon as possible（できるだけ早く）

**I'll let you know once it's been decided.**
→ once = as soon as; when

**I'll keep you posted.** →「ずいじ連絡します」との意。「ずいじお知らせください」とする場合は Please keep me posted. とする。 ⇒ posted → posted on the changes（変更があれば知らせる）

**It's not necessary to notify him about that.**

TRACK 174

**If there's something you don't know, look it up.**
→ look up（「言葉などを」調べる）

**I'll look it up.**

**Give me a second, I'll look it up for you.**

**I'll look into the matter.** → look into~（～を調べる、～をのぞき込む）

**How are you going to check that up?**
→ check up = investigate; examine; inspect; survey

**Consult your dictionary for the meaning of this word.**
→ consult = refer to; use

**I'll look it up online.** → online（オンラインで、ネットワーク上で） ⇒ online → on the computer（コンピュータで）

**I always look up words I don't know on the computer.**
⇒ on the computer → in the dictionary（辞書で）

地球温暖化についてネットで少し調べてみたよ。

彼の住所を地図で調べてるんだ。

この在庫があるかどうか調べてもらえますか？

論文を提出する前に調べて頂けますか？

## 知る

(諺) 衣食足りて礼節を知る。

(諺) 知者は一を聞いて十を知る。

神のみぞ知る。

彼のこと知ってる？

彼のことはよく知ってるよ。

彼の顔は知っているけど。

彼のことは知らないわ。

私が知るわけないでしょ。

僕の知る限りでは、彼女はまだ独身だよ。

それについては何も知らない。

この場所は知る人ぞ知るところですよ。

この地域のことはよく知りません。

僕の知ったことじゃないよ。

君は身の程を知るべきだ。

I did some research on global warming online.

I'm looking up his address on a map.

Could you check if you have this in stock?
→ in stock（在庫があって、在庫あり）

Could you please look over my thesis before I submit it? → look over（ざっと目を通す、～を一読する） → thesis =essay; paper; treatise → submit（提出する、投稿する）

TRACK 175

Well fed, well bred. / Fine manners need a full stomach.

A word to the wise is enough.

Only God knows.

Do you know him? ⇒ him → Spanish（スペイン語）

I know him very well. ⇒ very well → a little（少しだけ）

I know him by sight.
⇒ by sight → by name（名前は）、but not his name（でも名前は知らない）

I don't know him.

How should I know?

As far as I know, she is still single.

I know nothing of it.

This place is known to those in the know.
→ those in the know（よく知っている人たち、事情に通じている人たち）

I'm not familiar with this area.

It's no concern of mine. / It's none of my business.

You should know yourself. → yourself = your place

恥を知り給え。

## 信じる

(諺) 見ることは信じること（百聞は一見に如かず）

(諺) 人は願うことを信じる。

自分を信じなさい。

自分を信じることは大切だよ。

君の言うことを信じるよ。

もう一度あなたの言葉を信じてみる。

正しいと信じることをやりなさい。

あなた神を信じる？

私の言うことが信じられないの？

そんなの信じないよ。

あなたが何と言おうと信じない。

私がそんな話を信じるとでも思ってるの？

私、そんな話を信じるほどバカじゃないわ。

それを本当に信じる人はいないんじゃない。

それを信じるか信じないかはあなた次第よ。

彼の話を信じるべきじゃないよ。

**You ought to be ashamed of yourself.**

TRACK 176

**To see is to believe.** / Seeing is believing.

**We soon believe what we desire.**

**Believe in yourself.**
→ believe in ~（「~の存在、正当性などを」信じる、信頼する）

**It's important to believe in yourself.**

**I believe what you say.** / I believe you.
→ believe（「言ったことを」信じる）

**I'll believe you one more time.**

**Do what you believe is right.**

**Do you believe in God?**
⇒ God → ghosts（幽霊）、UFOs（UFO）、the immortality of the soul（魂の不滅）

**Don't you believe me?** ⇒ me → What I'm saying（私の言ってること）

**I don't believe it.** ⇒ don't believe → can't believe（信じられない）

**I don't believe you no matter what you say.**

**Do you think I believe those kinds of stories?**

**I'm not so stupid as to believe a story like that.**
/ I'm wiser than to believe a story like that.

**There will be no one who really believes that, I guess.**

**It's up to you to believe that or not.**
→ be up to you to~（~するのはあなた次第である）

**You ought not to believe him.**
→ ought not to~（~すべきでない、~しない方がいい）

### 親切にする

親切にしてくれてありがとう。

娘にとても親切にしてくれたことを感謝します。

お年寄りには親切にするようにね。

## す

### 吸う

大きく息を吸って。

新鮮な空気を吸うためにちょっと外に出るね。

タバコは吸うの？

1日に1箱吸うよ。

いつも電子タバコを吸ってるよ。

タバコは吸わないね。

ここでタバコを吸うのはやめていただけます？

### 過ごす

余暇をどのように過ごすの？

読書をしたり映画を観たりして過ごすんだ。

何もしないで過ごしたいな。

家でのんびり過ごすよ。

いつも通りに過ごすわね。

TRACK 177

Thank you for all your kindness.
/ I really appreciate your kindness.

I'm grateful that you were so kind to my daughter.

Try to be kind to the old. → the old = elderly people

TRACK 178

Take a big breath. → take a deep breath にすると「深呼吸する」

I'll go outside to get some fresh air.

Do you smoke?

I smoke a pack of cigarettes a day. ⇒ a pack of → five（5本）

I'm always smoking my vape. → vape=e-cigarettes

I don't smoke.

Would you please stop smoking here?

TRACK 179

How do you spend your free time?

I spend my time reading and watching movies.

I want to spend time doing nothing. → doing nothing = not doing anything ⇒ doing nothing → sleeping（寝て）

I'm going to take it easy at home.

I spend my time as always.

明日は午前中いっぱい寝て過ごすつもりさ。

休みの日はいつも家族と過ごすんだ。

残りの人生は田舎で過ごしたいね。

新年をどのように過ごすの？

週末はどこで過ごした？

週末は自宅で過ごしたよ。

夏休みはガールフレンドとハワイで過ごしたよ。

昨日は眠れぬ夜を過ごしちゃった。

## 進む

この時計は 3 分進んでいる。

この時計は 1 日に 2 ～ 3 秒進むんだ。

仕事は計画通り進んでる？

全て計画通りに進んでいるよ。

仕事はどんどん進んでいるよ。

例の計画は一歩前に進んだよ。

英語の進み具合はどう？

今日は 50 ページまで進んだんだ。

**I'm going to sleep away the whole morning tomorrow.** → sleep away~（～を寝て過ごす）

**I always spend time with my family on my days off.**
→ day off（休日）

**I want to spend the remainder of my life in the country.**
→ remainder of my life in the country → rest of my life with you（残りの人生を君と）

**How do you spend the New Year?**
⇒ the New Year → Christmas（クリスマス）、the vacation （休暇）

**Where did you spend the weekend?** ⇒ the weekend → your vacation（あなたの休暇）

**I spent the weekend at home.**
⇒ the weekend at home → useful time in Los Angeles（ロサンゼルスで有益な時間）、a meaningful time（意義ある時間） ⇒ at home → alone（一人で）

**I spent my summer vacation with my girlfriend in Hawaii.**

**I spent a sleepless night yesterday.**

TRACK 180

**This watch is three minutes fast.**

**This watch gains a couple of seconds a day.**

**Is your work progressing as planned?**

**Everything is going as scheduled.** ⇒ as scheduled → smoothly（順調に）

**The work is making steady progress. / The work is moving ahead rapidly.**

**That plan took a step forward.** ⇒ took a step forward → is making slow progress（ゆっくりと進んでいる）

**How are you getting along with your English?**
→ get along with = get on with ⇒ English → studies（研究）

**I got as far as page fifty today.**

教科書の60ページまで進むつもりさ。

自分が正しいと信じた道を進むことね。

自分を信じて進みなさい。

あなたが失恋したのはわかるけど、人生を前向きに進んでいかないと。

この通りに沿って進んで。

この道なりに進んで。

前に進んでください。

一列で進んで。

最寄りの出口に進んで。

今日、地球温暖化が進んでいる。

社会の様々な領域でグローバル化が進んでいる。

この国のIT化はまだ進んでいない。

最近、近視が進んじゃったよ。

この頃、食が進まないんだ。

胃ガンが進んでしまった。

君は考えが世間よりもかなり進んでいるね。

この映画は話が進むにつれてますます面白くなるよ。

**I'm going to get to page sixty in the textbook.**
⇒ page sixty → the end of the second chapter（第 2 章の終わり）

**You should go the way you believe is right.**

**Go forward believing in yourself.**

**I know you are heartbroken, but you need to move on with your life.** → be heartbroken（失恋している）= be crushed → move on with your life（「悲しみなどを忘れ」前を向いて自分の人生を生きる）

**Make your way along this street.**

**Follow this road.**

**Please move forward.** → move= proceed → Please continue moving forward.（「立ち止まらないで」前に進んでください）

**March in a single file.** → file（「縦の」列） ⇒ in a single file → by two and two/ two abreast（二列で）、shoulder to shoulder（並んで）

**Proceed to the nearest exit.**

**Today global warming is progressing.**

**Globalization is progressing in various areas of society.**

**This country is still backward in adopting IT.**
→ backward（遅れている、後進的な） → in adopting~（〜の導入において）

**My nearsightedness has gotten worse lately.**
→ get worse（より悪くなる）

**I have a poor appetite these days.** → a poor appetite = little appetite ⇒ have a poor appetite → have a good appetite（食が進む）

**My stomach cancer has reached an advanced stage.**
→ reach an advanced stage（「病気などが」進行した段階になる）

**You are way ahead of the times in your ideas. /** Your ideas are far ahead of the times. → way（はるかに、かなり、うんと）→ ahead of the times（時勢より進んだ、時代の先を）

**This movie gets more and more interesting as the story progresses.**

日が進むにつれてだんだん寒くなってくるね。

## 勧める

何がお勧めですか？

バニラ味がお勧めですね。

これは勧めませんね。

このDVD鑑賞を強くお勧めします。

彼にお茶を勧めたらどう？

彼にご飯のお代わりを勧めてみたらどう？

## 捨てる

これ捨てていい？

それはそこのゴミ箱に捨ててくれない？

昨日の残り物は捨てちゃった？

もう使わないものは捨てなさい。

思い込みや偏見は捨てるべきだよ。

その悪い癖は捨てたほうがいいね。

それ、捨てるなんてもったいないよ。

タバコの吸い殻を路上に捨てないで！

**It's getting colder as the day wears on.**
→ wear on（「時間が」ゆっくり過ぎる、経過する）= pass slowly

TRACK 181

**What do you recommend?** ⇒ What → Which（どちらが）

**I recommend the vanilla flavor.**
⇒ the vanilla flavor → the chocolate flavor（チョコレート味）、this one（こちらが）、this dish（こちらの料理）

**I don't recommend this.**

**I highly recommend you to watch this DVD.**

**Why don't you offer him a cup of tea?**

**How about encouraging him to have another bowl of rice?** → encourage（勧める）

TRACK 182

**Can I throw this away?**

**Will you dump it in the trash can over there?**
→ dump = put; toss → trash can=garbage box; dust bin（英）; rubbish bin（英）

**Did you throw away the leftovers from yesterday?**
→ leftover（料理の残り物、食べ残し）

**Get rid of the stuff that you no longer use.**
→ get rid of =discard; throw away; remove; dump → you no longer use=you don't use any more

**You should throw away your assumptions and prejudices.**
→ throw away = discard; abandon → assumption（仮説、憶測、仮定）

**You had better get out of that bad habit.**
→ get out of ~（~から抜け出す、~をやめる）

**It would be a waste to throw it away.**
→ waste（無駄、浪費、もったいない）

**Don't throw cigarette butts on the street!**

## 滑る

さっき滑って転んじゃった。

今朝、僕の車が凍った道路で滑ってさ。

入学試験に滑っちゃった。

俺のギャグ、滑っちゃったよ。

## 座る

座りませんか？

お座りください。

背筋を伸ばして座りなさい。

私、ここに座る。

あなたはそこに座って。

隣に座ってもいい？

私の右側に座って。

向かい合って座ってください。

みんな輪になって座ろうよ。

別々のテーブルに座るの？

ここはいつも僕が座る席なんだ。

お客さんに背を向けて座らないの。

私、車の後部座席に座るわ。

TRACK 183

I slipped and fell a while ago.

My car slipped on the frozen road this morning.

I failed in the entrance examination.

My joke landed with a thud. / My joke left them cold.
→ landed with a thud（俗）大失敗する　→ leave someone cold（人を冷たいままにしておく、「見ても聞いても」人に感銘を与えない、人に面白いと思わせない）

TRACK 184

Won't you sit down?

Please sit down. / Please have a seat.

Sit up straight. → up straight → at ease（楽に）

I'll sit here. ⇒ here → in my habitual seat（私のいつもの席に）

You go sit there.

Can I sit next to you? → next to you = beside you ; by your side

You can sit on my right. ⇒ on my right → on my left（左側に）

Sit face to face, please. ⇒ face to face → back to back（背中合わせで）

Let's sit in a ring. ⇒ in a ring → away from each other（互いに離れて）
⇒ sit in a ring → sit in a line（一列に座る）、sit in a semicircle（半円形に座る）

Do we sit at separate tables?

This is my accustomed seat.
→ accustomed（慣れた、いつもの）=habitual; usual; customary

Don't sit with your back to your guest.

I'll sit in the back of the car.
⇒ in the back of the car → in the passenger seat（助手席に）

# せ

## 成功する

君は必ず成功するよ。

君が成功することを願っている。

君が成功するチャンスは大いにあるよ。

君が全力を尽くせば、成功するさ。

成功するかどうかは君次第だよ。

最初、成功しなかったら、何度も挑戦してみなさい。

減量に成功するのって、難しいわね。

私、減量に成功したよ。

## 説明する

これを説明してください。

この単語の意味を説明していただけますか？

英語で説明してください。

それを英語ではうまく説明できません。

私が説明しましょうか？

どうしてそんなことを言ったか説明させてください。

TRACK 185

**You will surely succeed.** / You are sure to succeed. / You will **succeed without doubt.** → will surely = will certainly → succeed = make it → without doubt （疑いもなく）

**I hope you will succeed.** ⇒ succeed → succeed in your work（仕事において成功する）、succeed in your studies（研究において成功する）

**There is every chance that you will succeed.**
→ There is every chance~ （～のチャンスは大いにある）

**If you put your best foot forward, you will succeed.**
→ put your best foot forward（全力を尽くす）

**It's up to you whether you will succeed or not.**

**If at first you don't succeed, try, try again.**

**It's hard to succeed in weight loss.**

**I succeeded in losing weight.** / I was successful in losing weight.

TRACK 186

**Please explain this.** ⇒ this → this in detail（これを詳しく、詳細に）、how to eat this（この食べ方を）、your absence（欠席）、the results（結果）、the rules of this game（このゲームのルール）、the situation（状況）

**Could you explain what this word means?**
→ what this word means = the meaning of this word

**Please explain in English.** ⇒ in English → in Japanese（日本語で）

**I can't explain that well in English.**

**Would you like me to explain?**

**Let me explain why I said that.**
⇒ why I said that → a little further（もう少し）

この地図でそこへの行き方を説明しましょう。

グラフを使って説明しましょう。

## 責める

どうして自分を責めるの？

自分を責める必要はないわよ。

私を責めてるわけ？

あなたのミスで私を責めるのはやめてよ。

あなたを責めるつもりはないけど、でも…

## 世話をする

今週末は子供たちの世話をしなきゃいけないんだ。

私が子供の世話をしてるの。

今日は私たちのうちどっちが犬の世話をする？

私の留守の間に植物の世話をしてくれる？

お世話になりました。

## 洗濯する

毎日、洗濯してる？

私、ほぼ毎日洗濯してるわよ。

毎日洗濯するのは嫌だけど、でもやらないと洗濯物が溜まっちゃうからさ。

I'll show you on this map how to get there.

I'll explain using graphs.
⇒ using graphs → using figures（図を使って）、using diagrams（図表を使って）

TRACK 187

Why do you blame yourself?

You don't have to blame yourself.

Are you blaming me?

Stop blaming me for your mistake.

I don't mean to blame you, but……

TRACK 188

I have to take care of my children this weekend.
→ take care of~（～の世話をする、～を引き受ける）→ 大切に面倒をみるという意味合いで、人、物について一時的な面倒や世話をする際に使われる。

I look after my child. → look after~（～の面倒を見る、～の世話をする）
→ look after は毎日の習慣として面倒をみる、また世話をする、といった意味合い。

Which of us is going to take care of the dog today?

Can you take care of the plants while I'm away?

Thank you for taking care of me.

TRACK 189

Do you do your washing every day? / Do you wash clothes every day?

I wash clothes almost every day.

I hate doing my laundry every day, but it piles up otherwise. → do my laundry= do my washing → pile up（集積する、溜まる） → otherwise（さもないと、そうしないと）

今日は洗濯するにはいい日だわ。

今日はせんたくしよ〜っと。

洗濯した？

## 選択する

どちらか一方を選択して。

このリストから一つ選択して。

支払方法を選択してください。

間違った選択はしないこと。

人生とは絶えず選択することさ。

# そ

## 増加する

結婚詐欺事件が増加しているんだって。

コロナ感染者が増加しているね。

地震の発生数が増加してるんじゃない？

離婚率が急速に増加しているみたい。

それは今後も増加し続けると見込まれているんだ。

この町の人口はどんどん増加している。

It's a good day to do the laundry.

I'll do the laundry today.

Did you wash the clothes? / Have you done the laundry?

TRACK 190

Choose either one.
⇒ either one → your favorite color（あなたの好きな色）

Choose one from this list.

Please select the method of payment.
→ select= choose; pick out

Don't make a bad choice.

Life is to choose constantly.

TRACK 191

I hear marriage fraud cases are increasing.

The number of Corona infected people is on the increase. → is on the increase = is increasing

The number of earthquakes is increasing, isn't it?
⇒ earthquakes → people sixty-five and over（65 歳以上の人）

The divorce rate seems to be increasing rapidly.

That is expected to continue to increase.
→ be expected to~（～すると思われている、～するはずである）

The population of this town has been increasing.

## 掃除する

私は毎日自分の部屋を掃除するわよ。

私たち、誰がトイレの掃除をするかでいつも喧嘩してるの。

## 相談する

相談してもいい？

相談に乗ってほしいことがあるんだけど。

留学に関してあなたに相談に乗ってもらえるかなぁ。

いつでも相談に乗るよ。

そのことだったら彼女に相談したらいいと思うけど。

それは先生に相談してみたらどうかな？

まずはあなたに相談すべきだったわ。

## 注ぐ

カップに湯を注げば、3分でこのラーメンはでき上がるよ。

この川は海に注いでいるの？

俺、新しいプロジェクトにエネルギーを注がなきゃ。

## 育つ

あなたはどこで育ったの？

私は東京で生まれ大阪で育ったんだ。

TRACK 192

**I clean my room every day.**
⇒ every day → at least once a week（少なくとも週に一度は）

**We always argue about who cleans the bathroom.**
→ bathroom（浴室、トイレ）

TRACK 193

**Can I ask your advice?** / Can I talk to you about something?

**There's something I want to talk to you about.**

**I'm wondering if you could give me some advice on studying abroad.**

**I'm always here for you.** / You can come talk to me anytime.

**You should ask her for some advice about that.**

**Why don't you ask your teacher about that?**

**I should have consulted with you first.**
⇒ first → beforehand（前もって、事前に）

TRACK 194

**Pour the boiling water into the cup and the *ramen* will be ready in three minutes.**

**Does this river discharge itself into the sea?** / Does this river flow down to the sea? → discharge itself into~（川が～に注ぐ）

**I've got to concentrate my energies on the new project.** → concentrate ~on…（～を…に集中させる）= pour my efforts into

TRACK 195

**Where did you grow up ？** → grow up（育つ）

**I was born in Tokyo but raised in Osaka.**

## 育てる

子供を育てるのは大変な仕事だわ。

それに子供を育てるのはすごくお金がかかるもの。

私は 5 人の子供を育てたわ。

私は祖父母に育てられたの。

人材を育てるのは難しいよ。

うちの会社は従業員を一から育てているんだ。

わが校は運動選手を育てることで有名なんだ。

私は小さな庭で色んな花や野菜を育てているの。

この温室で何を育てているの？

## 卒業する

大学はいつ卒業する？

順調にいけば 2 年で卒業だよ。

いつ高校を卒業したの？

この 3 月に大学を卒業したんだ。

学資を稼ぎながら大学を卒業したわけさ。

卒業したらどうする？

学校を卒業したら留学するつもりよ。

TRACK 196

**Bringing up children is hard work.**
⇒ hard work → never easy（決して簡単じゃない）

**And it costs a lot of money to raise children.**
→ raise= bring up

**I raised five children.**

**I was raised by my grandparents.**

**It's difficult to develop human resources.**
→ develop= foster → human resources（人材）

**Our company trains employees from scratch.**
→ train = educate → from scratch=from the beginning; from the start

**Our school is famous for developing an athlete's ability.** → developing an athlete's ability = training an athlete

**I'm growing various flowers and vegetables in my small garden.**

**What are you growing in this greenhouse?**

TRACK 197

**When will you graduate from university?**

**I'll graduate in two years if things go well.**

**When did you graduate from high school?**

**I graduated from university this March.**
⇒ I graduated → I'll graduate（卒業する） ⇒ this March → three years ago（3年前）、with honors（優等で、優秀な成績で）

**I worked my way through university.**
→ work my way through ~（苦労して ~ を完了する、働きながら ~ を終える）

**What will you do after you graduate?**
→ after you graduate = after graduation

**I'll study abroad when I have finished school.**

今年は大学を卒業できなかったんだ。

卒業するためには論文を書かなきゃいけないんだ。

大学を卒業するためには後 20 単位必要なんだよ。

## 背く

その行為は明らかに法ならびに道徳に背きますよ。

どうして君はいつも上司に背くんだ？

## 染める

髪の毛を茶色に染めたいな。

私、白髪を黒く染めてもらったの。

彼女、髪の毛をブロンドに染めるんですって。

私は髪の毛を染めたことないの。

いいか。絶対に犯罪に手を染めるんじゃないぞ。

# た

## 退院する

私、いつ退院できますか？

私、もうすぐ退院するよ。

退院しました。

**I couldn't graduate from university this year.**

**I have to write a thesis in order to graduate.**
→ in order to~ （～するために）

**I need twenty more credits to graduate from university.**

TRACK 198

**It's obviously an act against laws and morality.**
→ obviously= clearly; evidently; plainly

**Why do you always rebel against your boss?**
→ rebel against（～に反抗する、～に逆らう）= disobey

TRACK 199

**I want to dye my hair brown.**
⇒ brown → red（赤）、pink（ピンク）、black（黒）

**I had my grey hair dyed black.**

**She is going to dye her hair blonde.**
→ blonde →男性に対しては blond.

**I have never dyed my hair before.**

**Remember. Never get involved in crime.**
→ get involved in~（～に巻き込まれる、～と関わり合いになる）

TRACK 200

**When can I be discharged?** → discharged = discharged from the hospital → イギリス英語では the hospital の the が省略され、from hospital となる。

**I'll be leaving the hospital soon.** / **I will be discharged soon.** ⇒ soon → on Monday（月曜日に）、tomorrow（明日）、next week（来週）

**I was discharged from the hospital.** / **Now I'm back home from hospital.**

## 耐える

君は耐えることを学ぶ必要があるね。

僕は何にでも耐えられるさ。

それには耐えられない。

もうこれ以上いじめには耐えられない。

震度 7 以上の地震に耐える家が欲しいよ。

## 絶える

彼との連絡が絶えちゃった。

恐竜は 6600 万年前に絶えたと言われている。

我が家では笑いが絶えない。

私、夫の浮気問題で苦労が絶えないわ。

## 倒れる

俺、今朝、仰向けに倒れちゃった。

彼、熱中症で倒れたよ。

彼はコロナウイルスで倒れたよ。

今日はすごく暑かったので、倒れるかと思ったわ。

TRACK 201

**You need to learn to endure.**

**I can stand anything.** → stand= bear; endure

**I can't bear it.** / It's more than I can bear. / It's too much for me.
⇒ it → his words（彼の言葉）、him（彼に）、this noise（この騒音）、her tears（彼女の涙）、this hard life（この苦しい生活）、this cold（この寒さ）、this heat（この暑さ）、this humidity（この湿気）

**I can't put up with bullying anymore.**
→ put up with = endure; bear; stand

**I want a house that can withstand an earthquake with a seismic intensity greater than seven.**
→ seismic intensity（震度）

TRACK 202

**I have lost contact with him.**

**It is said that dinosaurs died out 66 million years ago.**
→ die out（絶滅する、絶える）

**In my home there is no end to laughter.** / My house is always full of laughter.
→ there is no end to~（～に終わりはない、～が絶えない）

**I have no end of trouble because of my husband's affairs.** → no end of ~（限りない ~、とても多くの ~） → affair（「一時的で不純な」恋愛、浮気、不倫）

TRACK 203

**I fell on my back this morning.**
⇒ on my back → on my face（うつ伏せに）

**He collapsed from heatstroke.** → collapse（「病気、過労などで」倒れる） ⇒ from heatstroke → from his illness（病気で）、from exhaustion（疲れ切って）、from sleep deprivation（睡眠不足で）、from a heart attack（心臓発作で）

**He came down with coronavirus.** → came down = was laid up（病床にある、床についている） ⇒ coronavirus → the flu（インフルエンザ）

**It was so hot today, I thought I was going to collapse.**

塀が暴風雨で倒れちゃった。

地震の最中にタンスが倒れたんだ。

## 炊く

ご飯を炊いてくれる？

ご飯を美味しく炊くには水加減が大切なんだ。

## 確かめる

ちょっと確かめたいことがあるんだけど。

ドアが閉まっていることを確かめてくれる？

僕はいつも出かける前に天気予報を確かめるんだ。

それが本当かどうか確かめてみよう。

## 助かる

助かるよ。

君にはいつもすごく助かるよ。

すごく助かった。

その方が助かるよ。

手伝ってくれれば、すごく助かるよ。

本当に助かりました。ありがとう。

**The wall fell down in a rainstorm.**
→ fell down → fell down with a crash（すさまじい音をたてて倒れた）

**The chest of drawers fell over during the earthquake.**
→ chest of drawers（タンス）→ fall over（倒れる、倒壊する）= fall down

TRACK 204

**Can you cook rice?** → cook rice= make rice ⇒ rice → fluffy rice（ふわふわしたごはん）、rice al dente（硬めのごはん）

**The proper quantity of water is crucial for making good boiled rice.** → crucial =vital; important; essential; critical

TRACK 205

**I want to make sure of something.**
⇒ of something → of this with my own eyes（これを自分の目で）

**Can you check if the door is closed? / Please make sure that the door is closed.**
→ make sure ~（～を確かめる、～を確認する） ⇒ the door is closed → the door is locked（ドアに鍵がかかっている）、the window is shut （窓が閉まっている）、the fire is out（火が消えている）、the light is off（明かりが消えている）

**I always check the weather forecast before I go out.**

**Let's see if it is true or not.** → see if~（～かどうか確認する）

TRACK 206

**You are a lifesaver.** → lifesaver（命の恩人、苦境を救ってくれる人）

**You're always a great help.**

**That helped me a lot. / That really helped me.**

**That's more helpful to me.**

**If you could assist me, it would be a great help.**
→ assist = help; aid

**You've been very helpful. Thank you.**

## 助ける

助けてくれる？

お助けしましょうか？

助けて！誰か警察を呼んで！

待って。今、助けるから。

宿題を助けてくれる？

私、将来、人を助ける仕事がしたいんだ。

私、病気の人を助けるために看護師になったんだ。

この薬は消化を助けるんだ。

助けてくれてありがとう。

## 立つ

(諺) 火のないところに煙は立たない。

立て！

足がしびれて立てないんです。

僕の家は丘の中腹に立っているんだ。

今回は君の顔が立つよう言う通りにしよう。

私は今苦境に立っているんだ。

## 建てる

家を建てるの？

TRACK 207

Can you help me?

Can I help you?

Help me! Somebody call the police!

Hold on! I'm gonna help you!
→ hold on = wait; wait a minute; just a moment; stop; stay put

Will you help me with my homework?

I want a job in which I can help people in the future.
→ a job = to do a job

I became a nurse in order to help sick people.

This medicine helps the digestion.

Thank you for helping me out. → helping me out = helping me

TRACK 208

There's no smoke without fire.

Stand up! / On your feet!
⇒ up → on one leg（片足で）、on tiptoe（つま先で）、side by side（並んで）

I can't stand up because my legs have gone to sleep.
→ go to sleep（しびれる）

My house stands on the side of a hill.

I'll do as you say this time to save your face.
→ save your face（君の顔を立てる、君の顔をつぶさない）

I'm in a difficult situation now.

TRACK 209

Are you going to build a house?

新しい家を建てるために貯金してるんだ。

私の夢は東京の郊外に大きな家を建てることなんだ。

家を建てるために土地を買ったよ。

この地域では家は建てられないんだ。

新しい家を建てたよ。

悲しいことに、僕の家の隣に新しいアパートが建てられてるんだ。

僕は今のところ家を建てる余裕はないよ。

## 楽しむ

(諺) 楽しめるときに楽しめ。

楽しんでね。

みんなで楽しもう。

今日を楽しむぞ。

楽しんだ？

彼女との食事を楽しんだよ。

私の趣味は家庭菜園を楽しむことなの。

## 食べる

何か食べたいな。

**I'm saving up to build a new house.**

**My dream is to build a mansion in the suburbs of Tokyo.** → mansion（大邸宅、屋敷）

**I bought a piece of land to build a house.**
→ a piece of land= a plot of land

**Houses can't be built in this area.** / You can't build a house in this area.

**I had my new house built.** / I built myself a new house.

**To my sadness, they are constructing a new apartment complex next to my house.** → they are constructing a new apartment complex = a new apartment complex is being built → apartment complex（2棟以上のアパート、共同住宅、団地） ⇒ constructing a new apartment complex → building a factory（工場を建設している）、building a new school（新しい学校を建てている）、building a fence （フェンスを作っている）

**I can't afford to build a house now.**

TRACK 210

**Gather your rosebuds while you may.**

**Enjoy yourself.** / Have fun.

**Let's all have fun.**

**I'm going to enjoy today.**

**Did you have fun?** ⇒ have fun → enjoy the party（パーティーを楽しむ）、enjoy the concert（コンサートを楽しむ）

**I enjoyed dinner with her.** → dinner with her → lunch（ランチ）、talking with her（彼女との話）、the conversation with her（彼女との会話）、driving（ドライブ）、walking（ウオーキング）、shopping（ショッピング）

**My hobby is enjoying my home garden.**

TRACK 211

**I want something to eat.**

何を食べたい？

僕、何でも食べられるよ。

いつも腹いっぱい食べるんだ。

もう食べられないというぐらいチーズバーガーを食べたいな。

これどうやって食べるの？

これは何を使って食べるのかな？

フォーク、それともスプーンで食べる？

箸で食べるのよ。

この野菜は生で食べられるの。

よく噛んで食べなさい。

お皿のものは残らず食べなさい。

朝食は食べた？

朝食は何を食べた？

今朝はトーストとスクランブルエッグを食べたよ。

今朝はすごく忙しかったので、朝食を食べる時間がなかったんだ。

朝食は少ししか食べなかった。

朝食は余り食べないんだ。

朝食はたっぷり食べたよ。

今日は一日何も食べてないのさ。

What do you want to eat?

I can eat anything.

I always eat till I am full.

I want to eat a bunch of cheese burgers until I can't eat anymore. → a bunch of ~（たくさんの～、山ほどの ~）

How do I eat this?

What do you use to eat this ？

Do you use a fork or spoon to eat this?

You eat with chopsticks.
⇒ chopsticks → a fork（フォーク）、a spoon（スプーン）

We can eat this vegetable uncooked. → uncooked = raw

Chew well when eating.

Eat everything on your plate.

Did you eat breakfast?

What did you eat for breakfast?

I ate toast and scrambled eggs this morning.
⇒ scrambled eggs → a fried egg（卵焼き）

I was so busy this morning that I didn't have time to eat breakfast.

I only had a little breakfast.

I don't eat much breakfast.

I ate a lot of breakfast. / I had a huge breakfast.

I haven't eaten anything today.

昼ご飯は何を食べる？

誰とランチを食べるの？

これから彼とご飯を食べる予定なの。

これから食べるとこなんだ。

今日は外で食べようよ。

このレストランで食べないか？

私、一人でご飯を食べるのが好きなんだ。

これは食べる気がしない。

食べる前によく手を洗いなさい。

ここで食べ物を食べないでください。

## 溜まる

最近ストレスが溜まっちゃってさ。

この仕事はストレスが溜まるよ。

うちの上司にはストレスが溜まるよ。

入学試験のことでストレスが溜まってるんだ。

ストレスを貯め過ぎないように気をつけて。

仕事が溜まってるんだ。

ここの窓枠に埃が溜まっているよ。

What are you going to have for lunch?

With whom are you going to have lunch?

I'm going to eat with him.

I'm about to eat now.
→ be about to~（まさに～しようとしている、～するところ）

Let's eat out today. ⇒ eat out → eat in（家で食べる）

How about eating at this restaurant?

I like to eat meals alone. / I prefer to eat alone.

I don't feel like eating this. ⇒ this → today（今日は）

Wash your hands well before eating.

Please don't eat food here.

TRACK 212

I've been so stressed lately.

This work is stressful.

Our boss stresses me out.
→ stress someone out（人をストレスで参らせる、人をイライラさせる）

I feel so stressed out about my entrance examination.
→ feel stressed out（ストレスに苦しむ、ストレスで参る）

Take care not to get too stressed.

My work is piled up. / My work has been piling up.

Dust is piled up on this window frame. / This window frame is covered in dust. → is piled up = has accumulated

## 黙る

黙れ！

黙ってないで、何とか言ってよ。

あなたは都合が悪くなると、すぐ黙るんだから。

その件は黙っていたほうがいいよ。

他人のものを黙って使うなよ。

## 試す

試してみて。

これは試してみる価値があるね。

それ、試してみたらどう？

私の英語力を試してるんですか？

私、人を試すのは好きじゃない。

このアプリがどんなものか試してみたよ。

## 貯める

私、お金を貯めなきゃあ。

お金貯めてる？

夢を実現するためにお金を貯めてるんだ。

これから留学のためにお金を貯めるつもり。

TRACK 213

**Shut up!** / Zip your lips! / Save your breath!

**Don't just be silent, say something.**

**Whenever you are inconvenient, you give us the silent treatment.** → give someone the silent treatment（「一時的な怒りなどで」人に口をきかない）= become silent

**You had better keep it to yourself.**
→ keep ~ to oneself（～を口外しない、～を胸に秘めておく）

**Don't use other people's things without permission.**

TRACK 214

**Try it.** / Give it a try. ⇒ it → this *natto*（この納豆）、it again（それをもう一度）、it one more time（それをもう一回）、it if you have a chance（機会があれば）

**This is worth trying.**

**Why don't you try it?** → Why don't you…（～してはどう）

**Are you testing my English skills?**

**I don't like to test people.** / I hate to put a person to a test.

**I tried this application to see how it is.**

TRACK 215

**I've got to save money.**

**Are you saving money?** ⇒ Are you… → Why are you（どうして…）

**I'm saving money to realize my dreams.**
→ realize my dreams=make my dreams come true

**I plan on saving money for studying abroad.**
→ plan on ~ing = intend to~

私、アメリカへの旅費を貯めるためにアルバイトをしてるの。

## 保つ

(諺) 間の垣根は友情を新鮮に保つ。

若さを保つ秘訣を教えて？

若さは永遠には保てないわよ。

体型を保つために何してる？

私、体調を保つために毎日運動をしてるのよ。

健康を保つためには多くの野菜と果物を食べるといいわよ。

僕にとってモチベーションを保つことはすごく難しい。

## 頼る

君、頼りにしてるよ。

他人に頼るんじゃない。

頼れる人が欲しいんだ。

頼りになるのはあなただけよ。

君は他人に頼りすぎだよ。

自分の努力に頼るべきだと思うよ。

あなたは本当に頼りになるわ。

頼りになるボーイフレンドがいるのっていいわね。

**I'm working part-time to save up for a trip to America.**
→ save up for ~（～に備えてお金を貯める） ⇒ a trip to America → studying overseas（留学）、a rainy day（まさかの時）

TRACK 216

**A hedge between keeps friendship green.**

**Will you tell me the secret of keeping your youth?**
→ keeping your youth = staying young ; keeping you young

**You cannot stay young forever.** / You cannot retain youth forever. → retain=keep; keep possession of

**What do you do to stay in shape?**
→ stay in shape（体型を保つ、健康を保つ）

**I exercise daily to keep myself in condition.**
→ keep oneself in condition（良好な状態を保つ、健康な状態でいる）

**You had best eat plenty of fruits and vegetables to keep healthy.** → had best ~（～するのが一番いい）

**It's very difficult for me to maintain motivation.**

TRACK 217

**I'm counting on you**

**Don't rely on others.** → rely on = depend on; count on

**I want someone I can rely on.**

**You are the only one I can rely on.** / There is no one I can count on except for you.

**You rely too much on others.**

**You should rely on your own efforts, I think.**

**You are such a reliable person.**

**It's good to have a boyfriend you can depend on.**

# ち

## 誓う

私の秘密を人に言わないと誓う？

禁酒すると誓う？

神に誓う、嘘だったら死んでもいい。

君に永遠の愛を誓うよ。

## 違える

日付を間違えちゃった。

それを読み間違えた。

彼の名前を書き間違えた。

首を寝違えちゃった。

薬を飲み違えてしまった。

## 注意する

注意しなきゃだめよ。

もっと注意するよう何度も言ったでしょ。

何に注意すべきでしょうか？

言動には注意すること。

言葉にもっと注意すること。

TRACK 218

**Will you give me your word of honor that you will not tell my secret to anyone?** → give someone your word of honor（面目にかけて人に誓う） → tell my secret to anyone = give away my secret to others

**Do you swear to give up drinking?** → give up =quit
⇒ give up drinking → never leave me（私とは決して別れない）

**Cross my heart and hope to die.**

**I swear that I will love you forever.** / I vow to love you forever.

TRACK 219

**I got the date wrong.** / I got mixed up about the date. / I made a mistake about the date.

**I read it wrongly.** / I misread it. → wrongly = wrong

**I spelled his name wrong.** / I mistook his name's spelling.

**I sprained my neck in my sleep.**
→ sprain（捻挫する、くじく） → in my sleep = while I was sleeping

**I took the wrong medicine.**

TRACK 220

**You must be careful.**

**I've told you again and again to be more careful.**
→ again and again=over and over; repeatedly; frequently

**What should I be careful about?**

**You should mind your P's and Q's.**
→ mind your P's and Q's =mind your manners; mind your language（言動に注意する）→ p と q の文字が混同しやすいことから。

**Be more careful about your language.**
⇒ your language → your conduct（言動）、your health（健康）

車を運転するときは幾ら注意しても注意しすぎるということはないよ。

道路を横断するときは車に注意しなさい。

## 注射する

これから注射しますよ。

インフルエンザの予防注射をするところさ。

インフルエンザの注射をしたよ。

## 駐車する

ここに駐車しよう。

ここに駐車できますか？

この駐車場はバックで駐車してください。

僕はバック駐車が苦手なんだ。

バックで駐車するから誘導してくれる？

## 注文する

何を注文する？

何を注文するか決めた？

私、これを注文するわ。

このレストランではいつもカレーライスを注文するんだ。

これを電話で注文しようよ。

最近、僕は何でもネットで注文するんだ。

**You cannot be too careful when you drive a car.**
→ cannot be too ~（いくら～してもし過ぎることはない）

**Watch out for cars when you cross the street.**
→ watch out for~（～を見張る、～に気をつける、～に用心する）

TRACK 221

**I'm going to give you a shot.**
→ give someone a shot（人に注射をする）

**I'm having an injection to vaccinate against influenza.**
→ injection（注射） → vaccinate against ~（～のワクチン接種をする）

**I got a shot for influenza.** → a shot for influenza = a flu shot

TRACK 222

**Let's park here.** ⇒ here → in the station parking lot（駅の駐車場に）

**Can we park here?**

**Please reverse into this parking space.**
→ reverse into~（～へバックで入れる）

**I'm bad at parking in reverse.**
⇒ be bad at ~ → be good at ~（～が得意である）

**Can you lead the way while I try to back into the parking spot?** ⇒ back = reverse ⇒ back into…spot = park in reverse

TRACK 223

**What would you like to order?**

**Did you decide what to order?**

**I'll order this.** ⇒ this → salad（サラダ）、a glass of beer（ビール一杯）、a bottle of white wine（白ワインを１本）、the same（同じもの）

**I always order curry and rice at this restaurant.**

**Let's order this over the telephone.**

**Nowadays, I order everything online.**

僕はさっきピザをネットで注文したよ。

注文したいのですが。

マッシュルームオムレツを注文したいのですが。

料理を注文したがまだ来ないよ。

これは注文してないです。

これは注文したものとは違います。

別の料理を注文しました。

### 散らかす

その辺にものを散らかさないでよ。

部屋を散らかさないで。

部屋を散らかしっぱなしにしないで。

## つ

### 使う

今、これ使いますか？

これ、使ってる？

これ、いつ使います？

これは毎日仕事で使うんだ。

私は本にお金を使うの。

**I ordered a pizza online a little while ago.**
→ a little while ago（ちょっと前に、先ほど）

**I'd like to order, please. / Can I order, please?**

**I'd like to order a mushroom omelet.**

**I made an order but the food still isn't here.**

**I didn't order this.**

**This isn't what I ordered.**

**I ordered a different dish.**

TRACK 224

**Don't scatter your things about.**
→ scatter（あちこちに散らかす） ⇒ your things → toys（おもちゃ）、clothes（服）
⇒ about → about the house（家中に）

**Don't litter your room.**
→ litter（ごみを散らかす）= mess up; make a mess of

**Don't leave your room in a mess.** → in a mess = untidy

TRACK 225

**Do you use this now ?** → use は道具などを有効に使うこと。

**Are you using this?**

**When do you use this?** ⇒ this → a computer（コンピュータ）

**I use this for work every day.**

**I spend money on books.** ⇒ money → large sums of money（大金）
⇒ books → clothes（衣服）、make-up（化粧品）、accessories（アクセサリー）

一か月どれくらい本にお金を使ってる？

礼儀正しい言葉を使うようにしなさい。

汚い言葉を使うのはやめなさい。

二枚舌は使わないで。

彼女は男なら誰にでも色目を使うんだから。

彼はよく仮病を使うよね。

彼といるときは気を遣うわ。

## 捕まえる

捕まえた！

あの男にバッグがひったくられた。誰か、彼を捕まえて！

捕まえられるものなら捕まえてみろ。

子供の頃、よくカブトムシを捕まえたものだ。

タクシーが捕まらないよ。

## 掴む

(諺) 溺れる者は藁をもつかむ。

これ、しっかりつかんで。

夫の浮気の証拠をつかんだわ。

どうやって大金をつかんだんだ？

**How much money do you spend on books a month?**

**Try to use proper language.**
→ proper language（穏当な言葉）→ proper は「適切な、礼儀正しい、上品な」

**Stop using dirty words.**

**Don't keep two tongues in one mouth.**

**She casts sheep's eyes at every man.**
→ sheep's eyes（色目、流し目）

**He often fakes illness.** → fake illness（仮病を使う、病気のふりをする）

**I have to care for him when I'm with him.**
→ care for~ （～に気を遣う）

TRACK 226

**I got it!** / I caught it!

**That man snatched my bag! Somebody, catch him!**

**Catch me if you can.**

**I used to catch beetles when I was a kid.**
→ used to~（よく～したものだ、以前はよく～したものだった）→ 過去の習慣や状態を表す。→ kid= child

**I can't catch a taxi.**
→ catch= get ⇒ taxi → taxi on a rainy day（雨の日はタクシーが）

TRACK 227

**Drowning men clutch at straws.**

**Hold this tight.** → tight= tightly; firmly

**I seized proof of my husband's infidelity.**
→ I seized proof =I got evidence → infidelity =adultery; affair; cheating

**How did you acquire a large sum of money?**
→ acquire =obtain; get; earn; gain

## 疲れる

疲れたよ。

歩き疲れた。

最近、歩くとすぐに疲れるんだ。

心身共に疲れてるわ。

長時間の外出は疲れるね。

この仕事はすごく疲れるよ。

意地悪な同僚といると疲れるわ。

試験勉強はホント疲れるよ。

ラッシュ時の通勤は疲れるよ。

一日中ずっと英語を話すのって疲れちゃうよ。

コンピュータでの仕事は目が疲れるね。

疲れるのは暑さというより湿度よね。

## 尽くす

全力を尽くしなさい。

最善を尽くします。

僕は自分の仕事に全力を尽くしたよ。

TRACK 228

**I'm tired.**

**I got tired from walking.**

**These days I get soon tired from walking.** / These days walking soon tires me.

**My mind and body are both tired.**

**I get tired being out for a long time.**

**This work wears me out.** / This work is very tiring.
→ wear someone out（人を疲れさせる） → very tiring = exhausting; tiresome

**It's exhausting just to be with vicious coworkers.**
→ just to be with vicious coworkers= being around spiteful coworkers ⇒ just to be with vicious coworkers → having to listen to my boss complain all day（一日中ボスの文句を聞かなきゃいけない）

**Studying for exams really takes it out of me.**
→ take it out of a person = make a person very tired

**Going to the office during the rush hour is tiring.**

**Speaking English for a whole day makes me tired.**

**Working on a computer tires the eyes.**

**It is not so much the heat as the humidity that makes me tired.**
→ not so much A as B（A というよりむしろ B である、A ではなくむしろ B）

TRACK 229

**You should exert all your powers.**
→ exert all one's powers（全力を尽くす）

**I'll do my best. / I'll do all I can.** ⇒ my best → my best for our company（わが社のために最善を）

**I gave my all in my work.** →give one's all（全力を尽くす、精一杯やる）

どんなものでも全力を尽くさなければ成功しないさ。

私って、ボーイフレンドに尽くして、捨てられるタイプかな。

## 作る

何かを作りたいな。

良い思い出を作ろう。

この旅は思い出を作るためなんだ。

机を作ったよ。

それ自分で作ったの？

料理は作るの？

簡単な料理なら作るよ。

夕食は何を作る？

今夜の食事は誰が作る？

私、自分で弁当を作るんだ。

母と一緒にクッキーを作ったよ。

一緒にたこ焼きを作ろうよ。

私は卵焼きを作るのが得意なんだ。

明日午前 10 時までに会議用の資料を作ってくれます？

会議用の資料は作り終えましたか？

**You'll never succeed in anything unless you give it your all.**

**Maybe I'm the type who gets very devoted to my boyfriend, but then I get dumped.** → get devoted to ~（～に熱中する、尽くす、熱愛する） → get dumped（振られる、お払い箱になる）

TRACK 230

**I want to make something.**

**Let's make great memories.** ⇒ great memories → happy memories（楽しい思い出）、unforgettable memories（忘れえぬ思い出）

**This trip is all about making memories.**
→ be all about ~（～が大切である、～が重要な目的である、要するに～ということ）

**I made a desk.**

**Did you make it yourself?**

**Do you cook?** ⇒ cook → like to cook（料理を作るのが好き）

**I'll make a simple meal. / I'll make something simple.**

**What are you going to make for dinner?**
⇒ dinner → lunch（昼食）

**Who's going to cook dinner tonight?**

**I make a lunch box myself.**

**I made cookies with my mom.**

**Let's make *Takoyaki* .**
⇒ *Takoyaki* → stew（シチュー）、cookies（クッキー）

**I'm good at frying eggs.** ⇒ frying eggs → cooking sunny-side-up（目玉焼きを作ること）、making scrambled eggs（スクランブルエッグを作ること）

**Could you make meeting materials by 10 a.m. tomorrow?**

**Have you finished making materials for the meeting?**

現在、資料を作成している最中です。

この資料を作り直してください。

30 歳までには子供を作りたいな。

お二人で幸せなご家庭を作られるように。

チーズはミルクから作られる。

このテーブルは木から作られる。

この工場では冷蔵庫が作られている。

### 付ける

このメールに写真を付けます。

履歴書に写真を付けるべきだよ。

この子犬に一郎という名をつけるつもりだ。

次の一節にタイトルを付けなさい。

それは私に付けておいて。

### 漬ける

忘れずに食器を水に漬けておいて。

これ、一晩水に漬けておいて。

大根を漬けよう。

**I'm in the process of making materials.** / I'm making materials now. → be in the process of ~（～の最中である）

Please remake these materials.

**I want to have a child before I'm thirty.**

I hope you'll make a happy home together.

**Cheese is made from milk.**
→ be made from~（～からできている、～を原料とする）→ 何でできているか見た目でわかるものは be made of~ で、作られたものの形が変わり、何でできているかわからないものの場合は be made from~ が使われる。

This table is made of wood.

**Refrigerators are manufactured at this factory.**

TRACK 231

**I'll attach the pictures to this e-mail.** → e-mail = email

You should attach your photograph to your resume.
→ resume=curriculum vitae

**I'm going to name this puppy Ichiro.**

Give a title to the following passage.

**Charge it to my account.** / Put it down to my account.
→ charge（「支払い、代金など」請求する、回す、課す） → put ~ down to…（「～の費用を」…に付ける）→ account（勘定）

TRACK 232

**Make sure to soak the dishes.** ⇒ dishes → dishes in the sink（皿を流しに）→ make sure to~（必ず～する、忘れずに～する）

Please soak this overnight in water.

**Let's pickle Japanese radishes.**
→ pickle（「野菜などを塩水、酢などに」漬ける）

これらの野菜を味噌に漬けてみてはどうかな？

## 点ける

電気を点けて。

リビングルームの電気は点けたままにしておいてね。

タバコの火を点けてくれる？

## 伝える

あなたに伝えることがあるんだ。

このこと彼女に伝えてくれるかな。

彼女に伝言を伝えて欲しいんだけど。

後であなたへ電話するよう彼女に伝えておくわね。

私の気持ち、あなたに伝わった？

私の言ってること伝わってる？

彼女に自分の気持ちをうまく伝えられなかったよ。

この英語の文章で意味が伝わってます？

私のひどい英語ではあなたへの感謝の気持ちを伝えられそうにないな。

漢字は紀元前 3 世紀頃に中国から伝わったと言われているんだ。

この花瓶は曾祖父の代から伝わる家宝なんだ。

**How about preserving these vegetables in *miso*?**
→ preserve（保存する、漬ける）

TRACK 233

**Will you turn on the light?** ⇒ turn on the light =switch on the light
→ turn on the gas（ガスを点ける）、turn on the stove（ストーブの火を点ける）、turn on the radio（ラジオを点ける）、turn on the tap（蛇口を開ける）

**Keep the light on in the living room.**

**Can you give me a light?**

TRACK 234

**I have something to tell you.** ⇒ something to tell you → lots of things I want to tell you（あなたに伝えたいことが沢山ある）

**Can you tell her about this?**

**I'd like you to give her a message.**
→ give her a message= convey my message to her

**I'll tell her to phone you later.**

**Did my feelings get through to you?**
→ get through to ~（「言いたいことなどが」~に通じる、~に届く）

**Is what I'm saying getting through to you?**

**I wasn't able to convey my feelings well to her.**
→ convey=deliver; pass on; communicate

**Is the meaning conveyed with this English sentence?**

**It's hard to convey my gratitude to you with my poor English.**

**It is said that Chinese characters were introduced into Japan from China about 3rd century BC.** → were introduced into Japan from China = were brought from China; came from China

**This vase is a family treasure handed down from our Great-grandfather's time.**

銀は銅や鉄よりよく熱を伝えるんだよ。

## 続ける

続けてください。

まだ英語の勉強は続けてる？

英語の勉強はいつから続けてるの？

5 歳から英語の勉強を続けてるの。

現在の会社で働き続けたい？

夢を追い続けることは大切だよ。

こちらでは昨日、5 時間以上雨が降り続いたよ。

彼は 3 度続けて約束を破ったんだ。

## 包む

これ包みましょうか？

これを紙で包んでください。

このプレゼントをきれいに包んでいただけます？

これは割れ物なので、優しく、注意して包んでください。

それぞれ別々に包んでもらえます？

目覚まし時計をプレゼント用に包んでもらった。

それ、包む必要はありません。

**Silver conducts heat better than copper or iron.**
→ conduct（伝導する）

TRACK 235

**Please continue. / Please go on.** ⇒ continue → continue what you were saying（話を続けて）、continue your work（仕事を続けて）

**Are you still studying English?**
⇒ English → French（フランス語）、German（ドイツ語）、Spanish（スペイン語）

**How long have you been studying English?**

**I've been studying English since I was five.**
⇒ since I was five → for ten years（10 年間）

**Do you want to keep working at the current company?**

**It's important to keep chasing your dreams.**
⇒ keep chasing your dreams → keep practicing（練習を続ける）

**It kept raining for more than five hours here yesterday.**

**He broke his promise three times in succession.**
→ in succession= in a row

TRACK 236

**Shall I wrap this?**

**Please wrap this up in paper.** ⇒ up in paper → double（二重に）

**Could you please wrap this present neatly?**

**This product is breakable, so wrap gently and with care please.**

**Could you wrap each one separately? / Could you wrap them individually please?**

**I had the alarm clock gift-wrapped.**

**You don't have to wrap it up.**

彼女は謎に包まれているよね。

会場は笑いに包まれていた。

## 勤める

どちらにお勤めですか？

出版社に勤めています。

市役所に勤めたいと思っています。

## 積む

車にこの荷物を積める？

車にこれらの荷物を積むの、手伝ってくれる？

このトラックは明らかに荷を積みすぎだよ。

君はもっと経験を積む必要があるね。

冬、この地域では雪が高く積もるんだ。

それらの本を机の上に積んでくれる？

## 釣る

魚を釣りに行こう。

何が釣れた？

今日は良く釣れたよ。

一匹も釣れなかった。

余り釣れなかったね。

**She is veiled in mystery, isn't she?**
⇒ in mystery → in secrecy（秘密に）

**The hall was filled with laughter.**
⇒ laughter → enthusiasm（熱気）

TRACK 237

**Who do you work with?** / What company are you working for?

**I'm working for a publishing company.**
⇒ publishing company → bank（銀行）、law firm（弁護士事務所）、trading company（貿易会社）、department store（デパート）、prefectural office（県庁）

**I want to work at a city hall.**

TRACK 238

**Can I load the luggage onto the car?**
→ load（積む、積み込む）

**Could you help me load the car with these?**
→ load A with B（A に B を積む）

**This truck is obviously overloaded.**

**You need to have more experiences.**

**In winter, snow piles up high in this area.**

**Will you pile up those books on the desk?**
→ pile up= heap up

TRACK 239

**Let's go fishing.**

**What did you catch ?** ⇒ What → How many fish（魚を何匹）

**I had a great catch today.**

**I couldn't catch a single fish.** / I caught nothing.

**My catch wasn't good.** / I didn't catch much.

ここは釣れないよ。

足がつったぁ。

お金で私を釣ろうったって無理ですよ。

## て

### 出かける

出かけるの？

どこへ出かけるの？

誰と出かけるわけ？

食事に出かけるの。

ドライブに出かけようよ。

旅行に出かけるんだ。

出かける時間よ。

出かける準備はできた？

出かける前に化粧をしたいの。

今夜は出かけるには遅すぎるわ。

今日は出かける気がしない。

出かけるより家にいたほうがいい。

This is not a good fishing spot.

I've got a cramp in my leg. → cramp（痙攣、こむら返り）

You can't lure me with money. / You can't buy me.
→ lure（誘惑する、誘い込む、引きつける）

TRACK 240

Are you going out? ⇒ going out → going out now（今出かける）、going anywere（どこかへ出かける）

Where are you going out?

Who are you going out with?

I'm going out for dinner. ⇒ for dinner → to buy food（食べ物を買いに）、to eat lunch（ランチを食べに）

Let's go for a drive.

I'll go on a trip. / I'll get off on my journey. ⇒ on a trip → for a walk（散歩に）、for a ride in the car（車でドライブに） → get off on my = set out on a ⇒ a trip → a trip for the day（日帰り旅行）

It's time to go.

Are you ready to go out?

I want to put on makeup before I go out.

It's too late to go out tonight.

I don't feel like going out today.
⇒ today → on a cold day like this（こんな寒い日は）

I'd rather stay home than go out.

## できる

英語を話すことはできる？

多分できると思う。

英語を読むことはできるが、うまく話すことはできないんだ。

私にできることがあったら、知らせてね。

顔にニキビができちゃった。

胃にガンができたみたいだ。

急用ができたので、急いで帰らなくちゃぁ。

## 手伝う

ちょっと手伝って。

手伝おうか？

何か手伝うことある？

僕の宿題を手伝ってくれる？

僕は手伝うためにここにいるんだぜ。

手伝う必要はないよ。

## 出る

出ていけ。

何時に家を出るの？

TRACK 241

**Can you speak English?** ⇒ speak English → write English（英語を書く）、read English（英語を読む）、understand English（英語を理解する）、drive a car（車を運転する）、do that alone（それ一人でできる）

**I can probably do that.**

**I can read English, but I can't speak it well.**

**If there's anything I can do for you, please let me know.**

**I have a zit on my face.** → zit = pimple; acne

**A cancer seems to have formed in my stomach.**

**Something urgent came up, and I've got to rush home.**
→ urgent（緊急の、急を要する） → come up（「問題などが」生じる、持ち上がる）

TRACK 242

**Give me a hand.** / Help me for a minute. / I need your help.

**Can I help you?** / Can I give you a hand? ⇒ help you → help out around the house（家事を手伝う）

**Is there anything I can help you with?**

**Can you help me with my homework?**
⇒ with my homework → wash the dishes（皿洗いを）、make dinner（食事を作るのを）、move this（これ動かすのを）

**I'm here to help you.**

**You don't have to help me.**

TRACK 243

**Get out.** / Go out.
⇒ out → out of here（ここから）、out of my room（私の部屋から）

**What time do you leave home?**
→ leave home = leave the house

大抵は朝８時に家を出るんだ。

蛇口をひねったが、水も湯も出てこなかった。

その事件は新聞に出ているよ。

その情報は信頼すべき筋から出ているんだ。

電話に出てくれる？

彼女は大学を出たばかりだよ。

今日もまた宿題がどっさり出たよ。

## 電話する

警察に電話して。

後で電話するよ。

いつでも遠慮なく電話してね。

都合がつき次第電話してね。

家に着いたら電話して。

家に着いたらすぐに電話するね。

誰か電話に出て。

あなたに電話がかかってるよ。

電話を切らずに待ってて。

**I usually leave the house at eight o'clock in the morning.**

**I turned on the faucet, but neither water nor hot water came out.**

**That incident is in the papers.**
→ incident（「重大事件に発展する危険性を持つ」事件）→ 類似した語 accident は思いがけなく起こる「事故」、event は重要な「出来事、行事」。

**The information comes from a reliable source.**

**Will you answer the phone, please?**

**She is fresh from college.** / She just graduated from university.　→ be fresh from~（～から来たばかりである）

**We were assigned a lot of homework today, too.**
→ assign（「仕事など」割り当てる、あてがう）→ a lot of = plenty of

TRACK 244

**Call the police.** / （日本）Call 110.：/（アメリカ）Call 911./（イギリス）Call 999.

**I'll call you later.**
→ call=telephone; make a phone call to　⇒ later → back（折り返し）

**Feel free to call me anytime.**　→ feel free to~（遠慮なく ~ する）

**Call me at your earliest convenience.**
⇒ at your earliest convenience → back later（後で）

**Call me when you get home.**　⇒ when you get home → anytime（いつでも）、if something happens（何かあったら）、when you have trouble（困ったときは）　⇒ Call me → Don't fail to call me（必ず私に電話して）

**I'll give you a call as soon as I get home.**

**Will somebody answer the phone?**

**There's a phone call for you.** / You are wanted on the phone. / You have a phone call.

**Hold on, please.** / Please hold the line.

今、会社から電話してるんだ。

あなたに電話するよう彼に伝えます。

彼女に今すぐ電話するわ。

彼女に電話するのを忘れた。

久ぶりにボーイフレンドと TV 電話で話したんだ。

最近ラインを使ってお互い連絡できるから友人に電話することはほとんどないな。

## と

### 問う

賛否を問うてみよう。

彼の意図を問うてみよう。

経験は問わない。

### 到着する

いつ到着する？

そこへは何時に到着します？

いつ駅に到着するか教えて？

もうすぐ到着するよ。

駅には 10 時までに到着するはずよ。

私がそちらに到着するまで待ってくれる？

I'm now calling from the office.

I'll tell him to call you.

I'll call her straight away.

I forgot to call her.

I had a video chat with my boyfriend for the first time in a while. → for the first time in a while（久しぶりに）

I hardly ever call my friends on the phone these days because we can contact each other using LINE.

TRACK 245

Let's take eyes and noes. → eyes and noes （賛成と反対「の投票」）

Let's ask him what he intends to do.

No experience is necessary. → necessary = required

TRACK 246

When will you arrive?

What time will you be arriving there?
⇒ be arriving there → get to the restaurant（レストランに到着する）

Tell me when you'll arrive at the station.

I'll arrive shortly. ⇒ shortly → in ten minutes（10 分で）、twenty minutes ahead of time（定刻 20 分前に）→ ahead of time（定刻より早く、定刻前に）

I should arrive at the station by ten o'clock.

Could you wait until I get there? → get = arrive

たった今到着したよ。

東京行きの電車は何時に到着します？

列車は２時に到着します。

列車は定刻に到着したわ。

それらの商品は明日の朝到着します。

それらが明日の午後到着するよう送ります。

それらが到着するのが楽しみだ。

### 研ぐ

おコメを研いでくれる？

この包丁は研がないとだめだな。

### 溶ける

これは水に溶けるの？

10グラムの砂糖をお湯で溶かして。

砂糖が溶けるまでよくかき混ぜてね。

バターをフライパンで溶かしてくれる？

それ、早く飲まないと氷が解けて味が薄くなっちゃうよ。

太陽が出始めたので、雪が溶けてきたぞ。

暑すぎて、私、溶けちゃう。

**I've just arrived.**
⇒ arrived → arrived at the meeting place（待ち合わせ場所に到着した）

**What time does a Tokyo-bound train arrive?**
→ a Tokyo-bound train= a train bound for Tokyo

**The train will arrive at 2 o'clock.**
⇒ 2 o'clock → Track 2（2 番線に）

**The train arrived on schedule.** → on schedule = on time

**Those products will arrive tomorrow morning.**

**I'll send them so that they will arrive tomorrow afternoon.**

**I'm looking forward to receiving them.**

TRACK 247

**Could you rinse the rice?** → rinse = wash; wash out ⇒ rice → rice until the water gets clear（水が透明になるまで米を）

**I have to sharpen this knife.** → sharpen = make sharp

TRACK 248

**Does this melt into water?**
⇒ into water → at normal temperature（常温で）

**Dissolve ten grams of sugar in hot water.**
→ dissolve（溶かす、溶ける） = melt

**Stir well until the sugar dissolves.**

**Can you melt butter in the frying pan?**

**If you don't drink it soon, the ice will melt and the taste will get weaker.**

**We are getting some sun, so the snow is melting.**

**It's so hot I'm about to melt.**
→ be about to~（まさに ~ しようとしている）

## 解ける

この問題は解けないよ。

この問題は僕には難しすぎて解けないよ。

誰もこの問題は解けないと思うよ。

## 届く

その本はいつこちらに届きますか？

その本は明日あなたに届きます。

その本は届きましたか？

それはまだ届いていません。

それ、ここへ届くのにどのくらいかかる？

そのうち届くよ。

それは多分 13 日に届くだろう。

注文したものは何でも一日で届くので、いつもアマゾンから買うんだ。

この価格なら私にも手が届くよ。

これは手入れのよく届いた庭ですね。

## 飛ばす

難しいところは飛ばして結構です。

このエクササイズは飛ばして、エクササイズ3～4をしましょう。

10 ページから 20 ページまで飛ばしましょう。

TRACK 249

I can't solve this problem. → solve=work out; answer; explain

This problem is too difficult for me to solve.

Nobody can solve this problem, I guess.

TRACK 250

When will the book be delivered here?
→ be delivered = arrive

That book will be delivered to you tomorrow.

Has the book arrived?

It hasn't arrived yet. ⇒ It → What I ordered（私が頼んだもの）

How long will it take for that to arrive here?

It will arrive eventually. ⇒ eventually → soon（すぐに）

That will probably arrive on the 13th.

I always buy things from Amazon, because whatever I order arrives in just one day.

This price is within my reach. ⇒ within my reach → way beyond my reach（とても私の手には届かない） → way beyond~（～を遥かに超えて）

This is a well-kept garden, isn't it?
→ well-kept = clean, tidy and cared for

TRACK 251

You can skip the difficult parts.

Let's skip this exercise and do exercises 3 and 4.

Let's skip from page ten to page twenty.

受付が私の順番を飛ばして他の人を呼んだの。

彼は地方支店に飛ばされたってさ。

子供の頃、紙飛行機を飛ばして遊んだものだ。

ここでドローンを飛ばしてはいけません。

スポーツカーで高速道路を飛ばしたよ。

唾を飛ばさないで！

私に関するデマを飛ばさないでくれる。

君はいつも冗談をかっ飛ばしてるじゃない。

## 飛ぶ

見て。きれいな蝶がヒラヒラ飛んでる。

あそこ風船が飛んでるよ。

花粉が飛んでる時期は家の中にいたいよ。

明日、ニューヨークへ飛びます。

僕は君より高く飛ぶことができるよ。

空を飛ぶ夢を見たの。それって何か意味ある？

この本、2ページ飛んでるよ。

雷が電線柱に落ちて、電線から火花が飛んだよ。

**The receptionist skipped over my number and called someone else.** → skip over（飛ばす、無視する）

**I hear he was transferred to a branch office.**
→ be transferred to~（～へ転勤になる）

**I used to play flying a paper airplane when I was a child.** → used to~（よく ~ したものだ）

**You cannot fly drones here.**

**I drove my sportscar at top speed along the expressway.** / I breezed along the expressway in my sportscar.
→ breeze along= travel along casually, rapidly and happily

**Don't spit!** / You are spitting when you talk!

**Stop circulating a false rumor about me.**
→ circulating=spreading

**You are always cracking jokes, aren't you?**
→ crack a joke = tell a joke

TRACK 252

**Look. A beautiful butterfly is fluttering about.**
→ flutter（素早く羽ばたきする、ばたばたと進む）

**A balloon is sailing over there.**
→ sail（「鳥、飛行船などが」滑らかに進む、浮かぶ）

**When pollen is in the air, I want to stay home.**
→ pollen（花粉）

**I'll fly to New York tomorrow.**

**I can jump higher than you.**

**I dreamed of flying in the sky. Does that mean anything?**

**Two pages are missing from this book.**

**The utility pole got struck by lightning, and the electric wire gave off sparks.**
→ utility pole（「米」電柱） → give off（「光など」発する、放出する）

君を見たとたんに、心配事がすべて瞬時に吹き飛んじゃった。

## 止まる・止める

止まれ。

立ち止まらないで。

この時計止まっている。

大雪のため電車が止まっています。

電車が完全に止まるまで降りないでください。

バスが完全に止まるまで座席に座っていてください。

地震のため電気も水道も止まってしまった。

このバスはＡホテルに止まりますか？

前の車が突然止まった。

笑いが止まらないよ。

このところ物価の上昇が止まらないね。

タクシーを止めてくれる？

あの銀行の前で止めてください。

テレビを止めて。

車を止める場所がない。

**The moment I saw you, all my worries disappeared in an instant.** → the moment = as soon as → disappeared = vanished ⇒ all my worries → my uneasiness（私の悩み）

TRACK 253

**Stop.**

**Don't stop.** / Move along now.

**This watch is stopped.**

**The trains are stopped owing to the heavy snow.**
→ are stopped = are not running

**Don't get off the train till it stops completely.**

**Please remain seated until the bus comes to a complete stop.** → comes to a complete stop= stops completely

**Because of the earthquake, both the eletricity and the water supply were cut off.** → were cut off = failed

**Does this bus stop at A hotel?** / Will this bus be stopping at A hotel?

**The car in front came to a sudden stop.**
→ came to a sudden stop = stopped suddenly

**I can't stop laughing.** ⇒ laughing → coughing（咳）、crying（涙）

**Prices don't stop rising these days.**
→ don't stop rising= keep on rising

**Will you flag down a cab for me?**
→ flag down （「合図して」停止させる、手を振って止める）

**Please stop in front of the bank.** ⇒ in front of the bank → at the next corner（次の角で）、around the corner（あの角を曲がったところで）

**Turn off the TV.**
⇒ the TV → the water（水）、the gas（ガス）、the alarm clock（目覚まし時計）

**There is no room to park my car.**
→ room = space → park（駐車する）

妻に喫煙を止められているんだ。

## 泊まる・泊める

どこへ泊まるの？

君の所に泊まれる？

ところで、泊めてくれるかな？

よかったら僕のところに泊まっていいよ。

君が来て泊まるのは歓迎さ。

ここが君の泊まる部屋だよ。

泊まるホテルは決まった？

幾晩お泊りですか？

今晩、友だちを泊めていい？

悪いけど、うちには泊められない。

日本に来たら数日間泊めてあげるよ。

## 撮る

写真を撮るのが趣味なんだ。

どんな写真を撮るのが好きなの？

写真を撮るのは楽しい？

写真を撮ろう。

私たちの写真を撮ってもらえますか？

**I have been forbidden to smoke by my wife.**
⇒ smoke → drink（飲酒）

TRACK 254

**Where will you stay?** ⇒ Will you stay → shall we stay（泊まろうか）

**Can I stay at your place?**

**Can I stay over by any chance?**
→ stay over（「他人の家に一晩」泊まる） → by any chance=perhaps; probably

**You can stay at my place if you want.**

**You are welcome to come and stay over.**

**This is the room you'll be staying in.**

**Have you decided the hotel you'll stay at?**

**How many nights are you going to stay?**

**Can my friend stay over tonight?** / Is it okay if my friend stays over tonight?

**I'm sorry I can't have you at my place.**
→ I can't have you at my place= I can't have you stay over at my place

**I'll put you up for a couple of days when you come to Japan.** → put someone up（人を泊める）

TRACK 255

**My hobby is taking pictures.**
⇒ My hobby is → I'm good at（が得意なの）

**What kind of pictures do you like taking?**

**Is taking pictures fun?**

**Let's take a picture.** ⇒ a picture → a picture of this view（この景色の写真）、a commemorative photo（記念写真）→ photo= photograph; picture

**Would you mind taking our picture?**

君の写真を撮ってあげる。

あのタワーを背景に写真を撮ってあげましょうか？

あの建物の前で写真を撮るのはどう？

ここでは写真を撮るのは禁じられているんだ。

あなたが撮ったこの写真はすごく素敵ね。

動画を撮りに行こう。

スマホで動画を撮ろうっと。

撮ってる？

この動画は誰が撮ったんだ？

## 摂る

栄養を摂らないといけないよ。

お医者さんから鉄分を摂るように言われたわ。

朝食は摂りました？

## 取る

塩を取ってくれる？

紙を取ってくれるかな？

その英語の辞書を取ってもらえる？

今学期はスペイン語を取るつもりなんだ。

試験で何点取った？

**Let me take a picture of you.** ⇒ you → you two（君たち二人）

**Would you like me to take your picture with the tower in the background?**

**How about taking a picture in front of that building?**

**You aren't allowed to take pictures here.**

**This picture you took is so beautiful.**

**Let's go shoot a video.** → shoot a video= take a video; make a video
⇒ shoot a video → take a video for YouTube（YouTube 用に動画を撮る）

**I'll take a video on my phone.**
⇒ a video → a video of this（これをビデオに）

**Are you recording?**

**Who took this video?**

TRACK 256

**You need to take nutrients.** → take = get

**My doctor told me to take iron.** ⇒ iron → vitamins（ビタミン）

**Have you had breakfast? / Did you eat breakfast?**
⇒「食べる」の項参照。

TRACK 257

**Will you pass me the salt?** ⇒ the salt → the sugar（砂糖）、the mustard（からし）、the soy source（醤油）、the pepper（胡椒）

**Can you get me some paper?**

**Could you hand me the English dictionary?**

**I'm going to take Spanish this semester.**

**How many points did you get on the exam?**

私、英語で満点取っちゃった。

あなたはいつも良い成績を取るわね。

スピーチコンテストで一等賞を取ったよ。

車の運転免許を取りたいな。

このジャケットのシミが取れないんだ。

このインクのシミだけど、なかなか取れない。

ＡとＢのどっちを取ろうか迷っているんだ。

どちらでも好きな方を取ってください。

彼の言葉を文字通り取ってはだめだよ。

あなたに私の言葉をそんな風に取られたくないよ。

私のやることすべてをそんな風に悪く取るわけ？

近くのラーメン屋から味噌ラーメンを取ろうよ。

できたら席を取っておいて。

ごめんなさい、この席は友人のために取っているの。

新聞を取ってる？

この英語雑誌を取ろうかと思っているんだ。

来週、４日間の休暇を取るつもりなんだ。

**I got a perfect score in English.**
⇒ a perfect score → a passing score; a passing grade; a passing mark（合格点）、a mark of 80 = a 80 = 80 points（80 点）

**You always get good grades, don't you?**
⇒ good grades → bad grades（悪い成績）

**I got the first prize in the speech contest.** → got=won

**I want to get my driver's license.** ⇒ my driver's license → a degree（学位）、a bachelor's degree（学士）、a master's degree（修士）、a doctor's degree（博士号）

**I can't remove these stains from my jacket.**
→ remove= take out

**This ink spot will not come out.**
→ come out（「シミ、汚れなどが」落ちる、取れる、抜ける、消える）

**I'm torn between A and B.** / I'm at a loss which to choose.
→ be torn between A and B（AとBの間で迷う、悩む）

**You can take whichever you like.**
→ whichever（どちらでも、どれでも）

**Don't take his words literally.** → literally（文字通り）

**I don't want you to take my words that way.**

**You take everything that I do so badly, don't you?**

**Let's order *miso* ramen to be delivered from a nearby *ramen* shop.** → order A to be delivered（Aを注文して出前してもらう）

**Save me a seat if you can.**
⇒ a seat → a piece of cake（ケーキを一切れ）

**Sorry but I'm saving this seat for my friend.**

**Do you have a newspaper subscription?**

**I'm thinking of subscribing to this English magazine.**
→ subscribe to~（～を予約購読する）

**I'm going to take four days off next week.**

明日から有給休暇を取るんだ。

できるだけ食べて元を取らないとさ。

僕は元を取るために授業は絶対さぼらないんだ。

## な

### 流す・流れる

トイレを使った後は水を流して。

シャワーで汗を流しなさい。

食べカスを排水溝に流さないでくれる？

水を流しっぱなしにしないで。

それは聞き流したほうがいいよ。

私に関するデマを流したのは誰よ？

この地区のタクシーは夜遅くまで流しているんだ。

今日のサークルの集まりは流そうよ。

(諺) 過去のことは水に流そう。

(諺) 静かな川は深く流れる。

このパイプは詰まっていて、水が流れないんだ。

この村では時間がゆったりと流れる。

**I'll take a paid vacation starting tomorrow.**
→ paid vacation（有給休暇）

**I have to eat as much as possible to get my money's worth.** → get my money's worth（払った金に見合うものを得る）

**I never skip class in order to get my money's worth.**
→ skip = cut

TRACK 258

**Flush the toilet after using it.**
→ flush（「水などを」どっと流す、一気に流す）

**Shower off your perspiration.** → perspiration=sweat

**Don't throw food scraps down the drain, please.**
→ food scraps （食べカス、生ゴミ） → drain（下水管、排水管）

**Don't let the water run.**

**You had better let it go in one ear and out the other.**

**Who started the false rumor about me?** → false rumor（デマ）

**Taxis in this area are cruising about till late at night.**
→ cruise（「探したり監視しながら」ゆっくり進む、巡回する）

**Let's cancel our club gathering today.**
⇒ club gathering → social gathering（懇親会）、get-together（集まり）

**Let bygones be bygones.** / Let's forget past differences and conflicts.

**Still waters run deep.**

**This pipe is blocked and so the water doesn't flow through.**

**Time goes by slowly here in this village.**
⇒ slowly → very quickly（とても速く）

最後に会ってから20年の月日が流れましたね。

空をゆっくりと流れているあの不思議な雲を見て。UFOかも。

我々の試合が雨で流れちゃった。

講演会が流れた。

## 眺める

ずっと海を眺めていたい。

ここから綺麗な夜景が眺められるよ。

ここから眺める景色が好きなんだ。

海が眺められる家に住みたいな。

## 泣く・泣かせる

泣くなって。

泣くのはやめな。

そんなにすぐ泣かないの。

嬉しくて泣いているんだ。

嬉しくて泣いたんだ。

感動して泣いちゃうかも。

泣くのをこらえられないんだ。

泣きたいだけ泣きなさい。

**Twenty years have passed since we last met.**
→ we last met= I saw you last

**Look at that strange cloud drifting across the sky. It might be a UFO.**

**Our game got washed out.** → got washed out= was rained out

**The lecture was called off.**
→ call off（「計画、予定などを」中止する、取りやめる）=cancel; abort

TRACK 259

**I want to keep gazing at the ocean the whole time.**
→ gaze = look; stare ⇒ the whole time → from morning till night（朝から晩まで）、forever（いつまでも）

**You can see a beautiful night view from here.**

**I like the scenery that I can see from here.**
⇒ scenery → sea （海）、mountain（山）

**I want to live in a house with a view of the sea.**

TRACK 260

**Don't cry.**

**Stop crying.** ⇒ crying → crying for nothing（何でもないのに泣く）

**Don't be such a cry baby.** → cry baby（泣き虫、すぐ泣く人）

**I'm crying for joy.**

**I cried with happiness. / I cried tears of joy. / I wept with joy.**

**I may be moved to tears.** ⇒ may be → was にすると「感動して泣いた」→ be moved to tears（感動して泣く、感極まって涙を流す）

**I can't hold back my tears.**
→ hold back（「感情を」抑える、自制する）

**Have a good cry. / Weep to your heart's content.**
→ to one's heart's content（心ゆくまで、思いのままに）

泣いても笑ってもあと2日で今年も終わりだよ。

私、泣いちゃうからやめてよ。

君を泣かすことだけはしたくない。

これは泣かせる歌だよ。

## 鳴く

どこかで鳥が鳴いてる。

猫が遠くで泣いてるね。

## 慰める

私を慰めてくれる？

誰かに慰めてもらいたいの。

音楽を聴いて心を慰めたらどう？

酒で自分を慰めたって無駄だよ。

## 失くす

何を失くしたの？

車のカギを失くしちゃった。

あなたはよく物を失くすわね。

最近、いつも何かを失くしてるんだ。

**Like it or not, there's only two days left in the old year.**
→ like it or not（好むと好まざるとにかかわらず） → the old year（旧年、行く年）

**You are making me cry.**
→ 相手の優しさなどで泣きそうになる、といった意味。

**The last thing I want to do is to make you cry.**
→ the last thing I want to do is ~（私が最もしたくないことは ~）

**This is the song that makes me cry.**

TRACK 261

**A bird is chirping somewhere.**
⇒ chirp（さえずる） → sing（歌う、鳴く）

**A cat is meowing in the distance.**
→ meow（にゃ～と鳴く） → 犬が「吠える」は bark。

TRACK 262

**Would you console me?**
→ console（慰める、元気づける）=comfort; solace

**I want someone to console me.**

**How about finding solace in listening to music?**
→ find solace（慰めを見い出す）

**It's no use consoling yourself with *sake*.**
→ It's no use ~ing（～しても無駄である）

TRACK 263

**What did you lose?**

**I lost my car key.** ⇒ lost → might have lost（失くしたかも）
⇒ car key → my wallet（僕の札入れ）、my purse（私の財布）、my house key（家の鍵）

**You often lose things, don't you?**

**I have been losing something recently.**
→ recently この語は過去形、現在完了形、過去完了形で使用。

## 嘆く

(諺) こぼれたミルクを嘆いても仕方がない。

自分の不幸を嘆いてばかりいないで。

最近の政治腐敗を嘆かわざるを得ないよ。

## 投げる

おもちゃを投げるのはよしなさい。

犬に石を投げないの。

君、いい速球を投げるね。

日本には豆を投げる習慣があるのを知ってる？

豆を投げながら「鬼は外、福は内」って言うんだ。

## 怠ける

怠けるな。

勉強を怠けるなよ。

君、昨日学校を怠けたね？

僕は怠けてる余裕なんかないよ。

TRACK 264

**It's no use crying over the spilt milk**

**Stop grieving about your misfortunes.** → Stop → What's the use of ～?（～したところで何になる）→ grieve = lament; cry; sob; weep

**I can't help deploring the corruption of politics these days.** → can't help ~ing（～しないではいられない、～する他はない）→ deplore = bemoan; grieve; lament; mourn ⇒ the corruption of politics → the decline in moral standards（道徳の低下）

TRACK 265

**Stop throwing your toys around. / Don't throw your toys around.** → throw around（投げ散らかす）

**Don't throw stones at the dog.** ⇒ the dog → the window（窓）

**You throw a good fast ball.**
⇒ a good fast ball → a change-up（チェンジアップ）、a sharp curve ball（鋭いカーブ）、a mean curveball（いやらしいカーブ）、a ball at 150 km an hour, can't you?（時速 150 キロのボールが投げられるんだよね）

**Do you know we have a tradition of throwing dried soybeans in Japan?**

**As we throw soybeans, we say "Demons out, Fortune in."** → Demons out=Devil out; Evils out

TRACK 266

**Don't be lazy. / Don't be such a bum.**
→ bum（怠け者、能無し、役立たず）

**Don't neglect your studies. / Don't be lazy in your studies.**
→ neglect= ignore ⇒ studies → work（仕事）、homework（宿題）

**You played truant from school yesterday, didn't you?**
→ play truant from school（学校をさぼる、ずる休みをする）

**I can't afford to be idle.** → be idle= be lazy; idle away

## 悩む

何を悩んでるんだ？

くだらないことで悩んでるのさ。

隣の部屋の騒音に悩んでいるんだよ。

職場の人間関係で悩んでいるんだ。

そんな馬鹿げたことで悩むのはよせよ。

## 習う

（諺）習うより慣れろ。

何か習ってる？

車の運転を習ってるよ。

誰に英語を習ってるの？

毎週、バイオリンを習っているの。

テニスを習って 5 年以上よ。

子供の頃、水泳を習ったけど。

並んでください。

TRACK 267

**What are you worried about?**

**I'm worried about trifles.** → trifles（くだらないこと、つまらないこと） ⇒ trifles → my work（仕事）、my future（自分の将来）、my family（家族）、raising my children（子育て）、entrance examinations（入学試験）

**I've been disturbed by the noise coming from the room next door.** → disturbed = bothered

**I have trouble with interpersonal relationships at my workplace.** → have trouble with ～（～で苦労している、～に手を焼いている） → interpersonal relationships（対人関係、人間関係） → workplace（職場、仕事場）

**Stop worrying about such silly things.** → silly things = trifles

TRACK 268

**Practice makes perfect.**

**Are you learning something?**
⇒ learning something → practicing *judo*（柔道を習っている）

**I'm learning how to drive a car.** ⇒ how to drive a car → English three times a week（週3回英語）、English conversation（英会話）、how to speak English（英語の話し方）、how to paint（絵の描き方）、to play the piano（ピアノの弾き方）

**Who teaches you English?**

**I take violin lessons every week.**
⇒ take → decided to take（習うことにした）

**I've been taking tennis lessons for more than five years.**

**I took swimming lessons when I was a child.**
→ when I was a child = in my childhood

TRACK 269

**Line up, please. /** Please get in line. / Please form an orderly line.（きちんと並んで）
⇒ , please → against the wall（壁を背にして） → line（縦列）

2列に並んでください。

僕たち2時間も立って並んでいます。

椅子を横2列に並べてくれる？

これらの本を棚に並べてくれる？

テーブルに皿を3枚きれいに並べて。

## 慣れる

英語に慣れた？

まだそれに慣れているところよ。

それに慣れそうにないんだ。

そのうち慣れるよ。

英語を話すことに慣れる一番いい方法は何かな？

外国人と英語で話すのにどうにか慣れたかも。

ここの気候には慣れそうもないな。

# に

## 逃がす・逃げる

(諺) 好機は逃すな。

(諺) ためらう者は好機を逃す。

**Please stand in two lines.** → lines = rows ⇒ in two lines → next to him（彼の隣に）、by his side（彼の近くに）

**We've already been standing in line for two hours.**

**Will you line up the chairs in two rows?** → row（横列）

**Will you arrange these books on the shelf?**
→ arrange these books = line up these books → arrange（きちんと並べる、配列する）⇒ on the shelf → in alphabetical order（アルファベット順に）

**Put three plates neatly on the table.**

TRACK 270

**Did you get used to English?**
→ get used to~（～に慣れる） ⇒ English → your new work（新しい仕事）、the workplace environment（職場の環境）、living in the country（田舎での生活）、your new school（新しい学校）、Japanese food（日本食）

**I'm still getting used to it.** ⇒ getting used to it → not used to speaking English（英語を話すのに慣れていない）

**I can't seem to get used to it.**
⇒ it → speaking English（英語を話すこと）

**You'll get used to it someday.** ⇒ someday → right away（すぐに）

**What's the best way to get used to speaking English?**

**I somewhat got used to speaking with foreigners in English.**

**I can't seem to get used to the climate here.**
⇒ the climate here → this environment（この環境）

TRACK 271

**Make hay while the sun shines.**

**He who hesitates is lost.**

チャンスは逃がすな。

逃がしてやろう。

逃がした魚は大きい。

現実から逃げちゃだめ。

問題から逃げないで。

君はいつも苦手なことから逃げるんだから。

我々の上司は責任を私たちに押し付けて逃げちゃったのさ。

都会の喧騒から逃げたいと思わない？

## 握る

手すりを握って。

君の手を握りたい。

おにぎりを握るのはこれが初めてよ。

我々の上司は人事権を握っている。

財布のひもを握っているのはうちの奥さんなんだ。

## 濁す

言葉を濁さないで。

私たちの約束の話になると、いつも君は言葉を濁すんだから。

**Don't miss a good chance.**

**Let's let it go.** → let it go= release it ⇒ Let's → Don't（～しないで）

**You don't know what you've got 'til it's gone.**

**Never escape reality.** → escape reality= escape from reality

**Don't avoid your problems.**
→ avoid = escape; evade; dodge; avert

**You always run away from the things you are not good at.** → run away = avoid

**Our boss got off by shifting the responsibility onto us.**
→ get off（「仕事などを」やめる、逃げる、抜け出す） → shift the responsibility onto~（～に責任を押し付ける、～に責任転嫁する）

**Don't you think you want to get away from the bustle of the city?** → get away from ～（～から離れる、～から逃げる、～から脱出する） → bustle（喧騒、賑わい）

TRACK 272

**Hold onto the handrail.** → hold onto~（～をしっかりつかんでおく、～を手放さない） ⇒語尾に when riding the escalator（エスカレーターに乗るとき）

**I want to hold your hand.**

**This is my first time to press the rice into a ball.**
⇒ a ball → a triangle（三角形）

**Our boss has the power to shuffle personnel.**
→ power to shuffle personnel（人事権）

**It is my wife who holds the purse strings.**

TRACK 273

**Don't speak ambiguously.** → ambiguously（曖昧に、漠然と） ⇒ speak ambiguously（曖昧に、漠然と）→ give me an evasive answer（返事を濁す）
→ evasive = vague

**Whenever I refer to our promise, you start hedging.**
→ refer to~（～に言及する） → hedge（言葉を濁す）

お茶を濁さないでよ。

## 入院する

入院する必要があるの？

胃がんで入院するの。

私、7 月 20 日に入院することになっちゃった。

どのくらい入院することになるわけ？

月曜日に入院して土曜日に退院するの。

入院して一週間になるのよ。

## 煮る

これらのジャガイモを煮てくれる？

これらの野菜をとろ火で煮てちょうだい。

これらの野菜がドロドロになるまで煮てね。

あいつは煮ても焼いても食えないやつだよ。

## 妊娠する

あなた、妊娠してるの？

私、妊娠してる可能性があるの。

ガールフレンドを妊娠させちゃった。

**Don't dodge the subject.** → dodge = evade; avoid

TRACK 274

**Do you have to be hospitalized?**

**I'll be hospitalized for stomach cancer.** →⇒ I'll be → was（「入院して」いた） ⇒ stomach cancer → heart failure（心不全）、chest pains（胸の痛み）、pneumonia（肺炎）

**I'm going to stay in the hospital on July 20.**

**About how long will you be in hospital for?**
→ in hospital=（米）in the hospital

**I'll be admitted to hospital on Monday and discharged on Saturday.** / I'll be in the hospital from Monday until Saturday.
→ be admitted to（the）hospital（入院する、病院に収容される）

**I've been hospitalized for a week.**
⇒ for a week → in a private room（個室に）、in a shared room（大部屋に）

TRACK 275

**Will you boil these potatoes?**
→ boil は液体を「沸かす」、そこから食物を「ゆでる、煮る」

**Please stew these vegetables.**
→ stew は「とろ火でゆっくり煮る」こと。

**Boil these vegetables to a pulp, please.**
→ to a pulp（ぐにゃぐにゃになるまで、元の形をとどめぬまでに）

**I really don't know how to deal with him.**
→ how to deal with ~（~の扱い方、対応の仕方）

TRACK 276

**Are you pregnant?**

**There's a chance I'm pregnant.**
→ There's a chance = It's possible that

**I got my girlfriend pregnant.** / I impregnated my girlfriend / I got my girlfriend in the club. / I knocked up my girlfriend.

## ぬ

### 抜く

今日は朝食を抜いたんだ。

虫歯を抜いてもらわないといけないんだ。

今日は庭の雑草を抜かなきゃ。

この葡萄酒の栓を抜いてくれる？

後ろの車に抜かれた。

前の車を追い抜こう。

誰かにタイヤの空気を抜かれたよ。

お風呂の水を抜いてくれるかな？

### 脱ぐ

ここで靴を脱いでください。

ジャケットを脱いでもいい？

暑いようなら、ジャケットを脱いでもいいよ。

### 盗む

満員電車の中で財布を盗まれちゃった。

ここに自転車を置いていたら、誰かに盗まれたよ。

TRACK 277

**I skipped breakfast today.** ⇒ breakfast → lunch（昼食）

**I have to get my cavity pulled out.** ⇒ have to get → had（「抜いて」もらった） ⇒ cavity → wisdom tooth（親知らず） → pulled out = taken out ; removed

**Today I have to weed the garden. / I have to clear the garden of weeds today.** → weed（雑草を抜く）= pull out the weeds in → clear A of B（A から B を取り除く）

**Can you pull a cork out of this wine bottle?**
→ pull a cork out of = uncork; open

**The car behind passed mine.**

**Let's overtake the car in front.**

**Someone let the air out of this tire.**
→ let the air out of~（～から空気を抜く）

**Can you drain the water from the bathtub?**
→ drain（「液体を徐々に」流す、流し出す）

TRACK 278

**Please take off your shoes here.**
⇒ Please → You don't have to ～（～する必要はない）

**Is it okay if I take my jacket off?**
→ take my jacket off= take off my jacket

**If you feel hot, you can take off your jacket.**

TRACK 279

**My wallet was stolen on the crowded train.**
→ My wallet was stolen = Someone stole my wallet

**I left my bike here and someone stole it.**

ここに持ち物を置いていたら盗まれるかもしれないよ。

### 濡れる

雨で濡れちゃった。

雨の中を歩いたので、ずぶ濡れになったよ。

カバンが濡れるのは構わないさ。

## ね

### 願う

何を願った？

今年はサンタに何をお願いした？

星に願う。

世界の平和を願っています。

楽しいクリスマスと新年を迎えられることを願っています。

すぐに良くなられることを願っています。

お願いしたいことがあるのですが？

お手伝いをお願いできますか？

鈴木さんをお願いします。

今後とも宜しくお願い致します。

Someone might steal your belongings if you leave them here.

TRACK 280

**I got wet in the rain.**
⇒ in the rain → in the storm（嵐で）、from the heavy rain（激しい雨で）

**I got soaking wet, walking in the rain.**
→ get soaking wet（びしょ濡れになる）= get drenched to the skin; be soaked to the bone

**I don't mind getting my bag wet.**
⇒ bag → trousers（ズボン）、shoes（靴）

TRACK 281

**What did you wish for?** → wish for~（～を願う、～を望む） ⇒ did you → should I（「何を願おう」かな）

**What did you ask Santa for this year?**

**I wish on a star.** → wish on~（～に願いをかける）

**I wish for world peace.**
⇒ world peace → your happiness（あなたの幸せ）、your success（あなたの成功）

**I wish you a Merry Christmas and a Happy New Year.**

**I hope you get well soon.**
→ get well（「健康状態が」良くなる、「病気が」治る）

**May I ask a favor of you?** → ask a favor of ~（～にお願いする）

**Could I ask you to help me?**

（電話）**May I speak to Mr. Suzuki?** /（受付）May I see Mr. Suzuki?

**I look forward to working with you.** / I am looking forward to doing business with you.
→ look forward to ~（～を楽しみにしている）

これは願ってもないチャンスですよ。

これは願ったり叶ったりだ。

## 寝かす

子供を寝かすところよ。

毎晩、歌を歌って赤ちゃんを寝かせるのよ。

それを2時間ばかり冷蔵庫で寝かせよう。

## 寝る

何時に寝るの？

毎日、夜12時前には寝るんだ。

寝る時間よ。

今日はもう寝るよ。

よく眠れた？

ぐっすり眠れたよ。

昨夜はなかなか寝つけなかった。

全く眠れなかった。

一日中寝ていたいよ。

仰向けに寝てください。

## 練る

作戦を練ろう。

You couldn't ask for a better chance than this.

This is just what I wanted.

TRACK 282

I'm going to put my child to bed.

I sing my baby to sleep every night.

Let it stand in the refrigerator for about two hours.
→ let it stand =let it rest; let it sit; leave it ⇒ it → the carry（このカレー） ⇒ for about two hours → overnight（一晩）

TRACK 283

What time do you go to bed? → go to bed = retire to bed

I go to bed before twelve midnight every day.

It's time to go to bed. / It's time for bed.

I'll go to bed for today.

Were you able to sleep well? / Did you sleep well?

I slept like a log. / I was able to sleep soundly.
→ like a log = like a baby; soundly

I had a hard time falling asleep last night. / I had a tough time going to sleep.

I couldn't sleep a wink. → not sleep a wink = not sleep at all

I want to sleep all day long.

Please lie on your back. → on your back → on your stomach = on your face（うつ伏せに）、on your side（横向きに）

TRACK 284

Let's work out a strategy. → work out（「方法などを」考え出す、作り出す） ⇒ strategy → plan（計画）、strategy for future sales（今後の販売戦略）

いつも文章を練るの？

生地の練り方は知ってる？

まず、粉に水を入れて練るんだ。

生地が滑らかになるまで練ってね。

## の

### 残す

これ、残していい？

食べ物を残しちゃった。

食べ物を残すのはよくないわよ。

ケーキを一切れ残しておいてくれる？

彼女の留守電にメッセージを残しておいたよ。

### 残る

ここに残る？

ここにもう少し残る。

昨夜は会社に一人残って、仕事をしたんだ。

一番印象に残ってるのはなに？

一番印象に残ったのは、彼女がすごく頭がいいってこと。

**Do you always polish your writing?** → polish（「文体など」磨く、完全にする） ⇒ writing → speech（演説文）、style（文体）

**Do you know how to knead dough?**
→ knead（練る） → dough（「パンなどの」生地、こね粉）

**First, mix the powder with water and knead.**

**Knead the dough until it becomes smooth.**

TRACK 285

**Is it OK if I leave this?** / Do I have to eat this?
→ if I leave this= if I don't finish this

**I didn't eat all my meal.** / I left some food uneaten.

**It's not good to leave food on your plate.** / It's not nice to waste food.

**Will you leave me a piece of cake?**
⇒ a piece of cake → something to eat（何か食べ物を）

**I left a message on her answering machine.**

TRACK 286

**Are you going to stay here?** → stay =（フォーマルな表現）remain
⇒ here → in Tokyo after you graduate（卒業後は東京に）

**I'll stay here a bit longer.**
⇒ here a bit longer → home today（今日は家に）

**I stayed at the office alone and did work last night.**

**What left the biggest impression on you?**
→ leave the impression on~（～に印象を残す）

**What struck me the most was she's very intelligent.**
→ strike（「人の」心をうつ、印象を与える）→ struck は過去形。

去年あなたの言った言葉がまだ心に残っているわ。

それはいつまでも私の記憶に残ると思う。

記憶に残る一枚を撮るぞ。

発表が残っているのはあなただけです。

チョコレートケーキが 2 ～ 3 残っているけど、一ついる？

パソコンを使うと使用歴が残るのって知ってる？

僅かなお金しか残っていないよ。

5 から 3 を引くと 2 が残ります。

これ、売れ残ったの？

## 載せる

あなたの写真をインスタに載せてもいい？

これをネットに載せることにしたよ。

彼女の許可なくこれらの写真を載せたわけ？

私の名前がリストに載っていない。

私の名前をリストに載せてくれる？

このチーズピザに何か載せたい？

このピザにトマトのスライスを載せようよ。

The words you said last year still remain in my heart.
⇒ The words you said → What you said（あなたが言ったこと）

That I think will be in my memories forever.

I'm going to take a memorable photo.

You are the only one left to present. / You are the only one remaining who hasn't presented yet.

There are a couple of pieces of chocolate cake left. Do you want a piece?

Do you know that if you use a computer, your viewing history will remain? → your viewing history = your browser history; your user history → will remain= will be stored

There is only a little money left.

Taking three from five leaves two.

Did this remain unsold?

TRACK 287

Can I post your picture on Instagram? → post（「インターネットなどに情報を」載せる、掲載する）⇒ your picture → the pictures that we took at the alumni meeting（同窓会で撮った写真）

I decided to put this on the internet. → put=post

Did you upload these pictures without her permission?
→ upload（アップロードする）=transfer data from one computer to another

My name is not on the list.
⇒ is not on the list → is on the list（リストに載っている）

Can you put my name on the list?

Do you want anything on this cheese pizza?

Let's place slices of tomato on this pizza.

それをごはんの上に載せてくれます？

## 乗せる

車に乗せてくれる？

昨日、彼の車に乗せてもらったの。

## 除く

問5は除いてください。

あなたの答えは問1を除いてすべて正解です。

今日は寿司を除いて何も食べたくない。

僕はダンスを除いてスポーツは全部得意なんだ。

土曜日を除いて毎日、野球の練習さ。

私の名前をこの名簿から除いてください。

彼女をパーティの招待者リストから除いてください。

## 覗く

男の人が窓から中を覗いてるよ。

この店を覗いてみようよ。

あなた、いつも鏡を覗いているのね。

## 延ばす

締め切りを延ばせない？

締め切りを一週間延ばしましょう。

**Could you put that on top of rice, please?**

TRACK 288

**Can you give me a ride? / Can you give me a lift in your car?**
→ give someone a ride（人を乗せる）→ give someone a lift とするのはイギリス。

**He gave me a lift in his car yesterday.**
⇒ me a lift in his car → her a ride on his bike（彼女をバイクに乗せた）

TRACK 289

**Please leave out question 5.** → leave out（除外する、省く、抜かす）

**Your answers are all correct except question 1.**
⇒ all correct → all wrong（すべて間違って）

**I don't want to eat anything today except *sushi*.**
→ except = except for ⇒ don't want to → can（「食べ」られる）

**I'm good at all sports except dancing.**
⇒ be good at → be bad at~（～は不得意である）

**I practice baseball every day except for Saturday.**

**Please cross my name off this list.**
→ cross off（線を引いて消す）

**Please remove her from the list of the party invitees.**
→ remove =take off; take out; delete; get rid of

TRACK 290

**A man is looking in at the window.**
⇒ look in at the window → look out of the window（窓から外を覗く）

**Let's have a peep at this shop.** → have a peep at = have a look at

**You are always looking into the mirror, aren't you?**
→ looking into the mirror = looking at yourself in the mirror

TRACK 291

**Can't you extend the deadline?** ⇒ 文尾に for the report で「レポートの」→ extend= postpone → deadline=due date

**We'll extend the deadline for one week.**

健康寿命を延ばしたいな。

出発を 3 日延ばすことにしたよ。

滞在を延ばせますか？

東京滞在をあと 2 週間延ばす予定です。

今日できることは明日に延ばさないこと。

それをいつまでも延ばしておくわけにはいかないよ。

## 伸ばす

体を伸ばして。

両腕をまっすぐ伸ばして。

髪を伸ばしてるの？

この写真を伸ばそうよ。

売り上げを伸ばすには何をすべきかな？

## 伸びる

心配しないで。そのうち背は伸びるよ。

爪が伸びちゃった。切らないと。

口ひげが長く伸びたね。剃らなきゃ。

メンが伸びてるよ。

この蕎麦、伸びてしまった。

英語力を伸ばすにはどうしたらいい？

**I want to extend my healthy life-span.** → healthy life-span（健康寿命） ⇒ I want to → How can I …?（どうしたら〜）

**I decided to postpone my departure for three days.**
→ postpone= hold off; put off（延期する、遅らせる）

**Can you extend your stay?**

**I plan to extend my stay in Tokyo for two more weeks.**

**Never put off till tomorrow what you can do today.**

**We can't put it off forever.**

TRACK 292

**Stretch yourself.** ⇒ yourself → out your legs（足をまっすぐ「伸ばす」）

**Hold out your arms.** → hold out= extend

**Are you growing your hair out?** → growing your hair out=growing out your hair; letting your hair grow ⇒ out → long（長く）

**Let's enlarge this photograph.** → enlarge（引き延ばす）

**What should we do to increase sales?**
→ increase（「数、量などを」増加させる）

TRACK 293

**Don't worry. You will grow tall sooner or later.**
→ sooner or later = eventually; someday

**My nails have gotten longer. I have to trim them.**

**Your beard has grown long. You need a shave.**

**The noodles are getting soft.**

**The *soba* noodles have gotten soggy.**
→ get soggy（ふやける）

**What should I do to improve my English ability?**
→ to improve my English ability=to develop my English; to boost my English skills

この子の隠れた才能を伸ばしたいのよね。

### のぼせる

暑すぎてのぼせてるよ。

そんなに長く風呂に入っているとのぼせるよ。

彼は彼女にのぼせてるんだ。

### 登る

(諺) 豚もおだてりゃ木に登る。

富士山に登ったことある？

来月、富士山に登るんだ。

この長い石段を登らなきゃいけないのか？

この坂道を登るの？

東京スカイツリーに上ろうよ。

最近、運動のために階段を上るようにしてるんだ。

### 昇る

もうすぐ太陽が昇るよ。

僕が目を覚ました時にはすでに太陽は登っていた。

### 乗り換える

乗り換える必要はありますか？

**I want to develop his latent talents.** ⇒ latent talents（潜在能力）→ linguistic talents（語学の能力）、writing talent（文才）

TRACK 294

**I feel dizzy because it's too hot.**
→ feel dizzy（めまいがする、ふらふらする）

If you stay in the bath that long, you'll get dizzy.

**He's infatuated with her.** / He lost his head over her. / He's gone on her. → be infatuated with~（～にのぼせ上っている、～に心を奪われている）→ be gone on ~（～に夢中である）

TRACK 295

**Even a pig could climb a tree if praised.** → praised= flattered

Have you ever climbed Mt. Fuji?

**I'm going to climb Mt. Fuji next month.**

Do we have to climb up this long flight of stone steps? → flight of ~（一連の ~、一続きの ~）→ 階段、石段など階段状になっているものについていう。

**Are we going to climb this hill?**
⇒ 文尾に by bicycre ? で「自転車で」

Let's go up the Tokyo *Skytree*.

**I'm trying to go up the stairs for exercise these days.**
→ go up the stairs = take the stairs

TRACK 296

**It will not be long before the sun rises.** / The sun will soon rise.

The sun had already risen when I woke up.

TRACK 297

Do I have to change trains? ⇒ Do I → Where do I（どこで）

渋谷で乗り換える必要があります。

新宿へ行くには渋谷でA線に乗り換えてください。

この電車に乗って、A駅でB線に乗り換えてください。

池袋で丸の内線に乗り換えるよ。

梅田で乗り換えたほうが早いよ。

私、学校へ行くのに毎日4回電車を乗り換えるの。

この列車から乗り換えることはできません。

あなた、鈴木君から田中君に乗り換えたんだって。そうなの？

## 乗る

タクシーに乗ろう。

バスに乗ろうか？

最終バスに乗るなら急がないと。

自転車に乗れるの？

自転車に乗って通勤してるんだ。

いつもこの駅で列車に乗るのよ。

この電車に乗って新宿まで行くんだ。

エスカレーターに乗ろうよ。

**You need to change trains at Shibuya.**
⇒ need to → don't have to（～する必要はない）

**To go to Shinjuku, transfer to the A line in Shibuya.**
⇒ transfer to the A line in Shibuya → change trains at Shibuya（渋谷で乗り換える）

**Get on this train, and transfer to the B line at A station.**

**We'll change trains to the Marunouchi line at Ikebukuro.**

**It's quicker to change at Umeda.** / It takes less time if we change at Umeda.

**I change trains four times every day to get to school.**

**You can't transfer from this train.**

**I hear you dumped Suzuki for Tanaka. Is that right?**
→ dump（「恋人を」ふる、捨てる）

TRACK 298

**Let's take a taxi.** → take a taxi → take は「交通手段として用いる」ことで、go by taxi、use a taxi といった意味合い。

**Shall we get on a bus?**
→ get on → バス、電車、飛行機など大きな乗り物に「乗る」、また自転車やバイクのように「またがって乗る」場合。タクシーや乗用車に「乗る」は get in。

**We've got to hurry if we want to catch the last bus.**
→ catch →「つかまえる」という意味から、get より苦労してつかまえて「乗る」というニュアンス。

**Can you ride a bicycle?**
→ ride → ride a horse（馬に乗る）のように、またいで乗る、また ride a subway train（地下鉄に乗る）といった具合に、乗客としてものに乗るということ。

**I ride my bike to get to work.**
→ bike=bicycle ⇒ ride my bike → take the train（電車に乗る）

**I always get on a train at this station.**

**I ride this train to Shinjuku.**

**Let's take an escalator.** ⇒ an escalator → this train（この電車）

いつも JAL に乗るの？

たいてい 10 時 30 分の便に乗ってるんだ。

僕の車に乗って。

この車は 5 人乗れるよ。

飲んだら乗るな。

この儲け話に乗りたいかい？

その手には乗らないよ。

君はすぐおだてに乗るんだから。

図に乗るんじゃない。

## は

### 測る

熱を測ってみたら？

体重を量ったら、すごく太っちゃってた。

わたし、怖くて体重が量れないよ。

身長を測った？

毎日、血圧、測ったほうがいいよ。

この板の長さと幅を測ってくれた？

**Do you always fly Japan Air Line?**
→ fly → 飛行機で「飛ぶ」ということ。

**I usually take a ten thirty flight.**

**Get in my car.**

**This car can hold five people.** → hold（「人を」収容する）→ This room can hold 50 people.（この部屋は 50 人収容できる）

**Don't drink and drive.** / If you drink, don't drive.

**Do you want to be in on this profitable scheme?**
→ be in on ~（～に関与する、～に加わる） → scheme（計画、陰謀、悪だくみ）

**I won't fall for it.** / I won't fall into such a trap.
→ fall for~（「策略など」に引っかかる、～に騙される）

**You are easily flattered.** → be flattered → be tempted（誘惑に乗る）

**Don't push your luck too far.**
→ push one's luck（図に乗る、調子に乗る）

TRACK 299

**Why don't you try taking your temperature?**
⇒ taking your temperature → checking your body temperature with this thermometer（この体温計で体温を測る）

**I weighed myself and I have gotten so fat.**
→ weigh myself = check my weight

**I'm too scared to weigh myself.**
→ to weigh myself → to get on this scale（この体重計に乗る）

**Did you measure your height?** → measure = check

**You had better check your blood pressure every day.**

**Did you measure the length and width of this piece of wood?**

物差しでこの箱の寸法を測ったよ。

A から B までの距離を測ってみよう。

僕の 100 メートル走の時間を測ってみて。

## 吐く

吐きそう。

食べたものを全部吐いちゃった。

息を吐いて。

ここで唾を吐くのはだめよ。

あいつは僕に唾を吐きやがった。

弱音を吐くな。

そのことについて洗いざらい吐いたらどうだ。

## 履く

靴を履いてください。

この靴は履きたくないよ。きつ過ぎるんだ。

## 掃く

床を掃いてくれる？

## 始まる

あなたの学校はいつ始まるの？

私の学校は 9 時から始まるよ。

**I took the measurements of this box with a ruler.**
→ took the measurements of this box=measured this box

**Let's measure the distance from A to B.**

**Will you time me running 100 meters?**

TRACK 300

**I feel sick.** / I feel like throwing up. / I feel like I might puke.
→ puke = vomit; throw up

**I threw up all I had eaten.** → threw up = vomited

**Exhale.** / Breathe out. ⇒ Exhale → Exhale deeply（大きく息を吐いて）

**Don't spit here.**

**He spat at me.** → at= on

**Never say die.** / Chin up. / Cheer up.

**Why don't you make a clean breast of it?**
→ make a clean breast of~（～をすっかり打ち明ける）= confess

TRACK 301

**Please put on your shoes.** → put on your shoes=put your shoes on
⇒ your shoes → these slippers（このスリッパ）

**I don't want to wear these shoes. They are too tight.**
→ wear=put on ⇒ shoes → long boots（長靴）

TRACK 302

**Can you sweep the floor?**

TRACK 303

**When does your school start?** ⇒ When → What time（何時に）

**My school starts at nine o'clock.**

学校は4月10日から始まるんだ。

会議はあと3分で始まるよ。

急いで。もう始まる時間だよ。

例の展覧会がいつ始まるか知ってる？

それなら来週の木曜日に始まるよ。

物語は主人公がクラスメートと恋に落ちるところから始まるんだ。

梅雨は6月半ばに始まる。

この儀式は平安時代に始まったと言われているんだ。

私たちの不和は誤解から始まったの。

彼の遅刻は今始まったことではないさ。

ほらほら、また始まった。

(諺) 慈善は家庭から始まる。

## 始める

始めましょうか？

いつから英語を始めたの？

4月から英語を習い始めたのよ。

今日から英語の日記を書き始めるんだ。

今日からダイエットを始めるの。

Our school begins on April 10.

The meeting will start in three minutes.

Hurry up! It's already starting time.

Do you know when the exhibition will open?

It opens next Thursday.

The story begins with the hero falling in love with his classmate.

The rainy season starts about the middle of June.
→ starts= sets in

This ceremony is said to be originated in the *Heian* period. → originate（源を発する、起こる、始まる）

The ill feeling between us was caused by a misunderstanding. → ill feeling（悪感情、わだかまり）

His coming late is nothing new. / This isn't the first time that he has come late.

There you go again! → 相手の繰り返される発言、行動にうんざりしたときの表現。

Charity begins at home.

TRACK 304

Shall we begin? ⇒ Shall → Where shall（どこから…）

When did you start English? → start ＝ start learning

I started learning English from April.

I'll begin an English diary from today. / I'm going to start a diary in English from today.

I'm going to start my diet from today.
⇒ I'm going to start → I started（～始めた）

４月から東京で新しい仕事をはじめるのよ。

雨が降り始めた。

## 走る

運動のために走ってるんだ。

毎日、何キロ走ってる？

どの辺を走ってるの？

僕がクラスで走るのが一番早いんだ。

教室内を走ってはいけませんよ。

最寄りの駅まで走ってわずか３分ですよ。

この車はまだ走れるよ。

この通りは南北に走ってるのさ。

## 外す

寝る前にコンタクト外す？

コンタクトが外れた。

マスクを外してもいい？

どうして指輪を外したの？

彼はただいま席を外しております。

私のカン、外れたわね。

**I'll start my new job in Tokyo from April.**
⇒ my new job → living by myself（一人暮らしを）

**It started to rain.**

TRACK 305

**I run for exercise.**

**How many kilometers do you run every day?**

**Whereabouts do you run?** → whereabouts（どのあたりを）= where

**I'm the fastest runner in my class.** / I run the fastest in my class.

**Don't run in the classroom.** ⇒ in the classroom → down the hall（廊下を）、backwards（後ろ向きに）、across the street（通りを走って渡る）、up and down the stairs（階段を「走って」上がったり下りたり）

**It's only three minutes' run to the nearest station.**

**This car still runs all right.** / This car is still in running condition.

**This street runs south and north.**
⇒ south and north → east and west（東西に）

TRACK 306

**Do you take out your contacts before going to bed?**
⇒ take out your contacts → take off your glasses（眼鏡を外す）

**My contact lens came off.** / My contacts have come off.

**Can I remove my mask?** → remove = take off

**Why did you take off your ring?**

**He is not at his desk right now.**

**My hunch was wrong.** → hunch= intuition; guess

あの占い師の言ったことは外れたな。

この雑誌の星占いはいつも外れるよ。

最近、天気予報はよく外れる。

## 果たす

君は義務を果たすべきだよ。

君は約束を果たさないといけないよ。

目的を果たすまであきらめてはだめだ。

私はいま大きなプロジェクトで重要な役割を果たしているんだ。

## 働く

どこで働いているの？

A 社で働いているんだ。

金融業界で働いています。

ここで働いてどれくらいになりますか？

営業部で 20 年くらい働いているんだ。

社長秘書として働いているの。

朝のシフトで働いてるんだ。

昼寝て夜働いてるよ。

**What the fortune teller said was wrong.**

**Horoscopes in this magazine are always wrong.**
⇒ horoscopes → Birthday fortune-telling（誕生日占い）、Tarot fortune-telling/ Tarot reading（タロット占い）、Palm reading（手相占い）→ これらの be 動詞は is。

**These days, weather forecasts are often wrong.**

TRACK 307

**You should fulfill your duties.** ⇒ duties → responsibility（責任）

**You must keep your promise.**
⇒ must keep → never keep（全然果たさない）

**Never give up till you accomplish your purpose.**
→ accomplish= achieve → purpose= aim

**I'm now playing an important role in a big project.**
→ an important role = a key role

TRACK 308

**Where do you work?**

**I work for A company.** / I work for a company called A.
→ work for = work at

**I work in the financial industry.** → 業界や部門を示す場合は work in ⇒ financial industry → media industry（メディア業界）、human resources department（人事部）、advertising department（広告部）

**How long have you been working here?**

**I've worked in the sales department for about twenty years.**

**I'm working as a president's secretary.**
⇒ as a president's secretary → as a teacher（教師として）、as a freelancer（フリーランスとして）、as an editor（編集員として）、as a salesperson（販売員として）

**I work the morning shift.** ⇒ the morning shift → the night shift（夜のシフトで）= at night ⇒ the morning shift → from morning till night（朝から晩まで）→ till = to

**I sleep days and work nights.**

## 発表する

クラスの前で発表しなければいけないんだ。

授業で作文を発表するんだ。

授業で夏目漱石について発表するんだ。

僕の実験結果を発表します。

私の3週間の研修の結果を発表します。

遠慮なく意見を発表してください。

## 話す

英語が話せますか？

英語を流ちょうに話します。

あなたは立派な英語を話しますね。

ボソボソ話すのはやめなさい。

はっきりと話しなさい。

私は手話が話せます。

## 払う

キャッシュで払います。

10万円の月賦で払います。

TRACK 309

**I've got to give a presentation in class.**
⇒ a presentation → a presentation about global warming（地球温暖化についての発表）

**I'll read out my essay in class.**
→ read out = recite ⇒ in class → in front of everyone（みんなの前で）

**I'm going to present on *Soseki Natsume* in class.**

**I'll talk about the experimental results.**

**I'd like to speak to you about the results of my three-week training.**

**Please don't hesitate to express your opinion.**
→ don't hesitate to~（遠慮せずに～する）

TRACK 310

**Do you speak English?** → Do you → Can you より一般的

**I speak English fluently.** / I'm a fluent speaker of English.

**You speak good English.**
⇒ good English → bad English（ひどい英語）、in broken English（片言の英語で）、with a Kansai accent（関西訛りで）、in choice words（辛辣な言葉で）

**Don't speak in a mumble.**

**Speak plain.** ⇒ plain → in a loud voice（大きな声で）、in a whisper（声をひそめて）、in an undertone（小声で、ぼそっと）、in an audible voice（よく聞こえる声で、大声で）、more slowly（もっとゆっくり）、in plain English（平易は英語で）

**I can use sign language.** / I can communicate in sign language.

TRACK 311

**I'll pay in cash.** ⇒ in cash → by credit card（クレジットカードで）→ by =with; via、by bank transfer（銀行振り込みで）

**I'll pay in monthly installments of one hundred thousand yen.**

料金は後で払います。

割り勘で払おう。

割り勘は不公平なので、私が食べたものは払うよ。

これに幾ら払った？

自分の仕事にもっと注意を払うべきですよ。

### 晴れる

明日は晴れるだろう。

空が晴れてきてるよ。

朝は雨だったけど、今は晴れてきてる。

雨だと気分が晴れないな。

外に出て運動でもすれば、気分が晴れるよ。

何があったんだ。目を腫らしちゃって。

風邪でも引いたみたい。扁桃腺が腫れてるんだ。

## ひ

### 冷える

今朝は少々冷えるね。

夜は冷えるね。

最近は冷えてきたね。

**I'll pay the fee later.** ⇒ the fee → the tuition（授業料）、the rent（レンタル料）、utility bills（公共料金）、you for your work（あなたに仕事の報酬を）、the hospital（病院の費用）、my electricity bill（電気代）、everything（全部）、the remainder（残り）、the difference（差額）

**Let's split the bill.** → split the bill（割り勘にする）

**Splitting the bill isn't fair, so I'll pay for what I ate.**
⇒ what I ate → what I ate and drank（私が飲食したもの）

**How much did you pay for this?**

**You should pay more attention to your work.**
⇒ more attention … work → respect to your parents（両親に敬意を）

TRACK 312

**It will be fine tomorrow.**
⇒ fine → cloudy（曇）、rainy（雨）、snowy（雪）

**It's beginning to clear up.** / **The sun is coming out.**

**It rained in the morning, but it's clearing up now.**

**I don't feel well when it's rainy.**

**If you go outside and get some exercise, you'll feel better.**

**What happened? Your eyes are swollen.**

**I think I have a cold. My tonsils are swollen.**
→ tonsil（扁桃腺）

TRACK 313

**It's rather chilly this morning.** → chilly = cold; cool

**It cools down at night.**

**It's getting colder these days.**

足が冷えるよ。

冷たいものばかり食べてると、体が冷えるよ。

このビールを冷蔵庫で冷やしてくれる？

これさ、ギンギンに冷やしてよ。

頭を冷やせ！

## 控える

不要不急の外出は控えてください。

勝手な発言は控えてください。

わたし、今、塩分を控えてるの。

体重を落としたいなら、間食は控えることね。

健康のためにタバコは控えることにしよう。

## 光る

星が光っている。

今夜は月がこうこうと光っているね。

いま遠くでかすかに光ってるものが見えたけど。

彼は新入社員の中では光っているな。

**My feet get cold.** → get cold= become cold

**If you eat only cold foods, your body will get cold.**

**Can you chill this beer in the fridge?** → fridge=refrigerator

**Make this ice cold, please.**

**Cool it.** / Cool off. / Cool down. / Calm down.

TRACK 314

**Please refrain from any nonessential and non-urgent outings.** → refrain from~（~を控える、～をやめる）→ outing（外出、お出かけ）→ outings の後に for two weeks を付けて「2 週間は」

**Please refrain from speaking without permission.**
**/ Please don't talk without permission.**

**I'm cutting back on my salt intake now.** / I'm cutting back on my intake of salt.
→ cut back on~（～を減らす、～を削減する）= reduce; cut down on → my salt intake → my intake of sugar（糖質の摂取）

**If you want to lose weight, you should cut back on the between-meal snacks.**
⇒ the between-meal snacks → your mid-night snacks（夜食）

**I'm going to refrain from smoking for my health.**

TRACK 315

**The stars are twinkling.** → twinkle 星や光などが「キラキラ光る」。同意の glitter は星や宝石などが強い光で「ピカピカ光る」。

**The moon is shining brightly tonight.**
→ shine は光を出して「光る、照る」。

**I saw something gleaming in the distance.**
→ gleam は薄暗い場所などで「かすかに光る、ほのかに光る」。

**He stands out among the new employees.**
→ stand out（突出する、際立つ、人目を引く）

## 引く

値段を引いてくれますか？

風邪を引いちゃった。

熱があったが、今は引いてるよ。

5 から 2 を引いて。

7 引く 4 は 3。

君の失礼な態度、引く～。

この語を辞書で引いてください。

まずはフライパンに油を引いてちょうだい。

君はサムライの血を引いているんだってね。

この文を線を引いて消してください。

ページの中央に直線を引いてください。

ドアを手前に引いてください。

僕は一歩も後へ引くつもりなどない。

私もそろそろ身を引く時期だな。

## 弾く

ピアノを弾きますか？

毎日 2 時間ピアノを弾いてるよ。

昔はギターを弾きながら歌ったものだ。

TRACK 316

**Can you reduce the price?**
→ reduce = cut down ⇒ reduce → take 10 percent off（10%引く）

**I caught a cold.** ⇒ caught → have（引いている）

**I had a fever but it's gone now.**

**Subtract 2 from 5.**

**Four from seven leaves three.** / **Seven minus four equals three.**

**Your rude attitude turns me off.** ⇒ Your rude attitude → The words you just said（君の今の言葉）→ turn someone off（人に興味を失わせる）

**Please look up this word in your dictionary.**

**First oil your frying pan.**

**I hear you are descended from a *samurai* family.**
→ be descended from~（～の血筋を引いている）

**Please cross out the sentence.**

**Please draw a straight line in the center of the page.**
⇒ straight line → diagonal line（斜線）、broken line/ dashed line（破線）、wavy line（波線）、dotted line（点線）

**Please pull the door toward you.**

**I'm not going to budge an inch.**
→ budge（「意見、態度などを」変える、ちょっと動く）→ 否定形で使うことが多い。

**It's almost time I retire.** → retire（退職する、引退する）

TRACK 317

**Do you play the piano?**

**I play the piano for two hours every day.**

**I used to sing while playing the guitar.**

## 非難する

私のことを非難してるの？

自分の失敗で人を非難するのはやめてよ。

非難されることを恐れていては何もできないよ。

## 批判する

最近、ネットで他人を批判する人をよく見かけるね。

きっと彼らは他人を批判して楽しんでるんだね。

君は僕を批判する立場にはない。

人を批判する前に自分の問題を解決すべきだよ。

あなたを批判するつもりは全くありません。

## 響く

彼女の歌は心に響くね。

君の言葉は僕に響いたよ。

君の声はよく響くね。

この楽器はよく響かないな。

この部屋は思った以上に響くね。

## 冷やかす

僕のことを冷やかすなよ。

人前で彼女を冷やかすとはあなたも意地悪ね。

TRACK 318

**Are you criticizing me?** → criticize = accuse ; blame ⇒ me → me for not doing the job（仕事をしないといって私を）

**Don't accuse others for your own failure.**
⇒ failure → mistake（ミス）

**If you are afraid of being criticized, you can't do anything.**

TRACK 319

**Recently I've been seeing a lot of people criticizing others online.**

**I'm sure they are enjoying criticizing others.**

**You are in no position to criticize me.**

**You should resolve your own problems before criticizing others.** → resolve（「問題、困難などを」解決する）

**I don't intend at all to criticize you.**

TRACK 320

**Her songs are touching.** → touching=moving; stirring; impressive

**Your words touched my heart.**

**You have a sonorous voice.** / Your voice carries well.
→ sonorous（「音や声が」朗々とした、鳴り響く）

**This musical instrument doesn't sound good.**

**This room echoes more than I thought.**

TRACK 321

**Don't tease me.** → tease= make fun of; mock

**It's mean of you to ridicule her in public.**
→ ridicule = mock; taunt; tease ⇒ in public → in front of her friends（彼女の友人たちの前で）

## 冷やす

これ、冷蔵庫で冷やそう。

このビール、冷やしてくれる？

これ、冷蔵庫で冷やして食べて。

足を冷やさないように。

## 開く

この戸が開かないよ。

この戸は外側に開くんだよ。

つぼみがもうすぐ開きそうだ。

まだ教科書を開かないで。

教科書の 25 ページを開きなさい。

この添付ファイルはどうやって開くの？

緊急会議を開きますよ。

その会議はいつ開かれますか？

9 月に東京に店を開く予定です。

私は新宿でお店を開いています。

来週、ダンスパーティーを開きます。

## 拾う

落としたらちゃんと拾いなさい。

TRACK 322

**Let's cool this in the fridge.**
→ fridge= refrigerator　⇒ the fridge → the fridge overnight（冷蔵庫で一晩）

**Will you chill this beer?**
⇒ chill this beer → chill this beer a little bit more（このビールをもう少し冷やす）

**Eat this after cooling it in the fridge.**

**Don't let your feet get cold.**　⇒ feet → stomach（お腹）

TRACK 323

**This door won't open.**　⇒ won't → wouldn't（開かなかった）

**This door opens outward.**　⇒ outward → inward（内側に）

**The buds are going to unfold soon.**
⇒ are going to unfold soon → have opened into flowers（開いて花になった）

**Don't open your textbook yet.**

**Open your textbook to page 25.**

**How do I open this attachment?**
→ attachment = attachment file

**We'll call an emergency meeting.**　→ call（招集する）

**When will the meeting be held?**
⇒ meeting → panel discussion（公開討論会）

**We plan to set up a store in Tokyo in September.**
→ set up（設立する、創立する、開業する）⇒ store → new office（新しい事務所）

**I run a store in Shinjuku.**　→ run=have

**We are going to hold a dance party next week.**
→ hold= give; have; throw

TRACK 324

**If you drop something, pick it up.**

いま落としたごみを拾いなさい。

道でこの携帯電話、拾いました。

あそこで車を拾おう。

(諺) 捨てる神あれば拾う神あり。

## 広める

あなたはもっと見聞を広めるべきよ。

読書は私たちの知識を広げるのに役立つわよ。

日本で誰が仏教を広めたか知ってる？

この作品が彼女の名を世界中に広めたわけだ。

この歌はネットを通じてすぐに広まったんだ。

このガンが広がれば手遅れになる。

インフルエンザがいま職場で広がっている。

## ふ

## 増える

体重が増えちゃった。

ここ 1 か月で体重が 3 キロ増えちゃった。

年々年寄りの数が増えている。

**Pick up the rubbish you dropped just now.**
⇒ the rubbish…now → your socks off the floor（床の靴下を）→ off = from

**I picked up this cellphone on the street.**

**Let's get a taxi over there.**

**When one door shuts, another opens.** / The world is as kind as it is cruel.

TRACK 325

**You should broaden your knowledge more.**
→ broaden =widen; expand ⇒ knowledge → horizons（視野）

**Reading books helps us widen our knowledge.**

**Do you know who propagated Buddhism in Japan?**
→ propagated= spread

**This piece made her name known all over the world.**
→ piece（「美術、文学、音楽などの」作品）

**This song spread quickly through the internet.**

**If this cancer spreads, it will be too late.**
⇒ spreads → spreads to other organs（他の臓器に広がる）

**The flu is going around our office now.** → go around（「うわさ、病気などが」広まる） ⇒ our office now → this winter（この冬）

TRACK 326

**I gained weight.** → gained= put on

**I have put on three kilograms in weight in a month.** / I gained three kilos in a month.

**The number of old people is increasing year by year.**
⇒ The number of old people → The population of our city（私たちの町の人口） ⇒ old people → non-smoking restaurants（禁煙のレストラン）→ increasing= going up; rising

## 吹く

（諺）明日は明日の風が吹く。

今日は強い風が吹いているね。

口笛は吹ける？

僕、トランペットが吹けるよ。

ホラを吹くのはよせよ。

## 拭く

さあ、手を拭きなさい。

これらの皿を布巾で拭いてちょうだい。

テーブルにこぼした水を拭きなさい。

## 復讐する

わたし、彼のしたことに対して復讐してやるわ。

2年も浮気をしたことに対して、元カレに復讐してやるんだ。

## 復習する

これらの個所を復習しなきゃ。

復習はその日のうちにするのが肝心ですよ。

前の授業の復習から始めましょう。

TRACK 327

**Tomorrow is another day.** / Tomorrow is a new day. / Tomorrow's wind will blow tomorrow. / Every day is a brand new day. → brand new（真新しい）

**The wind is blowing very strongly today.** / There is a strong wind blowing today.

**Do you know how to blow a whistle?** / Can you whistle?

**I can play the trumpet.**

**Don't talk big.** / Don't make up bullshit.
→ make up bullshit（ホラを吹く）= brag

TRACK 328

**Wipe your hands now.**
⇒ your hands → the sweat off your brow（額の汗）、your tears（涙）

**Will you dry these dishes with a dish towel?**
⇒ a dish towel → a paper towel（紙タオル）

**Mop up the slops on the table.**
→ mop up = sponge up（ぬぐいとる） → slop（こぼれ水、はね水）

TRACK 329

**I'm going to revenge on him for what he did to me.**
→ revenge on ～ =revenge oneself on ～ ; take revenge on ～（～に仕返しをする、～に復讐する）

**I'll take revenge on my ex-boyfriend for cheating on me for two years.** → cheat on~（～を裏切る、～を裏切って浮気する）

TRACK 330

**I've got to review these parts.**
⇒ these parts → Chapter 5（第5章）、what I learned today（今日習ったことを）=the things I learned today

**It's best to review what you learned the same day.**

**Let's begin by reviewing the last lesson.**

先週やったことを復習しましたか？

膨らむ

この風船、膨らませてよ。

モチが膨らみ始めたぞ。

パンの生地が膨らみ始めたよ。

膨らんだけど、元に戻っちゃった。

桜のつぼみがすでに膨らんできてるね。

想像力を膨らませてみなさい。

太る

最近、太ってきちゃった。

犬に餌をやりすぎたので、太ってきたよ。

踏む

私の足を踏んでますけど。

ブレーキを踏んで！

Ring と Sing は韻を踏んでいますか？

Song と韻を踏む語を言ってみて。

増やす

英語の語彙を増やしたい。

何が何でも財産を増やしたいよ。

Did you review what we did last week?

TRACK 331

Will you blow up this balloon? / Inflate this balloon please.

*Mochi* started puffing up.
→ *mochi* = rice cake ; pounded rice → puff up =become bigger; enlarge; swell

The bread dough has started to rise.
→ rise（「大きさや容量が」膨らむ、増大する）

It got big, but it went back to what it was.

The buds on the cherry trees are already swelling.
→ swelling= growing bigger ⇒ already swelling → not swelling yet（まだ膨らんでいない）

Stretch your imagination.

TRACK 332

I recently got fat. → got fat = gained weight、put on weight
⇒ got fat → gained a lot of weight（ずいぶん太った）

My dog is getting fat because I gave it too much food.

TRACK 333

You are stepping on my foot.
⇒ are stepping → stepped（踏んだ） ⇒ my foot → my toes（私のつま先）

Step on the brakes! → Step on = Put on ; Hit

Do "ring" and "sing" rhyme? → rhyme（韻を踏む）

Give me a rhyme for "song." → rhyme（同韻語）

TRACK 334

I want to expand my English vocabulary.

I want to add to my fortune at any cost.
→ add to one's fortune（財産を増やす） → at any cost =no matter what

## 降る

雪が降る。

私の町では今、雪が降ってるよ。

明日雨が降るかしら。

今夜雨が降る？

雨が降りそうだね。

ここはよく雨が降る？

雨が降るといけないので、傘を持って行きなさい。

雨が降ってきたよ。

雨に降られちゃったよ。

どうしたんだ、太郎。しっぽをそんなに振っちゃって。

彼女、君に手を振ってるよ。

僕は首を縦に振ったりはしないぞ。

彼女は不賛成を表して首を横に振ってるよ。

彼女を振ったよ。

彼女に愛を告白したが、振られちゃった。

## 震える

手が震えるんだ。

TRACK 335

**Snow falls.** / It snows.

**It's snowing in my town now.**
⇒ snowing → raining（雨が降って）

**I wonder if it will rain tomorrow.** ⇒ rain → snow（雪が降る）

**Is it going to rain tonight?**

**It looks like rain.**
⇒ looks like → will probably（多分）、might（〜かも）、must（〜にちがいない）

**Does it often rain here?**

**Bring an umbrella just in case it rains.**
→ just in case ~（〜するといけないので） → just in case だけの場合は「万一に備えて、念のために」

**It started raining.**
⇒ started raining → suddenly started raining（急に降ってきた）

**I got caught in the rain.**

**What's the matter with you, Taro? Wiggling your tail like that.** → wiggle（「体の一部などを」小刻みに動かす）

**She is waving her hand to you.**

**I'm not going to nod my head.**
→ nod one's head（首を縦に振る、うなずいて賛成する）

**She is shaking her head in disapproval.** → shake one's head（不賛成を表して首を横に振る）

**I dumped her.** → dumped（「つき合っていたのに」振った） → dump = get rid of; leave; walk out on; jilt ; drop

**I confessed my love to her, but she turned me down.**
→ turn someone down（「no と言って」拒絶する、断る、振る）

TRACK 336

**My hands shake.**
→ shake は「震える」を意味する最も一般的な語。 ⇒ hands → legs（足）

震えが止まらないよ。

寒さでぶるぶる震えてるよ。

緊張しすぎちゃって足が震えてるよ。

唇も震えてるしさ。

あいつ、酒を飲み過ぎて手が震えてるぜ。

## 触れる

触れないで。

その件には触れないって約束するよ。

この本は地球温暖化には触れていないね。

悪いが、その件に触れる時間がないんだ。

過去のことは触れたくない。

色んな国の伝統や文化に触れてみたいな。

最近、英語に触れる機会が少ないんだ。

私は毎日英語に触れるようにしているよ。

アメリカへ行けば、本場の英語に触れることができるよ。

取り扱いに注意してください。これは空気に触れると急激に悪くなるから。

**I can't stop shaking.** ⇒ shaking → shaking all over （体中の震え）

**I'm shivering with cold.**
→ shiver は寒さ、恐怖のために瞬間的に体全体がブルッと震える → with=from

**I'm so nervous that my legs are shaking.**
⇒ legs → knees（膝）

**My lips are trembling, too.**
→ tremble は恐怖、疲労、寒さなどのために体の一部が無意識にぶるぶる震える。

**His hands are trembling from drinking too much.**

TRACK 337

**Don't touch.** / Keep your hands off. ⇒ 文尾に the goods（商品）、the exhibits（展示品）、my hand（私の手）、my shoulder（私の肩）、my back（私の背中）

**I promise I will not refer to that matter.**
→ refer to~ = touch on~; mention ~ （~ に言及する）

**This book does not refer to global warming.**

**Sorry, but I don't have time to touch on the subject.**

**I don't want to bring up the past.**
→ bring up （「問題などを」持ち出す）

**I want to experience the cultures and traditions of various countries.** → experience = have contact with

**These days I don't have many opportunities to be exposed to English.**
→ be exposed to~（~にさらされる、~に触れる） = come into contact with~

**I try to expose myself to English every day.**

**If you go to the United States, you can come into contact with real English.**

**Please handle with care. This will deteriorate rapidly on contact with air.**
→ deteriorate（悪くなる、劣化する） → on contact with~（~に触れて、~に触れたとたんに）

## 減らす

タバコの量を減らしなさい。

わたし、スイーツの量、減らすわ。

ご飯の量を減らしてくれる？

それ、量を減らしてもらえますか？

わたし、結婚式の前に体重減らさなきゃ。

いまダイエットで体重を減らしているところ。

食事の脂肪量を減らしてみてはどう？

ゴミを減らすよう頑張りましょう。

## 減る

腹が減った。

いつも昼食前に腹が減るんだよね。

今年、給料が減っちゃった。

コロナウイルス感染者の数が減るどころか増えている。

地球温暖化で日本の降雪量が明らかに減ってきているね。

日本の人口は減ってきているんだ。

TRACK 338

**Cut back on the cigarettes.** → cut back on~（～の量を減らす、～を削減する） ⇒ the cigarettes → your drinking（あなたの酒の量）

**I'm going to cut back on sweets.** ⇒ sweets → the sugar in this recipe（このレシピの砂糖の量）、late-night snacks（夜食のスナック）

**Can you decrease the amount of rice?**
→ decrease = reduce; lessen; diminish; cut back on

**Could you make it a smaller portion?**
→ portion（「料理などの」一人分の量、一人前）

**I've got to lose weight before the wedding.**
→ lose weight= reduce my weight

**I'm now reducing weight by dieting.** → reducing=losing

**How about cutting down on the amount of fat in your diet?** → cut down on ～（～を減らす）

**Let's try to reduce trash.**

TRACK 339

**I got hungry.** / I became hungry. / I'm hungry.

**I always get hungry before lunch.**

**My salary went down this year.** → went down = was decreased
⇒ this year → when I changed jobs（仕事を変えたら）

**The number of people who have COVID-19 has gone up instead of going down.**

**Due to global warming, the amount of snowfall is obviously decreasing in Japan.**

**The population of Japan is decreasing.**

## 変化する

世界は絶えず変化しているのさ。

外食産業を取り巻く状況は大きく変化したよね。

## 勉強する

秋は僕たちにとって勉強するには最高の季節だよ。

今日から勉強するぞ。

何を勉強するの？

私、英語の勉強してるんだ。

勉強する気になった？

もっとまじめに勉強しなさい。

毎日、夜遅くまで勉強してるの？

勉強することが一番好きだからさ。

もう少し勉強できませんか？

1000 円勉強できません？

わかりました。1500 円勉強しましょう。

## 返事する

返事ください。

返事しなさい。

TRACK 340

**The world is constantly changing.**

**Circumstances surrounding the food-service industry have greatly changed, haven't they?**
⇒ food-service industry → amusement industry（娯楽産業）

TRACK 341

**Fall is the best season for us to study.**

**I'll study from today.** ⇒ from today → from tomorrow（明日から）

**What are you going to study?**

**I'm studying English.**
⇒ I'm studying → I think I'll study ...（〜を勉強しようかな）

**Do you feel like studying?**
⇒ Do you → I don't（「〜する気に」なれない）

**Study more seriously.**
⇒ more → the basics of business（ビジネスの基本）

**Are you studying until late at night every day?**
⇒ until late at night → far into the night（夜更けまで）

**I like studying the best.**

**Can't you come down a little more?** / Can't you give me a better price? / Can't you lower the price a little more?
→ come down（「元の値段から」下げる、値下げする）

**Can't you take off one thousand yen?** → take off= knock off

**All right. I'll give you a discount of 1500 yen.**
/ I'll knock off 1500 yen.

TRACK 342

**Please reply.** ⇒ 文尾に → by e-mail immediately（メールですぐに）

**Answer me.** ⇒ 文尾に → when your name is called（名前を呼ばれたら）

返事をする前に少し考えさせて。

その件はゆっくり考えてから返事したほうがいいよ。

返事してない手紙がまだ 10 通もあるんだ。

返事をするのが遅くなってごめん。

## ほ

### 報告する

何か報告することはありますか？

結果を私に報告しなさい。

全ての結果をまとめ、それらを後で報告します。

会議の結果を報告します。

近況を報告します。

以下、報告致します。

### 干す

洗濯物を干すこと、忘れないで。

毎朝、洗濯物を干してる？

この布団を干そうか？

**Let me think before I give you an answer.**

**You had better think it over before giving your answer.**

**I still have ten more letters to answer.**

**Sorry for replying late.**

TRACK 343

**Do you have anything to report?**

**Report the result to me.**
⇒ the result → all of the progress（進捗状況を全て）

**I'll organize the conclusions and report them later.**
→ organize（整理する、まとめる）

**I'll report the result of the meeting.** ⇒ the result of the meeting → the research result（研究結果）、the result of the examination（検討の結果）、on the result（結果について）、on the damage situation（被害状況について）、on the new project（新しいプロジェクトに関して）、what I heard（聞いたこと）→文尾に sometime early next week（来週の早い時期に）

**Let me update on how things are going.**
→ update（更新する、最新のものにする） → how things are going = what's going on ⇒ how things are going → where we are now（現状を）

**Reported as below.**

TRACK 344

**Don't forget to dry the laundry.** → the laundry = the washing

**Do you hang the laundry out to dry every morning?**
→ hang the laundry out to dry= hang the laundry; dry out the laundry; hang out the laundry （洗濯物を外に干す）

**Shall we air this *futon*?**
→ air（「乾かしたりするために」空気に当てる、風に当てる）

彼はTV業界から干された。

## 褒める

今日、先生に褒められたよ。

先生から英語を褒められたんだ。

私はいつも自分の生徒を褒めるんです。

この新しいヘアスタイルを褒めてくれたのはあなただけ。

## 掘る

この木を植えるためにここに穴を掘ろう。

ジャガイモを掘りに行こう。

## 翻訳する

この文を日本語に翻訳して頂けますか？

このメールを英語に翻訳してくれる？

この仕様書を英語に翻訳するのを手伝ってくれますか？

コンピュータを使って英語を日本語に翻訳しているところ。

この資料は翻訳するのがすごく難しくてね。

この本を点字に翻訳してるの？

**He was ignored by the TV world.**
→ be ignored by~（～から無視される、～に相手にされない）

TRACK 345

**My teacher commended me today.**
→ commended = praised

**I received praise for my English from my teacher.**

**I always praise my students.**

**You are the only one who complimented me on my new hairstyle.** → compliment someone on = praise; flatter; admire

TRACK 346

**Let's dig a hole here to plant this tree.**
⇒ a hole → a hole about 1 meter deep（1 メートルくらいの穴）

**Let's go digging potatoes.**

TRACK 347

**Could you translate this sentence into Japanese?**

**Can you translate this e-mail into English?**

**Could you help me translate this specification document into English?**
⇒ specification document（仕様書）→ Japanese novel（日本の小説）

**I'm translating English into Japanese using a computer.**

**It's too difficult for me to translate this material.**
**/ Translating this material is too much for me.**

**Are you transcribing this book into Braille?**
→ Braille（点字）→ フランスの視覚障害者ルイ・ブライユ（Louis Braille, 1809 – 1852）が 1821 年に考案し、世界標準となった点字。

## ま

### 舞う

桜の花が風に舞っている。

ここ、ほこりが舞ってるよ。

### 負かす

彼を負かすのは簡単だ。

さっき彼を負かしたよ。

彼を負かすつもりで、逆にやられちゃった。

### 曲がる

あそこを左に曲がって。

交差点を右に曲がって。

次の交差点を左に曲がると郵便局があります。

この通りをまっすぐ行って、突き当りを左に曲がってください。

三つ目の角を左に曲がるんだっけ？

### 紛らわす

悲しみを紛らわすためにたいていは何をしてる？

悲しみを紛らわすためにいつも酒を飲んでいるよ。

TRACK 348

**Cherry blossoms are dancing in the wind.**
→ dancing in the wind=rambling through the wind ⇒ cherry blossoms → cherry blossom petals（桜の花びら）

**Dust is floating in the air here.** → float（「空中に」浮かぶ、漂う）

TRACK 349

**I can beat him easily.** → beat = defeat → easily=hands down; any day

**I defeated him a while ago.** ⇒ defeated him → argued him down（彼を言い負かした）⇒ a while ago → at English（英語で）、in a debate（討論で）、in his favorite game（彼の好きなゲームで）

**I meant to beat him, but got beaten instead.** → mean to~（～するつもりである）→ instead（それどころか、あべこべに）

TRACK 350

**Turn to the left over there.** → turn to the left = turn left

**Turn right at the intersection.**
⇒ intersection → next corner（次の角）

**When you turn left at the next intersection, you'll find a post office.**

**Go straight down this street, and make a left turn at the end.** → at the end（突き当りで）

**Do we have to turn left at the third corner?**

TRACK 351

**What do you usually do to distract yourself from being sad?** → distract oneself from~（～から気を紛らす）

**I always drink to distract myself from being sad.**
⇒ drink → listen to classical music（クラシックを聴く）、play computer games（コンピュータゲームをする）

## 巻く

これを紙で巻こう。

この箱に赤いリボンを巻くのはどう？

寒い。マフラーを首に巻こうっと。

足に包帯を巻くの手伝ってよ。

僕はいつも腕時計のねじを巻くの、忘れるんだ。

## 撒く

芝に水を撒くのを忘れないで。

ここにひまわりの種を撒こう。

この肥料を撒いてくれる？

彼女さ、彼にはとびっきりの笑顔を振りまくのよ。

## 負ける

君の負けだ。

負けたくない。

僕は誰にも負けないさ。

プレッシャーに負けるんじゃないぞ。

うちのチーム、負けそう。

いいか、時には負けるが勝ちだぞ。

TRACK 352

**Let's wrap this in paper.** ⇒ paper → seaweed（海苔）

**How about wrapping a red ribbon around this box?**

**It's cold. I'm going to put a scarf around my neck.**
→ put=wear; tie; have; wrap

**Can you help me wrap a bandage on my leg?**
→ wrap a bandage on my leg=bandage my leg; bind my leg with a bandage → put a dressing on the wound（この傷口に包帯を巻く）

**I always forget to wind my watch.**

TRACK 353

**Don't forget to water the lawn.**
→ lawn 公園や庭などのきれいに刈り込んだ芝生で、turf に同じ。grass は植物としての芝生。

**Let's plant sun flower seeds here.**

**Can you spread this fertilizer?**

**She flashes her sweetest smile at him, you know.**

TRACK 354

**You lose.**

**I don't want to lose.** ⇒ I don't want to → I'm not going to（〜はしないぞ）⇒ lose → lose to you（君に負ける）、lose to you at golf（ゴルフで君に負ける）、lose at *pachinko*（パチンコで負ける）

**I am second to none.** / No one can beat me. / I am unbeatable.
→ second to none（誰にも負けない → 誰に対しても 2 番目にはならない、から）

**Don't lose to the pressure.** → lose to= succumb to

**Our team is losing.** / Our team is losing this game. ⇒ is losing → lost the game（試合に負けた）、by one point（一点差で）、in the finals（決勝で）

**Remember, sometimes you win by losing.**

少しまけてくれますか？

1000円にまけてよ。

二割負けましょう。

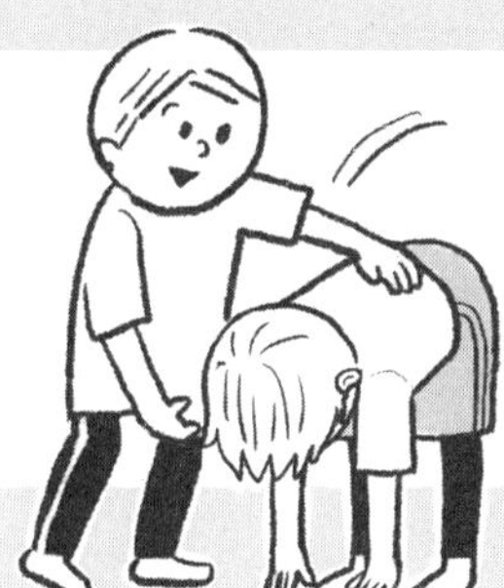

## 曲げる

腰を曲げて。

手首を曲げて。

僕は、自分の信念は絶対に曲げないよ。

何と言われようと、規則は曲げられません。

誰にも事実は曲げられないさ。

## 混ぜる

私、ときどきコーヒーにブランデーを混ぜるんだ。

これをスプーンでかき混ぜて。

卵をよく混ぜて。

今度は醤油と砂糖を混ぜてくれるかな。

ボウルのサラダを軽く混ぜ合わせてちょうだい。

## 待たせる

ごめん、待たせた？

**Can you reduce the price a bit?** / Can you take a little bit off the price?

**Bring the price down to one thousand yen, please.** / Make it one thousand yen, please.

**I'll reduce the price by twenty percent.** / I'll take twenty percent off the price.

TRACK 355

**Bend over.** / Bow.
⇒ over → your knees（あなたの膝）、your elbows（あなたの肘）、your body forward（体を前に）、back（腰を後ろに）、this spoon（このスプーン）

**Flex your wrists.** → flex（「手足などを」曲げる、「筋肉を」ほぐす）

**I never bend my conviction.**

**We can't bend the rules no matter what you say.**
⇒ bend the rules → bend the law（法律を都合よく変える）

**Nobody can falsify the facts.**
→ falsify the facts = pervert the truth; twist the truth

TRACK 356

**Sometimes I lace my coffee with brandy.**
→ lace（「飲食物にアルコールなどを」少し加える、少量混ぜる）

**Stir this with a spoon.** ⇒ this with a spoon → till it gets sticky（粘り気が出るまで）、it well and enjoy（それをよく混ぜて召し上がれ）

**Beat the egg thoroughly.** → beat（「卵などを」強くかき混ぜる）
⇒ thoroughly → until it becomes foamy（それが泡立つまで）

**Can you mix soy sauce and sugar this time?**
⇒ soy sauce and sugar → all the ingredients in the bowl well（ボウルの中の全ての材料をよく）→ ingredient（「料理の」材料）

**Toss the salad in the bowl, please.**
→ toss（「サラダなどを」軽くかき混ぜる）

TRACK 357

**Sorry, did I keep you waiting?**

待たせてごめんね。

お待たせしました。

お客様を待たせないようにして。

あとどれくらい待たせるつもり？

お待たせしちゃったかな。

## 間違える

間違えた。

誰でも間違えるさ。

間違えることが必ずしも悪いとは限らないよ。

間違えることを恐れてはだめ。

テストで5問間違えたよ。

授業時間を間違えちゃった。

9時と10時を間違えたよ。

日付を間違えたかも知れない。

わたし、計算をよく間違えるの。

いつもケタを間違えちゃうんだよね。

間違えてこのメッセージをあなたに送っちゃいました。

道を間違えたかも。

**I'm sorry to have kept you waiting.** / Sorry to keep you waiting.

**Thank you for waiting.**

**Try not to keep our customers waiting.**

**How much longer are you going to make me wait?**
⇒ How much longer → How long（どのくらい）

**Sorry, you had to wait long, huh?**

TRACK 358

**I made a mistake.** / I messed up.

**Everyone makes mistakes.** / Nobody is perfect.

**Making mistakes is not always bad.** → not always~（いつも～とは限らない、必ずしも～とは限らない）→ bad = a bad thing

**Don't be afraid of making mistakes.**
→文尾に in speaking English（英語を話す際に）

**I missed five questions on the test.**

**I got the lesson time wrong.**
→ get the time wrong = make a mistake with the time

**I mistook 9 o'clock for 10.** → mistake A for B（A を B と間違える）

**I might have gotten the date wrong.**

**I often make a mistake in calculation.** / I often commit an error in calculation. ⇒ in calculation → with English grammar（英文法を）、in spelling（綴りを）、with the date（日付を）

**I always mess up the number of digits.**
→ mess up（間違える、しくじる）→ number of digits（桁数）

**I sent this message to you by mistake.**

**It looks like we've come the wrong way.**

電車に乗り間違えるなんて、僕って、なんとも不注意だな。

## 待つ

（諺）待つ身は長い。

ちょっとお待ちください。

待ってます。

どこで待ってる？

ここで待つわ。

あなたからの連絡を待ってます。

あなたからの便りを指折り数えて待ってます。

待つのは構わないけど。

どのくらい待たなければいけませんか？

もう待てないよ。

待つの、疲れちゃった。

だいぶ待った？

何を待ってるんだ？

電車を待ってるの。

これを待ってたんだよ。

並んでお待ちください。

それは待つかいがあるね。

It's careless of me to take the wrong train.

TRACK 359

A watched pot never boils.

Wait a minute, please. / One moment, please. / （電話）Please hold on a minute.

I'll be waiting.

Where will you wait for me?

I'll wait here. ⇒ here → for you to come（あなたが来るのを）、for your answer（あなたの返事を）、at the usual place at 11 o'clock（いつもの場所で 11 時に）

I look forward to hearing from you.

I'll be counting the days till I hear from you.
→ hear from~（~から連絡をもらう）

I don't mind waiting.
⇒ don't mind waiting → can only wait（待つしかない）

How long do I have to wait?

I can't wait any longer.

I'm tired of waiting.

Have you been waiting long?

What are you waiting for? →何をグズグズしてるんだの意も表す。

I'm waiting for the train. ⇒ the train → my friend（私の友人）、the shop to open（開店を）、my turn（私の番）

This is what I've been waiting for.

Wait in line, please.

It's worth the wait.

## まとめる

君は考えをまとめる必要があるね。

まだ自分の意見をまとめていません。

今日の授業の内容をまとめてみよう。

次回の会議のために私たちの意見をまとめよう。

それらを１ページにまとめてくれる？

これらをまとめると以下の通り。

それらの書類をまとめてくれる？

メールをまとめてファイルしておきました。

あなたの荷物をまとめてください。

## 招く

これは混乱を招くかもしれない。

君、批判を招きたいのか？

うっかり口を滑らせるとしばしばよくない結果を招くものだ。

わたし、彼女の誕生パーティに招かれちゃった。

## 守る

約束は守るよ。

TRACK 360

**You need to get your ideas in shape.**
→ get your ideas in shape = put your thoughts together; get your ideas properly organized; get your ideas properly worked out

**I still haven't formed an opinion.**

**Let me sum up the contents of today's class.**
→ sum up（まとめる、要約する）

**Let's put our ideas together for the next meeting.**
→ put together（寄せ集める、まとめる）

**Can you turn them into a one-pager?**
→ one- pager（1ページにまとめた文書）

**These can be summarized as follows.**
→ as follows（次の通り、以下の通り）

**Will you gather those documents together?**
→ gather together（ひとまとめにする）

**I gathered the mail and kept them on file.**
→ keep ～ on file（～をファイルにしておく）

**Please gather your things.** ⇒ things → belongings（持ち物）

TRACK 361

**This might cause confusion.**
⇒ confusion → a misunderstanding（誤解）、unhappiness（不幸）、a disaster（災い）

**Do you want to invite criticism?**

**A slip of the tongue often brings about dismal consequences.**
→ a slip of the tongue（舌のすべり、失言、言い間違い）→ bring about（引き起こす、もたらす）→ dismal = dark; gloomy; dreary; grim → consequences（結果）

**I was invited to her birthday party.**

TRACK 362

**I'll keep my promise.**
→ promise=word ⇒ my promise → your secret（あなたの秘密）

交通ルールは守ってください。

ルールはちゃんと守りましょうね。

約束の時間は守ってください。

時間を守るのは立派な社会人としてマナーです。

私たちは自分たちの権利を守らねばならない。

紫外線から肌を守ってる？

日光から肌を守るために帽子をかぶってるよ。

## 迷う

道に迷うかも。

道に迷った。

そこでは道に迷うことなんてないよ。

どれにしようか迷ってるんだ。

どれを買うか迷うな。

A と B で迷ってるんだ。

## 丸める

背中を丸めないの。

背中を丸めて歩くのはよしなさい。

**Please observe the traffic rules.** → observe = keep; follow; obey → traffic rules= traffic regulations ⇒ the traffic rules → the speed limit（制限速度）、the school regulations（校則）、the social codes（社会のルール）

**Please follow the rules properly.**
→ follow the rules = abide by the rules; obey the rules; respect the rules ⇒ the rules → the guideline（ガイドライン）、the schedule（スケジュール）

**Please be punctual for the appointment.**

**Being punctual is part of being a respectable member of society.** → punctual（時間を守る）

**We must protect our rights.**
⇒ our rights → the environment（環境）、nature（自然）

**Are you protecting your skin from the UV rays?**
→ UV ray= ultraviolet ray

**I wear a hat to protect my skin from the sun.**

TRACK 363

**I might get lost.** / I might lose my way.

**I got lost.** / I lost my way.

**There is no risk of losing your way there.**

**I can't make up my mind which one to choose.** / I'm not sure which one to choose. → make up one's mind = decide

**I can't decide which to buy.** ⇒ which to buy → whether to go for a walk（散歩に行くかどうか）、what to cook（何を料理するか）、which movie to watch（どっちの映画を見るか）、which dish to order（どの料理を注文するか）、what to do（何をするか）、when to go（いつ行くか）、what to eat（何を食べるか）

**I can't decide between A and B.** → decide = choose

TRACK 364

**Don't stoop.** → stoop（体を前方に曲げる、かがむ）

**Stop walking with a stoop.**

## 回す

カギを右に回して。

110 番を回して。

これらの書類を回して。

これらの書類を担当のセクションに回してくれる？

一枚取って、残りを後ろの列に回してください。

彼は本社から大阪の支店に回されたんだってね。

彼は販売促進部へ回されたよ。

車を１台ゲートに回してくれます？

# み

## 見える

あれ見える？

何が見えるの？

見えない。

ほとんど見えないな。

眼鏡をかけていてもよく見えない。

TRACK 365

**Turn the key to the right.** → to the right= clockwise → to the left（左に）=counter-clockwise ⇒ the key → the wheel（ハンドル）

**Dial 110 please.** ⇒ 110 →（米）911、（英）999

**Pass around these documents.**
→ pass around =pass round（順に回す、回送する）

**Will you send round these papers to the section in charge?** → send round（回す、回覧する）

**Take a sheet and pass the rest on back rows, please.**
→ pass ~on …（～を…に移す、～を…に伝える）

**I hear that he was transferred from the head office to a branch in Osaka.**
→ be transferred to~（～へ転勤になる、～へ所属が動く）

**He was transferred to the Sales Promotion Department.** ⇒ the Sales Promotion Department → the Information Systems Department（情報システム部）、the Sales Division（営業部）、R&D Department（研究開発部）、the Overseas Department（海外事業部）、another section（別の課）

**Could you send a car round to the gate?**
→ send round = send over

TRACK 366

**Can you see that?**

**What do you see?**

**I can't see it.**

**I can barely see it.** → barely=hardly

**Even with my glasses, I can't see very well.**

私、目が見えなくなるかも。

晴れた日には、ここから富士山が見えるんだよ。

富士山が見えてきた。

物が二重に見えるよ。

これ何に見える？

リンゴのように見えるけど。

それらはみな同じにみえるけどなぁ。

どうした？疲れて見えるよ。

彼女、若く見えるよね。

彼女、10 歳以上は若く見えるよ。

## 磨く

わたし、食後のたびに歯を磨くの。

特にこの表面をきれいに磨いてね。

君は人格を磨く必要がありそうだね。

僕はマジで男を磨きたいんだ。

わたし、毎日、英語力を磨いているんだ。

ニューヨークへ行く前に英語力を磨きなおさないと。

**I might go blind.** / I might lose my eyesight.
⇒ go blind= become blind

**On a fine day, you can see Mt. Fuji from here.**

**Mt. Fuji came in sight.** → came in sight= came into view

**I see double.**

**What does this look like?**

**It looks like an apple.**

**They all look the same.**

**What happened? You look tired.**

**She looks young, doesn't she?** ⇒ young → cute（かわいく）、scary（こわそう）、cheerful（陽気に）、childish（幼く）、younger than 20（20歳より若く）

**She looks ten years younger than she really is.**

TRACK 367

**I brush my teeth after every meal.**

**Polish especially this surface clean.** ⇒ this surface clean → these leather shoes（これらの革靴）

**It seems that you need to cultivate your character.**
→ cultivate = build up

**I really want to improve myself as a man.**
→ improve oneself（自分を成長させる、自分を高める）

**I'm polishing up my English every day.** ⇒ polish up my English = improve my English skills ⇒ English → music playing skills（音楽の演奏技術）、skill on the piano（ピアノの腕）

**I have to brush up on my English before I go to New York.** → brush up on ～（～の能力を磨きなおす、～を学びなおす）⇒ my English → my communication skills（コミュニケーション能力）

君、ずいぶん腕を磨いたね。

## 見せる

そこのネクタイを見せてください。

あなたに見せたい写真があるんだ。

その写真見せて。

これをあなたに見せたかったの。

これは誰にも見せられないよ。

彼女は自分をかわいく見せる方法を知っているよ。

彼らに君の熱意を見せることが重要だよ。

君は彼らに良い手本を見せるべきだ。

彼女は本当の自分を見せないね。

先日、彼女は意外な一面を見せたんだ。

## 乱れる

なんだ？映像が少し乱れ出したぞ。

髪が乱れてるよ。

強風で髪が乱れちゃった。

**You have certainly improved your skill.**
⇒ your skill → your English skills（英語力）

TRACK 368

**Could you show me that necktie?** / Let me see that necktie, please.

**I have some pictures I want to show you.** / I have some pictures to show you.

**Show me the pictures.** / Can I look at the pictures? / Can I have a look at the pictures?

**I wanted to show this to you.** ⇒ show this to you= show you this

**I can't show this to anyone.**
⇒ can't show → am not going to show（見せるつもりはない）

**She knows how to show herself in a cute way.**
⇒ in a cute way → in a good way（良く「見せる」）

**It's important to show them your enthusiasm.**
→ enthusiasm = passion; eagerness

**You should set them a good example.**
→ set them a good example = set a good example to them

**She never shows her true self.**
⇒ true self → emotions（喜怒哀楽）

**The other day, she showed an unexpected side.**

TRACK 369

**What's up with this? The image is becoming a bit fuzzy.**

**Your hair is messed up.** / Your hair is a mess.

**My hair got disarranged by the strong wind.** / The strong wind messed up my hair.

大地震のせいで列車のダイヤが乱れているのよ。

酔っ払っても僕は決して乱れないんだ。

## 見つける

失くしたカバンを見つけた。

君の家を見つけるのに苦労したよ。

いい仕事を見つけるのに少々時間がかかっちゃった。

新しい彼女を見つけてね。

タイプミスを見つけたら、訂正してください。

この報告書の中に間違いを見つけました。

## 認める

あなたは自分が間違っていることを認める？

間違っていたことを認めるよ。

私は自分のミスを認めるつもりは全くありませんからね。

君は負けを認めるべきだよ。

いさぎよく負けを認めなよ。

それを認めることはできない。

上司はわたしの業績を認めてくれないのよ。

**The train schedule is disrupted because of the massive earthquake.** ⇒ The train schedule is → Bus services are（バスのダイヤが）⇒ the massive earthquake → a heavy snowfall（大雪）、the strike（ストライキ）

**Even when I get drunk, I never lose control of myself.**

TRACK 370

**I found my missing bag.**
⇒ my missing bag → the key under the desk（カギを机の下で）

**I had a hard time finding your house.**
⇒ your house → the right man for this job（この仕事に適任の人物）、a parking space（車を止める場所）、the solution to that problem（その問題の解決策）、a red jacket（赤いジャケット）、his whereabouts（彼の居場所）

**It took me a little time to find a good job.**
⇒ good job → plum job（割のいい仕事）、juicy job（おいしい仕事）

**I hope you'll find a new girlfriend.**
⇒ girlfriend → boyfriend（ボーイフレンド）、lover（恋人）

**If you find any typos, please correct them.**
→ typo（タイプミス、誤植）

**I found a mistake in this report.**
⇒ a mistake in this report → his weak point（彼の弱点）

TRACK 371

**Do you admit you are wrong?** ⇒ wrong → mistaken（間違って）

**I admit I was wrong.** ⇒ I was wrong → it was wrong（それが間違っていた）、he is sincere（彼が誠実である）、I lied（私が嘘をついた）

**I'm never going to admit my mistakes.**

**You should acknowledge your defeat.**
→ acknowledge=admit

**Be a good loser.**

**I can't approve of it.** → approve of~（～を認める、～を承認する）

**My boss doesn't approve of my performance.**
→ performance（業績、実績、功績）

## 見る

これ見てよ。

（店で）見ているだけです。

サッカーの試合をテレビで見よう。

テレビは見ないんだ。

日本のアニメを見るのが大好きなんだ。

僕と一緒に映画を見に行かない？

僕はネットを見て時間を過ごすのが好きなんだ。

桜を見に京都へ行きたいな。

左を見て。金閣寺が見えますよ。

ここは見るべきものは何もないね。

人の顔をじっと見ないでよ。

彼を見るのもいやだわ。

昨夜、変な夢を見たよ。

一般的に言って、見るのと聞くのでは大きな違いがあるものだ。

今に見ていろ。

しばらく様子を見てみよう。

私の論文をざっと見て頂けますか？

TRACK 372

Look at this.

I'm just looking.

Let's watch a soccer game on television.

I don't watch television.

I love watching Japanese anime.

How about going to see a movie with me?

I like to spend time doing net surfing. → net surfing → インターネットのサイトをあちこち見ること。単に surfing ともいう。

I want to go to Kyoto to see the cherry blossoms.

Look to your left. You can see *Kinkakuji* Temple.
⇒ look to your left → look to your right（右を見る）、look to the side（横を見る）

There is nothing to see here.
⇒ to see → worth seeing（見る価値がある）

Don't look me square in the face. → look a person in the face（人の顔をまともに見る） → square （「副詞句の前に置いて」まともに、じっと）

I can't bear even the sight of him. → can't bear= hate

I had a strange dream last night.
⇒ a strange dream → a nightmare（悪夢）

Generally speaking, there is a great difference between what you see and what you hear.
→ generally speaking = generally; overall

Just you watch. / You'll pay for this.

Let's wait and see for a while.

Could you look over my research papers?

今、気候変動に関する文献を見ているところなんだ。

## む

### 向かう

どこへ向かってるの？

今、向かってるよ。

駅へ向かってるんだ。

九州へ向かいます。

これは西に向かう列車ですか？

南に向かう列車に乗りたいのですが。

事態は悪い方向に向かっていますね。

親に向かって口答えするのはやめなさい。

### 迎える

わたし、来週誕生日を迎えるの。

もうすぐ20歳を迎えるのよ。

もうすぐ新年を迎えます。

蕎麦を食べながら新年を迎えようよ。

**I'm looking into the literature on climate change now.**
→ look into（〜の中を見る、調査する） → literature=documents

TRACK 373

**Where are you headed?** / Where are you heading? / Where are you going?

**I'm on my way.** ⇒ on my way → on my way home（自宅に向かって） ⇒ 文尾に to my friend's house を付けて「友だちの家に」→ on one's way to~（〜へ向かっている途中で、〜に向かって進んでいる）

**I'm heading for the station.**
⇒ the station → the café（カフェ）、the restaurant（レストラン）、the bank（銀行）、the post office（郵便局）

**I'm off to Kyushu.** / I'll head towards Kyushu.
→ be off to ~（〜へ行く）→ head towards（〜に向かって進む）

**Is this a westbound train?** ⇒ westbound → eastbound（東行きの、東に向かう）

**I want to take the southbound train.**
⇒ southbound → northbound（北行きの、北に向かう）

**The situation seems to be taking a turn for the worse.**
→ take a turn for the worse（「事態、状況が」悪い方向に向かう）

**Stop talking back to your parents.** / Don't talk back to your parents.

TRACK 374

**My birthday is next week.** / It's my birthday next week.
⇒ next week → on the 28th of March（3 月 28 日に）

**I'll soon become twenty.** / I'll be twenty soon. / My 20th birthday is coming soon.

**We'll soon greet the New Year.**
→ greet（挨拶する、迎える） = welcome

**Let's see in the New Year with *soba*.**
→ see in the New Year（新年を迎える）

この春わが校は開校 100 周年を迎えました。

今週木曜日に私の好きなテレビドラマが最終回を迎えるの。

とうとう一か月のイベントの最終日を迎えたね。

旧友を迎えるために駅へ向かっているところさ。

## 蒸す

今夜は蒸すよね。

サツマイモを蒸そうよ。

## 群がる

アリが砂糖に群がってる。

君も彼女に群がる男性の一人か？

# め

## 面倒をみる

2 日間、犬の面倒をみてもらえる？

犬の面倒をみてくれてありがとう。

⇒「世話をする」の項目参照

We celebrated the 100th anniversary of the opening of our school this spring. → opening = founding

My favorite TV drama will reach the last day of its run this Thursday. → run（続演）

Finally, we have come to the last day of the month-long event.

I'm on my way to the station to meet my old friend.

TRACK 375

It's muggy tonight, isn't it?
→ muggy=sultry; humid; sticky ⇒ tonight → these days（最近）

Let's steam some sweet potatoes.
⇒ sweet potatoes → these vegetables（これらの野菜）

TRACK 376

The ants are swarming to sugar.

Are you one of the men who swarm to her, too?

TRACK 377

Could you take care of my dog for two days?

Thank you for taking care of my dog.

## 申し込む

ねえ、留学プログラムに申し込む？

私、交換留学生プログラムに申し込むつもりよ。

昨日、カナダの夏季語学研修に申し込んだんだ。

A 社のインターンシップに申し込もうよ。

ついさっきジムに申し込んだよ。

明日、花子に結婚を申しこむつもりなんだ。

## 燃える

私、いま向学心に燃えてるんだ。

どんな時に燃えるの？

わたし、逆境に燃えるタイプかな。

この大プロジェクトに燃えてきたぞ。

## 用いる

この機械は世界中で用いられているんだ。

この薬はガン治療に用いられている。

TRACK 378

**Say, are you going to apply for a study abroad program?**

**I'm going to apply for an exchange student program.**
⇒ an exchange student program → a summer language program（夏季語学プログラム）

**Yesterday I applied for a summer language program in Canada.** ⇒ a summer language program in Canada → the TOEIC（トーイック）、the English proficiency test（英検）

**Let's apply for an internship at A company.**

**I signed up for the gym a little while ago.**
→ sign up for ~（「署名して」~を申し込む、～に参加する）⇒ the gym → the yoga class（ヨガのクラス）、the swimming club（スイミングクラブ）

**I'm going to propose to Hanako tomorrow.**
→ propose to =propose marriage to

TRACK 379

**I'm burning with the desire to learn now.** ⇒ with the desire … now → with anger（怒りに）、with jealous（嫉妬に）、with high hopes（希望に）

**When do you feel the most motivated? / What makes you motivated?** → feel motivated（やる気を感じる、やる気になる）

**Maybe I am the type who thrives on adversity. / I might be a person who is driven by adversity.**
→ thrive on adversity（逆境をこやしに成長する）= stare down adversity → thrive on~（～ですくすく育つ）→ adversity （逆境、困難）

**I'm fired up about this big project.**
→ be fired up（燃え上がる、気合が入る）

TRACK 380

**This machine is used all over the world.**

**This medicine is used to treat cancer.**

今度は別の方法を用いてみよう。

これは仏教で用いられる表現だね。

## 持つ

ちょっとこれ持ってくれる？

君のカバン持ってあげるよ。

辞書を持ってくるのを忘れないで。

身分証明書はお持ちですか？

君は強い意志を持ってるね。

私たち、同じ興味を持ってるみたいね。

そんな大金を持ち歩いていると危ないよ。

私、現金は持ち歩かないんだ。

これは冷蔵庫に入れないと 2 日以上はもたないよ。

ガソリンはあとどれくらいもつかな？

この天気は、数日はもちそうだな。

自慢するつもりはないけど、この会社は私でもってるんだ。

**Let's employ another method this time.**
→ employ=adopt　→ another method → a new method（新しい方法）

**This expression is used in Buddhism.**
⇒ Buddhism → period dramas（時代劇）⇒ is used in Buddhism → is still often used in America（今でもアメリカでよく用いられている）

TRACK 381

**Just hold this for me, will you?**
→ hold は手を使うときに使われる。

**Let me carry your bag.** / I'll carry your bag for you.
→ carry は持ち歩くときに使われる

**Don't forget to bring your dictionary.**

**Do you have your identification card with you?**
→ identification card = identity card　→ with you=on you　⇒ your identification card → your driver's license（あなたの運転免許証）

**You have a strong will, don't you?**
→ 同じ「持つ」でも have は手を使わないものに用いる。⇒ a strong will → many faces（多くの顔）、something comical about you（ひょうきんな面）

**Sounds like we have the same interests.**
→ Sounds like = It seems like

**It's not safe to carry so much cash around.**
→ It's not safe =It's dangerous

**I don't carry cash with me.**

**This will not keep for more than two days unless you put it in the fridge.** → keep（「食物が腐らないで」もつ）

**How much longer will our gas last?** → last= hold out

**It looks as if this good weather will hold for a few days.** → hold（「天気などが」もつ、持続する）

**I don't mean to brag, but I am the prop of this company.** → I don't mean to brag = If I say so myself（自分で言うのもなんだが）→ brag=boast　→ prop　（支柱、支え、頼り、つっかい棒）

## 戻す

この本を書棚に戻しなさい。

このおもちゃを元の場所に戻しなさい。

それ、元の状態にもどしてくれる？

座席を元の位置に戻してください。

この本を金曜日までに戻してください。

その肉の冷凍を戻してくれる？

この干しシイタケを水に戻しましょう。

時計を 5 分戻さないといけないな。

できるだけ早く体力を取り戻したいよ。

元カレとよりを戻したい。

元の体重に戻したいな。

それ、元の設定に戻してくれる？

削除された電子ファイルを元に戻すにはどうすればいい？

## 求める

ボーイフレンドに求めるものはなに？

TRACK 382

**Put this book back on the bookshelf.** / Return this book to the shelf.

**Put this toy back where it was.** / Return this toy to where it came from.

**Can you put it back the way it was?**
⇒ the way it was → in its place（元の位置に）

**Please put your seat in the upright position.** → put your seat in the = return your seat to the → upright position（直立位置）

**Please return this book by Friday.**

**Can you defrost that meat?** → defrost（「冷凍食品を」解凍する）

**Let's soak this dried *shiitake* mushroom in water.**
→ soak（「水などの液体に」浸す）

**I have to put back the clock by five minutes.** / I've got to turn back this clock five minutes.
→ put back=turn back; set back

**I want to recuperate my strength as soon as possible.**
→ recuperate（「元気、活力などを」取り戻す、「病気、疲労などから」回復する）
⇒ recuperate my strength → recover my health（健康を取り戻す）

**I want to get back with my ex-boyfriend.**
→ get back（「振られた後などで」もう一度好きになってもらう、よりを戻す）

**I want to return to my previous weight.** ⇒ want to return → returned（戻った） ⇒ weight → shape（体形）

**Can you return it back to the original settings?**

**What should I do to restore the deleted electronic files?**

TRACK 383

**What do you expect from your boyfriend?**
→ expect from~（～に期待する、～に要求する）

結婚相手に求めるものはなに？

誰もが幸せを求めていると思うよ。

私たちが求めているものは同じね。

私が求めているものとあなたが求めているものは違うよ。

この三角形の面積を求めよ。

## 戻る

すぐ戻るよ。

急いで戻ろう。

もと来た道を戻ろう。

自分の席に戻ってください。

彼女、いつ戻ります？

彼女はすぐ戻るはずです。

いつ戻ってくるか定かではありません。

彼女が戻ってくるまで待ちます。

私が戻るまで待ってもらえます？

私、もうここには戻らない。

元の関係に戻りたいよ。

**What qualities do you look for in a marriage partner?**
/ What are some qualities you look for in a marriage partner? → quality（「人などの」特質、特性）この意の場合は可算名詞 → do you look for = are you after

**I believe everybody seeks happiness.**
→ seek = demand; ask for; search; look for ⇒ happiness → stability（安定）

**What we are looking for is the same.**

**What I'm looking for is different from what you are looking for.**

**Find the area of this triangle.**
⇒ area … triangle → volume of this cube（この立方体の体積）

TRACK 384

**I'll be back soon.**

**Let's go back quickly.** / Let's hurry back.

**Let's go back the way we came.** / Let's retrace our steps.

**Please go back to your seat.**

**When will she be back?**

**She should be back soon.** → should be ~（～のはずである）

**I'm not sure when she'll be back.**

**I'll wait till she comes back.**

**Could you wait till I return?**

**I won't be back here anymore.** / I'm never coming back here.

**I want to go back to how it was before.**
→ how it was before= what we used to be; the way we used to be ⇒ I want to go back to → We can't go back to（私たちは戻れない）⇒ how it was before → the good old days（古き良き時代）、my childhood（子供の頃）、the days when we were good friends（仲の良かったころに）

過去には戻れないよ。

はっきり言って、何事も元に戻ることはないわよ。

本題に戻ろう。

## 燃やす

火を燃やそう。

これを燃やそう。

元カレの写真は全部燃やしたわ。

わたし、運動して脂肪を燃やさなきゃあ。

今、新しい仕事に情熱を燃やしてるんだよ。

## もらう

彼にプレゼントもらったよ。

これ、タダでもらったんだ。

初めて給料をもらったよ。

毎月いくら小遣いをもらうの？

毎月一万円もらうよ。

何か飲み物をもらえますか？

このシャツをもらいます。

この勝負はもらったよ。

**We can't go back to the past.**
→ We can't go back = There is no returning

**To put it clearly, nothing could be the same again.**
→ To put it clearly= obviously

**Let's get back to the subject.** / Let's return to what we were talking about.

TRACK 385

**Let's make a fire.** / Let's kindle a fire.

**Let's burn this.** ⇒ this → wood（マキ）、a candle（ロウソク）、waste paper（紙屑）、fallen leaves（落ち葉）

**I burned all the photos of my ex-boyfriend.**

**I've got to burn away some flab by exercising.**
→ flab（「体についた」脂肪、ぜい肉） ⇒ burn away some flab → burn my belly fat（お腹の脂肪を燃やす）

**I'm burning with passion for my new job.**
→ burning with =fired up with → passion=enthusiasm

TRACK 386

**I received a present from him.** / He gave me a present.

**I got this for free.** → for free = for nothing ; without charge

**I received a salary for the first time.** / I got my paycheck for the first time.

**How much money do you get as a monthly allowance?**

**I get ten thousand yen every month.** → get=receive

**Can I have something to drink?** ⇒ something to drink → a cup of coffee（コーヒー一杯）、two cups of coffee（コーヒー２杯）

**I'll take this shirt.** ⇒ this shirt → the bigger one（大きい方）

**This game is mine.**

どこかで風邪をもらっちゃった。

### もらす

私たちの計画を彼らに漏らさないように。

この秘密は洩らさないでね。

このことは洩らさないで。

SNS を無頓着に使うと個人情報が洩れるかもよ。

もれそ～。

君、ついに本音を漏らしたね。

### 漏れる

その話が漏れると、私は困ったことになる。

管からガスが漏れてないか？

わたしの名前が名簿から漏れてるわ。

### 焼く

この魚を焼こう。

卵を焼こうよ。

それ弱火で焼いて。

僕がギョーザをフライパンで焼こう。

**I picked up a cold somewhere.** → picked up=contracted

TRACK 387

**Don't leak our plan to them.** → leak = divulge

**Don't let this secret out.** / Don't give this secret away. / Don't let the cat out of the bag. → let out = give away; leak out; reveal

**Keep this to yourself.**
→ keep ~to oneself（～を口外しない、～を自分の胸にとどめておく）

**If you use social networking sites carelessly, your private information might be exposed.**

**I'm going to pee in my pants.** / I have to pee really bad.
→ pee（おしっこをもらす）=urinate; pass water

**Finally, you revealed your true intentions.**

TRACK 388

**I'll be in trouble if the story gets out.**

**Isn't gas leaking from the pipe?**
→ leaking= escaping ⇒ gas → water（水）

**My name is missing from the list.**
→ is missing from = is left off → be left off ～（から除外されている）

TRACK 389

**Let's grill this fish.**
⇒ this fish → 文尾に thoroughly（徹底的に、しっかりと）

**Let's fry eggs.** → fry（「油で」焼く）→「揚げる」は deep-fry、French-fry。

**Fry it over low heat.** ⇒ low heat → high heat（強火）

**I'll pan-fry the dumplings.** → pan-fry（フライパンで炒める）

オーブンでパンを焼くのはどう？

トースターでパンを焼くよ。

ステーキはよく焼いてね。

あなた、私にやきもちを焼いてるの？

やきもちを焼くなんてあなたらしくないわよ。

## 訳す

次の英語を日本語に訳しなさい。

これを日本語から英語に訳してほしいの。

この５ページ分を日本語に訳すのにどれくらいかかった？

## 約束する

約束する？

約束するよ。

禁煙すると約束して。

二度とあんなことしないって約束する。

彼はいつも口約束する。

## 役に立つ

何かお役に立てることはありますか？

**How about baking bread in the oven?** → bake（「オーブンで」焼く、調理する） ⇒ bread in an oven → an apple pie（アップルパイ）、cookies（クッキー）

**I'll toast bread in the toaster.** → toast（「パンなどを」焼く）

**I like my steak well done.**
⇒ well done → medium（ミディアム）、rare（レア）

**Are you jealous of me?**
→ be jealous of~（～を嫉妬している、～に焼きもちを焼いている）

**It's not like you to be jealous.**

TRACK 390

**Translate the following English into Japanese.**
→ translate は書き言葉を翻訳することで、interpret は話し言葉を訳すこと。

**I want you to translate this from Japanese into English.**

**How long did it take for you to translate these five pages into Japanese?** ⇒「翻訳する」の項目参照

TRACK 391

**Do you promise?**

**I promise.** / You have my word.
⇒ promise → can't promise（約束できない）

**Promise me to stop smoking.** ⇒ to stop smoking → to abstain from drinking（禁酒する）、to come back early（早く帰る）、to marry me（私と結婚する）、to love me forever（永遠に私を愛する）、that you will behave（良い子にすると） → behave（行儀よくする、大人しくしている）

**I promise I'll never do that again.**
⇒ I'll never do that again → I won't tell anyone（誰にも言わない）

**He always makes a verbal promise.**

TRACK 392

**Can I be of any help to you?**

少しでもあなたのお役に立てれば嬉しいのですが。

このフレーズはあなたにはとても役に立つと思うよ。

この本はこれらの本の中で英語学習に一番役に立つよ。

この資料が君の役に立ってくれるといいけどなぁ。

この情報は私には大いに役に立ちますよ。

お役に立ててうれしいです。

お役に立てなくてすみません。

君は色んな点で役に立つねぇ。

## 焼ける

日焼けしちゃった。

わたし、すぐ日に焼けるの。

昨日ビーチでひどい日焼けしちゃった。

日に焼けて皮がむけたよ。

パンがちょうどよく焼けてる。

魚が焼けたよ。

もうすぐ肉が焼けるよ。

鳥がいい具合に焼けてきたね。

**I hope I can be of any help to you.**

**I think this phrase will be very helpful to you.**

**This book is the most helpful out of all these books for studying English.**

**I hope you'll find this material useful.**
⇒ material = document

**This information is very useful to me.**
⇒ This information → This knowledge（この知識）、This machine（この機械）、Your advice（あなたのアドバイス）⇒ useful to me → helpful for me（私の助けになる、役に立つ）

**I'm glad I could help you.** / I'm happy that I could be of help.
→ help you = help you out

**I'm sorry I couldn't be of help.**
→ be of help = be helpful; help out

**You are helpful in many ways.**

TRACK 393

**I got sunburned.** / I got tanned. / I got a suntan. → sunburned はひりひりする日焼けのことで、suntan は健康に焼けたこと。⇒文尾に and it really hurts（で、本当に痛い）

**I tan easily.** / I easily tan.

**I got a nasty sunburn at the beach yesterday.**
→ nasty（「怪我、症状などについて」ひどい、たちの悪い）

**My skin peeled when I got sunburnt.** → sunburnt（英）

**The toast is done just right.**

**The fish is done.** → done= grilled; broiled

**The meat will be roasted soon.** → roasted → roast はあぶり焼きすることで、直火で焼く、あるいはオーブンで強く熱すること。

**The chicken is roasting nicely.**

友人の家が一昨日の火事で焼けちゃった。

このカーテンの色が焼けちゃった。

この生地は日焼けするかもね。

## 休む

（号令）休め。

ゆっくり休んで。

彼はもう休みました。

彼は今、休んでいます。

昨夜はよく休みましたか？

明日お休みをいただきたいのですが。

今日は具合が悪いので、休みます。

具合が悪かったら休むって連絡しなきゃ。

先ほど彼から病気で休むとの連絡があったよ。

昨日は仕事を休んだよ。

わたし、絶対仕事は休まないから。

今日は学校を休むよ。

彼はよく学校を休むね。

数学の時間を休んじゃった。

**My friend's house was burnt down in the fire.**
→ burnt down=burned down ⇒ in the fire → in the great fire（大火で）

**This curtain has discolored.**
→ has discolored=became discolored（変色した）

**This material might get faded from the sun.**

TRACK 394

**At ease.** / Rest.

**Have a good rest.**
⇒ a good rest → a good night's rest（一晩ゆっくり休む）

**He has already gone to bed.** → gone to bed=retired

**He is in bed now.**

**Did you sleep well last night?** / Did you have a good night's rest?

**I'd like to take the day off tomorrow.**
⇒ I'd like to ~ → Would it be possible to ~?（～は可能でしょうか）

**I'm not feeling well today, and so I'm going to take the day off.**

**If you are not feeling well, you should call in sick.**
→ call in sick （病欠の電話をする、病気で欠席すると電話で伝える）

**He called in sick a little while ago.**

**I took the day off work yesterday.** → took the day off = was absent from ⇒ work → school（学校）

**I never miss work.** / I never take time off from work.

**I'll take the day off school today.** / I will be absent from school today.

**He is often absent from school, isn't he?**

**I did not attend the math class.**
⇒ did not attend → cut（さぼった）

この喫茶店で休もうか？

ちょっと勉強を休もうよ。

## 破る

わたし、約束は絶対破らないから。

彼女は決して約束を破るような人じゃない。

彼は約束を破ることを何とも思わないやつだよ。

ルールを破らないで。

このルールを破ると何か罰則があるわけ？

法を破れば、罰せられるよ。

あの国は平気で国際協定を破るからさ。

彼はこの世界記録を破るかもしれない。

この本からページを破り取ったのは一体どこのどいつだ？

その写真を破らないで！

我がチームは大阪ジャイアンツを 3 対 1 で破ったよ。

## やめる

止めろ。

わたし、いつも 5 時きっかりに仕事を止めるんだ。

仕事を辞めたよ。

**What do you say to taking a rest at this coffee shop?**
→ What do you say to ~（「提案」～はどうですか）⇒ coffee shop → restaurant（レストラン）

**Let's take a break from our study.**
→ take a break（休憩する、一休みする） ⇒ study → work（仕事）

TRACK 395

**I never break my promise.** → promise= word

**She is definitely not someone who would break her promise.** → definitely（絶対に）

**He thinks nothing of breaking his promise.**
→ think nothing of~（～を何とも思わない）

**Don't break the rule.** ⇒ rule → law（法律）

**Is there any punishment for breaking these rules?**

**If you break the law, you'll be punished.**

**That country breaks the international agreement without hesitation.**
→ without hesitation（躊躇なく、何のためらいもなく）

**He might break this world record.**

**Who the hell tore some of the pages out of this book?**

**Don't tear that picture!**

**Our team defeated the Osaka Giants three to one.**

TRACK 396

**Stop it.**
⇒ it → talking（話し）、singing（歌うこと）、playing the piano（ピアノの演奏）

**I always finish work at five o'clock sharp.**
→ sharp（きっかり、ちょうど）

**I quit my job.**
→ quit=threw up ⇒ my job → drinking（飲酒）、smoking（喫煙）

先月、四菱銀行の仕事を辞めたよ。

あと 3 か月で、定年で仕事を辞めるんだ。

会社を辞めて今は家事手伝いをしてるの。

学校を辞めたよ。

ダイエットをやめたんだ。

その爪を噛む悪い習慣はやめなさい。

今月の終わりで英語のレッスンを辞めるんだ。

彼は仕事を辞めさせられたんだ。

## ゆ

### 優勝する

今年は優勝するよ。

この美人コンテストで優勝したいな。

私の目標は県大会で優勝することなの。

その大会で誰が優勝すると思う？

今年は阪神ジャイアンツが優勝すると思うけど。

I quit working for *Yotsubishi* bank last month.

I'll retire at the official retirement age in three months. / I'll retire from my job in three months.
→ official retirement age（法定退職年齢）

I left the company and now I help with the housework. ⇒ left the company = walked away from the company

I left school. / I gave up school.
→ leave（現在形）=give up; quit; drop out of ⇒ school → college

I went off my diet. → go off one's diet（ダイエットをやめる）

Drop that bad habit of biting your nails.
→ drop the habit of ~（〜の習慣をやめる、〜の癖を治す）

I'll be quitting my English lesson at the end of this month. → I'll be quitting my English lesson = I'll stop going to the English lesson

He was forced to quit his job. / He was fired from his job.

TRACK 397

We will win the championship. / We will become the champion. ⇒ the championship = the victory; the pennant; the cup

I want to win this beauty contest.
⇒ this beauty contest → in this competition（この競技で）

My goal is to be a champion in our prefectural tournament. / My goal is to become the prefectural champion.

Who do you think will win that tournament?

I think that the Hanshin Giants will be the champion this year.

## 譲る

込み合った電車の中では私たち、若い人はお年寄りに席をゆずるべきじゃない？

僕はいつもお年寄りには席を譲るね。

ここは歩行者に道を譲らないといけないんだよ。

## ゆでる

これらの卵をゆでよう。

これら何分ゆでる？

それら熱湯で 1 分ゆでて。

沸騰したら弱火にして 3 分ゆでてね。

## 夢見る

どんな夢を見る？

昨日の夜、変な夢を見ちゃった。

彼女のことをよく夢で見るんだ。

正月に富士山の夢を見たら、幸運が訪れるっていうよ。

## ゆるめる

このベルトをゆるめなきゃ。

TRACK 398

**Shouldn't we young people like us offer our seats to the old in a crowded train?**

I always offer my seat to the elderly. ⇒ the elderly → the disabled（障害者）

**You must give way to pedestrians here.**
→ pedestrian（歩行者） ⇒ pedestrians → buses（バス）

TRACK 399

**Let's boil these eggs.**

How many minutes do we boil these for?

**Boil them for one minute.**
⇒ for one minute → until they are soft（柔らかくなるまで）

When it comes to a boil, turn the heat to low and cook for three minutes.

TRACK 400

What kind of dreams do you have?

**I had a weird dream last night.** ⇒ weird dream → nightmare（悪夢）、dream of being rich（金持ちになった夢）、dream of being a hero（英雄になった夢）、dream that I passed the exam（試験に受かった夢）

I often dream of her. ⇒ her → flying in the sky（空を飛んでいる）、my mother who died last year（去年亡くなった母）

**It is said that if you dream of Mt. Fuji on New Year's Day, it will bring you good luck.**

TRACK 401

**I've got to loosen this belt.** ⇒ this belt → my tie（ネクタイ）、my collar（襟元）、this knot（この結び目）、the purse strings（財布のひも）、this screw（ネジ）

運転中は少しでも気をゆるめるんじゃないよ。

試験が近づいているので、いま気をゆるめるわけにはいかないよ。

連休が控えているために気が緩んできちゃった。

## 揺れる

地面が揺れてるよ。

わが家が左右に揺れたよ。

地震で家が揺れたね。

建物が揺れるのを感じたね。

# よ

## 酔う

酔っちゃった。

もう酔っちゃったの？

僕は酒に気持ちよく酔うんだな。

僕は酔っても乱れないよ。

僕はどんなに飲んでも酔うことがないんだ。

君は酔うと怒り出す傾向があるよね。

**Don't let your mind wander for even a brief moment when you are driving.** / You should stay focused the whole time you are driving.

**The examination is approaching, and I can't let my guard down now.** → let one's guard down（気をゆるめる、油断する）

**I'm starting to slack because I've got consecutive holidays coming up.** → I'm starting to slack = I'm losing focus

TRACK 402

**The ground is shaking.**
→ shake は小刻みに揺れるとき。大きな揺れの場合は move。

**My house swayed from side to side.**
→ sway は大きくゆらゆらと揺れる場合。→ from side to side（左右に）⇒ swayed from side to side → shook（小刻みに揺れた）

**The earthquake shook my house.**

**I felt the building shake.**

TRACK 403

**I got drunk. / I became intoxicated.** ⇒ got drunk → got dead drunk（泥酔した）、got drunk on *sake*（酒に酔った）、get drunk easily（すぐ酔う）

**Are you drunk yet?** → yet（「疑問文で」もう）

**I get moderately drunk.** → moderately（適度に、程よく）

**I can take my drink.** / I can carry my liquor.
→ take= hold → can take one's drink（酒に強い）

**I can hold my liquor no matter how much I drink.**

**You have the inclination to lose your temper when drunk, haven't you?** → have the inclination to~（～する傾向がある）
→ lose one's temper = get very angry; blow up; fly into a rage; rage ⇒ lose your temper → start crying（泣き上戸になる）、start laughing（笑い上戸になる）

あの男は酔うと手がつけられないんだよ。

車に酔ったわ。

車で長旅するといつも酔っちゃうのよ。

彼は自分に酔ってるのさ。

## 予習する

わたし、明日の授業の予習をしなきゃ。

わたし、予習しないで学校へ行くことなんてないもん。

第 5 章の途中までしか予習してないや。

忙しくて次の授業の予習ができなかったんだ。

## 呼ぶ

（諺）類は友を呼ぶ。

助けを呼ぼう。

タクシーを呼んで。

友だちを呼んでもいい？

夕食に彼女を呼んでいるんだ。

あなたをファーストネームで呼んでもいいですか？

僕を負け犬と呼ぶのはやめろ。

**That man is out of control when drunk.**
→ is out of control → chops logic（理屈をこねる）

**I got carsick.** → got = felt ⇒ got carsick → got seasick（船に酔った）、got airsick（飛行機に酔った）

**I always get carsick during road trips.**

**He's so self-satisfied.** / He's so narcissistic.
⇒ so self-satisfied → intoxicated with his success（自分の成功に酔って）、intoxicated with delight（歓喜に酔って）

TRACK 404

**I've got to prepare for tomorrow's lessons.**
→ lessons = classes ⇒ I've got to prepare → I'm preparing（予習している）、I prepared（予習した）、Did you prepare ...?（予習はした…？）

**I don't go to school without doing my preparation.**

**I've only studied half of Chapter five.**

**I was too busy to prepare for the next class.**
⇒ the next class → that chapter（その章）

TRACK 405

**Birds of a feather flock together.** / Like attracts like. / Like will to like.

**Let's call for help.** ⇒ for help → an ambulance（救急車）、the police（警察）

**Call a taxi for me.** / Call me a taxi.

**Can I have my friends come over?** / Can I have my friends over?

**I'm having her over for dinner.**
→ having= inviting

**Can I call you by your first name?**
⇒ first name → nickname（あだ名）

**Stop calling me a loser.** → a loser = an underdog ⇒ a loser → a problem child（問題児）、stupid（間抜け）、dumb（うすのろ）

## 読む

本を読むのは好き？

何よりも本を読むのが好きなの。

自分の知識を増やすために読んでるんだ。

1 か月に 4 冊くらい読んでるよ。

どんな本を読むの？

主に探偵小説を読んでるね。

江戸川乱歩の小説をちょうど読み終えたところだよ。

この本を一日で読み終えたよ。

高校時代にヘミングウエイの小説をむさぼり読んだね。

彼の小説を買ったけど、読まなかったわ。

このページを読んでください。

1 行飛ばして読みましたよ。

これは何て読むの？

彼女の字は読めないよ。

行間の意味を読みなさい。

この文章はいろいろに読めるね。

TRACK 406

**Do you like reading books?**
⇒ reading books → to read this book（この本を読むのは）

**I like reading books better than anything else.**
⇒ books → *manga*（漫画）、the paper（新聞）

**I read in order to increase my knowledge.**

**I read about 4 books per month.** → per=a

**What kind of books do you read?**

**I read mainly detective novels.**
⇒ detective novels → romantic novels（恋愛小説）、coming-of-age novels（青春小説）、science fiction novels（SF 小説）、fantasy novels（ファンタジー小説）、horror novels（ホラー小説）、mystery novels（ミステリー小説）

**I've just finished reading *Ranpo Edogawa*'s novel.**

**I finished reading this book in one day.**

**I read Hemingway's novels greedily when I was in high school.** → greedily（貪欲に）
→ when I was in high school = when I was a high school student

**I bought his novel, but never read it.**

**Please read this page.**
⇒ read this page → read this page silently（このページを黙読する）、read this page aloud（このページを音読する）、read chapters 5 through 6（5 章から 6 章まで読む）

**You skipped one line.**
→ skipped = skipped over ⇒ skipped one line → skipped over a few lines（数行飛ばした）、skipped over three chapters（3 章飛ばした）

**How do you read this?**

**Her writing is impossible to read.**

**Read between the lines.**

**This sentence can be read in various ways.**
→ can be read = can be interpreted

英語を読むのは疲れるよ。

英語を読むことはできるけど、うまく話せないんだ。

## 予約する

予約したいのですが。

予約できますか？

席を予約したいのですが。

今夜7時に二人の予約をしたいのですが。

このレストランで食事をしようと思ったら、3か月前から予約しないと無理なんだ。

予約なさってますか？

7時の予約をしています。

## 喜ぶ

彼女、喜ぶと思うな。

彼女、君のアドバイスを喜んでたよ。

彼女、僕たちの突然の訪問を喜ぶかなぁ。

君は彼女が喜ぶようなことばかり言うよね。

それって、喜ぶべきこと？

誰もこの人事異動を喜んでいないよ。

Reading English makes me tired.

I can read English, but I can't speak it well.

TRACK 407

（ホテル、レストランなど）I'd like to make a reservation. /（病院、美容院など）I'd like to make an appointment.

Can I make a reservation?

I'd like to reserve a table.

I'd like to make a reservation for two people for tonight at 7 pm.

You have to make a reservation three months ahead of time if you want to eat in this restaurant.

Do you have a reservation?

I have a reservation for 7 o'clock. ⇒ for 7 o'clock → at this hotel（このホテルで）、for tonight（今夜の）、for three nights from today（今日から三晩）

TRACK 408

I think she'll be happy.
⇒ happy ＝ glad →文尾に to hear that（それを聞いたら）

She was happy with your advice.

I wonder if she'll be happy with our sudden visit.
⇒ our sudden visit → this present（このプレゼント）

You always say something that will make her happy.

Is that something to be happy about?

No one is pleased with the personnel changes.
→ personnel changes（人事異動）

## 弱る

最近、足が弱ってきたよ。

彼はだんだん弱ってきてるみたいだ。

雨が弱まったね。

風が弱まったね。

# ら

## 羅列する

自分の長所を羅列してください。

この文は文字が羅列してあるだけで、何の意味もないよ。

これは単なる数字の羅列だと思うよ。

## 乱用する

上司に権力を乱用するのはやめてもらいたいよ。

あの俳優は薬物を乱用してるって噂だよ。

# り

## 理解する

私の言ってることが理解できますか？

TRACK 409

**Recently my legs have started to weaken.** / I've begun to lose strength in my legs recently. → weaken （弱まる）

**He is getting weaker, it seems.**

**The rain has died down.** / The rain has let up.

**The wind has dropped.** / The wind has abated.
⇒ The wind → The storm（嵐）

TRACK 410

**Please list your virtues.** / Please cite your good points.
→ virtues（形式ばった語）=good points; strong points; merits → list = cite; arrange ⇒ virtues → bad points；weak points; demerits（短所）

**This sentence is just a collection of letters and has no meaning.** → letter（文字）

**I guess this is merely a meaningless row of numbers.**
→ merely=only

TRACK 411

**I want our boss to stop abusing his power.**
→ abuse（乱用する）⇒ power → privileges（特権）

**It is whispered that the actor is abusing drugs.**

TRACK 412

**Do you understand what I'm talking about?**
→ understand = get ⇒ what I'm talking about → the meaning of this sentence（この文章の意味）

君の言おうとしてることは理解できる。

君の説明のおかげでこの謎が理解できたよ。

その論文を理解するにはこの参考文献が役に立つよ。

彼はすごく頭がいい。何でもすぐに理解するよ。

君の発言の主旨が理解できない。

君のジョークが理解できなかったよ。

## 離婚する

夫と離婚するの。

私たち離婚することになったの。

彼らが離婚するなんて考えられないね。

彼らが離婚しないことを願うね。

彼らは子供が大きくなってから離婚するそうだ。

わたし、夫から離婚されちゃった。

二人は協議離婚したよ。

## リサイクルする

それ、捨てちゃだめ。リサイクルしなきゃ。

もっと資源ごみをリサイクルする必要があるね。

**I understand what you mean.** / I understand the point you are trying to make. ⇒ what you mean → your situation（君の事情）、everything（全て）

**Thanks to your explanation, I could understand this enigma.** → enigma（謎、謎めいた言葉）

**This reference book is helpful to understand that essay.**

**He's very smart. He understands everything right on the spot.** → right on the spot = immediately; straight away; instantly

**I don't understand the point of your remark.** ⇒ the point of your remark → what you are trying to say（君が言おうとしていること）

**I didn't get your joke.** ⇒ joke → point（主旨）

TRACK 413

**I'll divorce my husband.** / I'll get a divorce from my husband.
⇒ husband → wife（妻）

**We decided to get a divorce.**
→ decided to get a divorce=ended up getting a divorce

**I can't even think of them getting divorced.**

**I hope they do not get divorced.**

**I hear they'll divorce after their children are grown up.**

**I was divorced by my husband.**

**They got a divorce through mutual agreement.**
→ got a divorce= got divorced; became divorced; were divorced

TRACK 414

**Don't throw that away. You've got to recycle it.**

**We need to recycle recyclable waste more.**
⇒ recyclable waste（資源ごみ）→ plastic（プラスチック）

ほら、リサイクルするのは当たり前のことになっているから。

このトイレットペーパーがリサイクルされた新聞からできてるって知ってる？

## 利用する

彼は人を利用するやつだ。

上司は僕を利用して手柄を独り占めしたのさ。

僕を利用するんじゃない。

このクーポンを利用して携帯電話を買うつもりだよ。

この図書館は４月１日から利用できるそうだ。

私たちはもっと太陽エネルギーを利用すべきだね。

## 料理する

料理できる？

簡単な料理ならするよ。

家でよく料理するわ。

料理することが好きなの。

君が料理しているところを見てみたいな。

ときどきストレス発散のために料理するわね。

今、一人暮らしだから、料理はするよ。

毎日三食料理するわ。

**Recycling has become an obvious thing to do, you know.** → an obvious thing to do = the norm

**Do you know that this toilet paper is made from recycled newspapers?**

TRACK 415

**He takes advantage of people.** / He is a user.
→ take advantage of = use

**My boss took advantage of me and took all the credit.**
→ take all the credit（手柄を独り占めする）

**Don't take advantage of me.**

**I'm going to use this coupon to buy a cellphone.**

**It seems that this library will be available from April 1st.** / It appears that you may use this library starting April 1st. / Apparently you can start using this library after the first of April.

**We should utilize solar energy more.** → utilize = use

TRACK 416

**Can you cook?** / Do you know how to cook?
→ cook（熱を用いて料理すること）

**I do simple cooking.**

**I often cook at home.**
→文尾に by using leftovers（残り物を使って）→ leftovers（「料理の」残り物）

**I like to cook.** / My hobby is to cook.

**I want to see you cooking.**

**I sometimes cook to release my stress.**

**I'm on my own now, so I cook for myself.**
→ be one one's own （自力で、単独で、自活して）

**I cook three meals daily.** → daily = every day

出前を取らないで、料理することに決めたんだ。

料理するのを手伝ってくれる？

忙しすぎて料理する時間がないんだ。

料理をする気がしないの。

一緒に料理しよう。

この牛肉は母のレシピ通りに料理するつもりよ。

## 旅行する

よく旅行をする？

一人で旅行するのが好きなの。

よく車で旅行をするんだ。

どこへ旅行するの？

毎年、国内旅行をたくさんしてるよ。

よく日帰り旅行に行くよ。

至る所を旅行するつもりよ。

どこかへ旅行したいな。

旅行する暇がないんだ。

**I decided to cook rather than order in.**
→ order in = order out（出前を取る） ⇒ order in → order in *sushi*（寿司の出前を取る）=order out for *sushi*

**Will you help me cook?**

**I'm too busy to cook.**

**I don't feel like cooking.**

**Let's cook together.** ⇒ together → this with wine（ワインを使ってこれを）

**I'm going to prepare this beef according to my mother's recipe.** → prepare（「食事などを」調理する、作る）

**TRACK 417**

**Do you often travel?** → travel= go on a trip; take a trip

**I like traveling by myself. / I enjoy going on trips alone. / I like taking trips by myself.**

**I often travel by car. / I often go on a road trip.**
⇒ by car → by bicycle（自転車で）、on foot（徒歩で）、by rail（鉄道で）

**Where are you going for your trip?** ⇒ for your trip → on vacation（休暇は）

**Every year I do a lot of domestic travel.** → domestic travel = national travelling ⇒ do a lot of domestic travel → take trips overseas（海外旅行をする）、travel locally（近場を旅行する）、travel light（軽装で旅行する）、travel business class（ビジネスクラスで旅行をする）、travel economy class（エコノミークラスで旅行をする）

**I often go on a day trip.**
⇒ go on a day trip → travel inside Japan（日本国内を旅行する）

**I'm going to travel far and wide.**
⇒ travel far and wide → travel to all parts of the globe（世界中を旅する）、travel around the world（世界一周旅行をする）、travel abroad=travel to a foreign country（海外旅行をする）、travel to New York（ニューヨークへ旅行する）

**I want to take a trip somewhere.**

**I have no time to travel.** → to travel= for traveling → traveling はアメリカ英語 ⇒ no time → no opportunity（機会がない）、no money（お金がない）

## る

### 留守番する

いい子でお留守番してね。

今日は私が留守番なの。

今日は私が留守番です。

## れ

### 冷凍する

この残り物を冷凍してくれる？

これ、家に帰ったらできるだけ早く冷凍してね。

それ冷凍保存して、1か月以内に食べてね。

わたし、ときどきパンを冷凍保存するよ。

これって冷凍保存できる？

### 恋愛する

恋愛したい。

いつか魅力的な人と恋愛したいな。

わたし、今、ちょ～イケてる男性と恋愛してるの。

わたしは遠距離恋愛をしてるんだ。

TRACK 418

**Be a good boy and stay at home.** / Be a good boy and watch the house for me. ⇒ a good boy → a good girl（女の子の場合）

**I stay at home today.** / I watch the house today.

**I'm house-sitting today.** / I am the house-sitter.
→ house-sitter（よその家の留守番する人）

TRACK 419

**Will you freeze this leftover food?**

**Freeze this as soon as possible after you get home.**

**Keep it in a freezer and eat it within a month.**

**I sometimes keep bread in a freezer.**

**Can this be preserved by freezing?**

TRACK 420

**I want to experience love.** / I want to fall in love.
→ experience love = experience romance → fall in love（恋に落ちる、恋をする）

**Someday I want to fall in love with an attractive person.**

**I'm currently in a relationship with an amazing guy.**
→ be in a relationship with ～（～と交際している、～とつき合っている）

**I'm in a long distance relationship.** / I'm doing the long distance thing.

彼女は数人の男性と恋愛してるって噂だよ。

### 練習する

毎日サッカーの練習をしてるの？

明日はダンスの練習なの。

### 連絡する

連絡するね。

連絡取りあおう。

家に帰ったらすぐに連絡する。

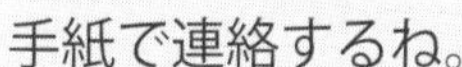

手紙で連絡するね。

彼から連絡はあった？

彼からついさっき連絡があったよ。

どれくらいの頻度で彼と連絡取ってる？

時々お互い連絡取ってるよ。

最近、彼とは連絡取ってないな。

まだ彼から連絡がないんだ。

**Rumor has it that she is romantically involved with a few men.**
→ Rumor has it that=It's rumored that; People say that → be romantically involved with~（～と恋愛関係にある、～と深い仲である、～と性的な関係を持つ）

TRACK 421

**Are you practicing soccer every day?**
⇒ every day → after school（放課後）

**I've got to practice dancing.** ⇒ practice dancing → practice singing（歌の練習をする）、practice playing the piano（ピアノの練習をする）、practice speaking English（英会話の練習をする）、practice driving（運転の練習をする）

TRACK 422

**I'll be in touch.** / I'll contact you. / I'll let you know. / I'll text you.（携帯メールで連絡する）/ I'll e-mail you.（パソコンで連絡する）

**Let's keep in touch.** / Let's stay in touch.

**I'll contact you as soon as I get home.**
⇒ contact you → contact you by phone（電話で連絡する） ⇒ as soon as I get home → when I get to the hotel（ホテルに着いたら）、when I get there（そこに着いたら）

**I'll get in touch with you by mail.**

**Was there any contact from him?** / Any contact from him? / Did he contact you? / Did you hear from him?

**I received contact from him just now.** / I got contacted by him just now.

**How often do you contact him?** → contact him=make contact with him; get in touch with him ⇒ him → each other（互いに）

**We contact each other sometimes.**
⇒ sometimes → quite often（頻繁に）

**Recently I haven't contacted him.** / I haven't been in touch with him.

**There is still no contact from him.** / I have heard nothing from him yet. → contact= word

# ろ

## 老化する

男性の方が女性より早く老化するっていうよ。

睡眠が短いと脳の老化が早くなるらしいよ。

気をつけて。紫外線は肌を老化させるんだよ。

このサプリメントは老化するのを防いでくれると言われているんだ。

## 浪費する

お金を浪費しないで。

僕に時間を浪費する余裕はないよ。

## 録音する

私たちの会話を録音してもいい？

この授業を録音してもいいですか？

## 録画する

この授業をビデオ録画してもいいですか？

わたし、毎週お気に入りの TV ドラマを録画してるんだ。

2 日前に放送された例の TV ドラマを録画した？

1 か月前に録画したドラマをまだ観てないんだ。

TRACK 423

**They say men age more rapidly than women.**

**I hear that lack of sleep causes brains to age faster.**

**Be careful. UV radiation will age your skin.**

**This supplement is said to prevent aging.**

TRACK 424

**Don't waste your money.** / Don't be wasteful with your money. / Don't spend your money prodigally. → prodigally = wastefully
⇒ waste your money → waste electricity（電気を浪費する）、waste time（時間を浪費する）

**I can't afford to waste time.**
→ can't afford to~（「経済的、時間的に」~する余裕がない）

TRACK 425

**Can I tape our conversation?** / Do you mind if I record our conversation? / （丁寧に）May I have your permission to tape our conversation? ⇒ Can I tape → Is it a problem if I tape（録音して問題がありますか、録音してもいいですか？）

**May I record this lesson?** / Is it okay if I record the lesson?

TRACK 426

**Can I video record this lesson?**
⇒ this lesson → this lesson to review later（この授業を後で復習するために）

**I record my favorite TV dramas every week.**

**Did you record that drama aired two days ago?**

**I still haven't watched the TV drama I recorded one month ago.**

## わ

### 沸かす

湯を沸かしてコーヒーを飲もうよ。

お風呂沸かしてくれる？

彼女の演説は聴衆を大いに沸かせたよね？

### わかる

わかる？

わたしの言ってること、わかる？

良いことと悪いことがわからないの？

答えがわかる人は手をあげて。

それはわかるよ。

君の言いたいことはわかる。

君が何を考えているかわかるよ。

他の人の気持ちがわかるようになったよ。

そんなことは子供でもわかるさ。

本当にわかってるのかなぁ。

何でわかるの？

時が経てばわかるよ。

TRACK 427

**Let's boil some water and drink coffee.**

**Can you heat the bath?** / Can you prepare the bath? / Will you run the bath?

**Her speech stirred the audience, didn't it?**
→ stir（「人を」興奮させる、感激させる）= move; excite

TRACK 428

**Do you see?** / Do you understand? / Get it?

**Am I making sense?** / Am I making myself clear?/ Do you understand what I'm trying to say?

**Don't you know right from wrong?**
→ Don't you know = Can't you tell

**Raise your hand if you know the answer.**

**I understand that.**
⇒ understand that → think I understand that（それわかるような気がする）

**I know what you mean.** / I can figure out what you are trying to say. → figure out（わかる、理解する）

**I know what you are thinking.**
⇒ what you are thinking → how you feel（君の気持ちは）

**I came to understand other people's feelings.**

**Even children can understand that.**

**I wonder if you really understand.**

**How do you know?** ⇒ How → How did you know?（何でわかった？）

**Time will tell.**

好きな花からあなたの性格がわかるんだ。

(諺) 人はつき合う人によってわかるもの。

日本語がわかる人と話したいのですが。

これがわかる人はいますか？

これがわかるなんてすごいね。

私にわかるわけないでしょう。

あなたが何を言ってるのかわからない。

あなたが何を言おうとしているのか全くわからないわ。

何が不満なのかわからないけど。

あなたの考え方はわからないな。

あなたが何であんな馬鹿なことをしたのかわからない。

それ、私にはとうていわからないよ。

わたし、どうしていいかわからない。

私の言ってることがわかってもらえなかった。

## 別れる

あなたと別れるわ。

別れよう。

**I can tell your personality from your favorite flowers.**
⇒ from your favorite flowers → by your everyday behavior（日々の行動から）

**A man is known by the company he keeps.**

**I want to speak with a person who understands Japanese.**

**Is there anyone who understands this?**

**It's amazing that you can understand this.**

**How should I know?**

**I don't understand what you are saying.**
⇒ what you are saying → what you are talking about（なたが何を話しているのか）

**I haven't the slightest idea what you are trying to say.**
→ slightest=faintest; foggiest　⇒ what you are trying to say → what you are trying to do（何をしようとしているのか）

**I don't see what you are complaining about.**
→ complain（不平・不満を言う、愚痴をこぼす）

**I cannot follow your line of thinking.**
→ follow（「議論、説明などに」ついていく、理解する）　→ line of thinking（考え方）
⇒ line of thinking → logic（「発言、行動などの」理屈、わけ）

**I don't understand why you did such a stupid thing.**
→ stupid = foolish; silly（ただし、silly はしばしば親しみを込めて、「おばかな」といった意味合いで使われる）

**It's beyond my comprehension.** / It's beyond me.

**I don't know what to do.** / I'm at my wits' end.
→ at one's wits' end（途方に暮れて）

**I could not make myself understood.**
⇒ understood → understood in English（英語では理解して「もらえなかった」）

TRACK 429

**I'm leaving you.**

**Let's break up.** / Let's call it a day on our relationship.
→ break up（「関係を」断ち切る、別れる）→ call it a day（終わりにする）

彼女と別れることにしたよ。

わたしたち、上手くいかなくなったので、別れたの。

遠距離が原因で彼と別れたわ。

別れたくないよ～。

友人とは駅で別れたよ。

## 沸く

お風呂が沸いたわよ。

湯が沸くのを待っているんだ。

お湯が沸いてるよ。

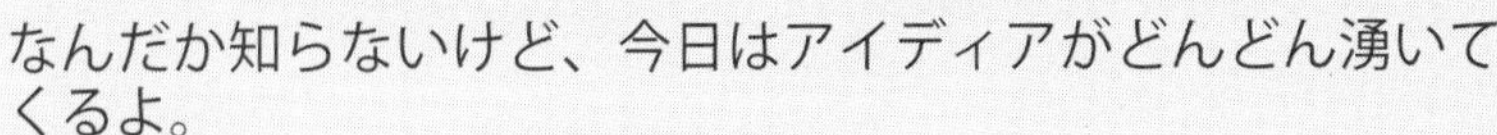

なんだか知らないけど、今日はアイディアがどんどん湧いてくるよ。

## 分ける

このケーキを均等に分けよう。

このケーキを人数分に分けてください。

彼らを４つのグループに分けましょう。

それらを色ごとに分けて。

この問題は初級、中級、上級の３段階に分かれています。

**I decided to break up with her.** / I made up my mind to end the relationship with her.

**We were not getting on anymore, so we split up.**
→ split up（別れる、離婚する）

**I broke up with him because of the distance.**

**I don't want to end our relationship.**

**I said goodbye to my friend at the station.** / We parted at the station.

TRACK 430

**The bath is ready.**

**I'm waiting for the water to boil.**

**The water is boiling.** ⇒ is boiling → is not boiling yet（まだ沸いていない）

**I don't know why, but I'm coming up with lots of ideas today.**
→ come up with ~（「アイディアなど」を思いつく、～を考えつく、～が浮かぶ）

TRACK 431

**Let's divide this cake equally.**
⇒ divide this cake equally → divide this cake in half（このケーキを半分に分ける）、divide this cake into three parts（このケーキを 3 つに分ける）、divide this cake into four parts（このケーキを 4 つに分ける）

**Please divide this cake by the number of people.**
/ Please cut this cake for the number of people.

**Let's divide them into four groups.** ⇒ divide them into four groups → divide them into two groups（2 つのグループに分ける）

**Sort them by color.** / Divide them by color.
→ sort（「種類、大きさなどで」分類する）

**The problems are divided into three levels: novice, intermediate, and advanced.** → novice=beginner

彼らは能力に基づいてクラス分けされているんだ。

髪を右から分けたら、もっとよくなると思うよ。

儲けを二人で分けようぜ。

### 忘れる

何か忘れてない？

もう少しで教科書を忘れるとこだった。

何か買うのを忘れた。

僕、一つ覚えると、一つ忘れちゃうんだよね。

どこかへ傘を置き忘れたよ。

午前中に約束があるのを忘れてた。

人の名前をよく忘れるんだ。

僕の得意技は物を忘れることかな。

君は物を忘れすぎるよ。

約束は忘れないで。

あなたのことは決して忘れないよ。

出かける際にドアにカギをかけるの、忘れないで。

**They are divided into classes based on their abilities.**
⇒ are divided into classes based on their abilities → are divided by skill level into classes (技能レベルでクラス分けされている)

**If you part your hair on the right, you'd look better.**
⇒ on the right → on the left (左で)、in the middle (真ん中で)

**Let's divide the profit between the two.**
⇒ between the two → among the three (三人で)、among us (俺たちの間で)

TRACK 432

**Aren't you forgetting something?** / You haven't forgotten anything, have you?

**I almost forgot my textbooks.**
⇒ textbooks → driver's license (運転免許証)、cell phone (携帯電話)

**I forgot to buy something.**
⇒ to buy something → what I had to do (しなければならないこと)、what I ate yesterday (昨日食べたもの)、my wallet (財布)、his name (彼の名前)、her e-mail address (彼女のメールアドレス)、your birthday (君の誕生日)、to do my homework (宿題するのを)、my umbrella (私の傘)

**When I memorize one, I forget another.** / When I learn something new, I tend to forget something I learnt before

**I've left my umbrella somewhere.**

**I forgot I had an appointment in the morning.**
⇒ I had an appointment → to hand in my report (レポートを提出するのを)
→ hand in~ (~を提出する、~を差し出す) = submit

**I'm apt to forget people's names.**
→ be apt to ~ (~しがちである、~しやすい)

**My specialty is forgetting things, maybe.**

**You are too forgetful.** ⇒ You are → I am (私は)

**Don't forget your promise.** ⇒ your promise → about me (私のこと)

**I'll never forget you.** ⇒ you → seeing you (あなたに会えたこと)

**Don't forget to lock the door when you go out.**
⇒ lock the door → turn off the water (水道の水を止める)、turn off the light (電気を消す)、turn off the TV (テレビを消す)、turn off the gas (ガスを止める)

彼のことは忘れて、前に進みなよ。

**渡す**

それを私に渡しなさい。

このメモを彼女に渡して。

この包みを彼女に渡してもらえる？

**渡る**

この通りを渡ろう。

向こう側へ渡ろうよ。

通りを渡るときは左右を確かめること。

信号のところを渡らなきゃだめだよ。

赤信号で通りを渡ってはだめだよ。

青信号になったら通りを渡りなさい。

横断歩道を渡りなさい。

問題冊子は全員に渡りましたか？

**笑う**

ただ笑うしかないね。

笑いが止まらないよ。

何を笑ってるんだ？

どうして笑ってるんだ？

Just forget him and move on.

TRACK 433

Give it to me.

Pass this note to her.

Could you give this parcel to her for me? / Please give this parcel to her for me. ⇒ parcel → package（包み）

TRACK 434

Let's cross the street here.
⇒ Let's → It's dangerous to（～するのは危険だ）

Let's get over to the other side.

Look both ways crossing the street.
→ crossing the street=when you cross the street

You must cross at the light.
⇒ at the light → at the pedestrian crossing（横断歩道を）

Don't cross the street at a red light. → at a red light = when the light is red ⇒ at a red light → against the red light（赤信号を無視して）

Cross the street on the green light.
→ on the green light = when the traffic light is green

Go across the crosswalk. / Cross at the pedestrian crossing.
→ crosswalk（横断歩道）

Has everyone received a question sheet?
⇒ a question sheet → an answer sheet（解答用紙）

TRACK 435

All I can do is just laugh.

I can't stop laughing.
⇒ I can't stop ~ ing → I can't help ~ ing（笑わずにはいられない）

What are you laughing at?

Why are you laughing?

このコメディドラマは笑えるね。

彼が出演するTV番組を観るたびに大笑いさ。

先週放送されたバラエティー番組はすごく面白くて大爆笑したよ。

これは笑いごとじゃないんだ。

俺のことを笑うなよ。

陰で俺のことを笑ってんのか？

人のミスを笑うのはよくないよ。

彼女はよく笑うね。

彼女が笑っているのを見ると、こちらも自然と笑いたくなるよ。

彼女、笑うと本当に可愛いよ。

笑わせないで。

（諺）来年のことを言うと鬼が笑う。

## 割る

この窓を割ったのはだれ？

この板を2つに割ってくれる？

オムレツを作るので卵を3個割ってちょうだい。

このウイスキーを水で割ってくれるかな？

**This comedy drama makes me laugh.**
→ makes me laugh= cracks me up

**I laugh out loud whenever I watch a TV show with him.** → laugh out loud（大笑いする）

**The variety show aired last week was so funny that I laughed my head off.**
→ laugh one's head off（頭が転げ落ちるほど笑う、大爆笑する）

**This is no laughing matter.** ⇒ no laughing matter → not a time for laughing（笑うときじゃない）

**Don't laugh at me.** ⇒ me → my misfortune（私の不幸）

**Are you laughing at me behind my back?**
⇒ behind my back → for having no ear for music（私の音痴を）

**It's not nice to laugh at other people's mistakes.**
⇒ It's not nice to ～ → It's awful to ～（～するなんて最低だ）

**She laughs a lot.** ⇒ a lot → at everything（すべてのものに、何を見ても）

**When I see her laugh, I naturally want to laugh.**

**She is really cute when she smiles.**

**Don't make me laugh.** →よく言うよ、ばかばかしくて信じられない、の意。

**Next year is the devil's joke.** / **We know not what a year may bring forth.**

TRACK 436

**Who broke this window?** ⇒ broke this window → smashed this windowpane（窓ガラスを粉々に割った）、broke this vase（この花瓶を割った）、broke this expensive cup（この高価なカップを割った）

**Can you split this board in two?**
⇒ in two → completely in two（真っ二つに）、vertically（縦に）

**Would you break three eggs to make omelets?**
→ omelets =（英）omelettes

**Will you water down this whisky?** / **Can you mix this whisky with water?** → water down=dilute

勘定をみんなで割ろう。

6 人で割ると一人につき 1000 円だね。

8 割る 2 は 4 です。

5 は 2 で割れますか？

奇数は 2 で割れない。

10 を 3 で割ると 1 が余る。

1 ドルが 100 円台を割ったよ。

我が大学は入学定員を割ってしまった。

## 悪口を言う

あいつ、陰で君の悪口を言ってるぜ。

陰でこそこそ私の悪口を言うのはやめてよ。

良子と花子は友だちに見えるけど、お互い悪口を言いあってるよね。

友だちの悪口を言うのは良くないよ。

**Let's split the check among us.**

**If you split it six ways, it's one thousand yen per person.** → split it six ways = divide it among six people

**Eight divided by two is four.** / Divide eight by two and you get four. → is=makes; gives

**Can you divide five by two?**

**Odd numbers cannot be divided by two.**

**Ten divided by three equals three, with 1 left over.**

**The dollar dropped below the 100 yen mark.**
→ mark = level ⇒ the 100 yen mark → 100 yen（100円を）

**Our university didn't get our full quota of students.**
→ full quota（割り当て、「学生などの」定員、定数）

TRACK 437

**He's talking badly about you behind your back.**
⇒ He is talking → He was talking（彼は言っていた）→ talk badly about = bad mouth

**Stop talking about me behind my back.**
→ talk behind someone's back（人の陰口を言う）

**Yoshiko and Hanako seem like friends, but they talk behind each other's back.**

**It's not good to speak badly of your friends.**
→ speak badly of = speak ill of

著者紹介

**曽根田 憲三**（そねだ・けんぞう）

立教大学大学院修了。現在、相模女子大学名誉教授、HSU 客員教授。UCLA（カリフォルニア大学ロサンゼルス校）客員研究員（1994、1997、2000）。アメリカ映画文化学会名誉会長、映画英語アカデミー学会名誉会長。著書に『今日のアメリカ小説』『アメリカ文学と映画』『ハリウッド映画でアメリカが読める』（開文社出版）、『一日の会話のすべてを英語にしてみる』『一日のすべてを英語で表現してみる』『ニュアンスそのまま！日常のこんな日本語を英語で言いたい』『和英対訳　英語で日本昔ばなし 丁寧な語句解説付き』『書きたいことがパット書ける英語表現集』『暮らしの英会話表現辞典』『シンプルな英語で日本を紹介する』『数・単位・計算の英語表現集』『教室で使う英語表現集』（ベレ出版）、『日常生活ですぐに使える英語表現集』「昔話で英会話シリーズ」『桃太郎』『かぐや姫』『つるのおんがえし』（勉誠出版）など。また、スクリーンプレイ出版の『おもてなしの英語表現集』『映画で学ぶ英語ことわざ・慣用表現辞典』をはじめ『風と共に去りぬ』『オズの魔法使い』『ローマの休日』『サウンド・オブ・ミュージック』など、50 タイトルを超える名作映画完全シナリオシリーズの翻訳・解説等を含めると、出版した書籍の数は 170 冊に及ぶ。

◉── カバーデザイン　田栗 克己
◉── DTP　三松堂株式会社
◉── 本文イラスト　いげた めぐみ
◉── 収録音声　4時間2分／ Chris Koprowski, Jennifer Okano

**［音声 DL 付］〈50 音順〉一日の会話で使う動詞のすべてを英語にしてみる**

2021 年 7月 25 日　初版発行

| | |
|---|---|
| 著者 | 曽根田 憲三 |
| 発行者 | 内田 真介 |
| 発行・発売 | ベレ出版<br>〒162-0832　東京都新宿区岩戸町12 レベッカビル<br>TEL.03-5225-4790 FAX.03-5225-4795<br>ホームページ　https://www.beret.co.jp/ |
| 印刷 | 三松堂株式会社 |
| 製本 | 根本製本株式会社 |



ISBN 978-4-86064-663-9 C2082　　編集担当　綿引ゆか

CD BOOK 2枚付き

## 一日のすべてを英語で表現してみる

曽根田憲三／ブルース・パーキンス 著

四六並製／本体価格 2000 円（税別）■ 312 頁

ISBN978-4-86064-372-0 C2082

朝「私は早起きです」という表現から夜「すぐ眠りに落ちる」まで、身のまわりのさまざまな行動、遭遇する状況、頭の中を駆け巡る思いや考えを、シンプルで短い英語表現にして紹介していく。英語の上達に必要なのは日常的に英語に触れること。毎日聴いて、つぶやいてみることは、ネイティブと話す機会のない学習者が、ひとりで簡単に、すぐに実践できる効果的な学習法。細やかで豊富なバリエーションを収録してあるので、文の形や語彙、フレーズもたくさん身につけていける。

## [音声 DL 付] 一日の会話のすべてを英語にしてみる

曽根田憲三／上原寿和子 著

四六並製／本体価格 2000 円（税別）■ 368 頁

ISBN978-4-86064-601-1 C2082

起きてから寝るまでの一日に交わす会話を全部英語にして紹介します。「まだ寝てるの？」「もうちょっと」、「明日忙しい？」「午後なら大丈夫」、「今日はいい天気だね」「久しぶりじゃない？」というように日常会話でよくあるやりとりがたくさん集めてあります。会話形式なので、話しかけ表現にあいづち表現、質問表現に返しの表現、とセットで覚えることができます。また、決まり表現やイディオムが頻出するため表現の幅も広がります。ダウンロード音声には本書にある会話表現のすべてを収録。ネイティブの自然な英語を聞くことで、正しい発音が身につき、暗唱トレーニングにも活用できます。